WOMEN'S SPACE

CRITICAL EXPLORATIONS IN SCIENCE FICTION AND FANTASY
(a series edited by Donald E. Palumbo and C.W. Sullivan III)

Earlier Works: www.mcfarlandpub.com

Recent Works: 42 *The Heritage of Heinlein* (Thomas D. Clareson and Joe Sanders, 2014)

43 *The Past That Might Have Been, the Future That May Come* (Lauren J. Lacey, 2014)

44 *Environments in Science Fiction: Essays* (ed. Susan M. Bernardo, 2014)

45 *Discworld and the Disciplines: Critical Approaches to the Terry Pratchett Works* (ed. Anne Hiebert Alton, William C. Spruiell, 2014)

46 *Nature and the Numinous in Mythopoeic Fantasy Literature* (Christopher Straw Brawley, 2014)

47 *J.R.R. Tolkien, Robert E. Howard and the Birth of Modern Fantasy* (Deke Parsons, 2014)

48 *The Monomyth in American Science Fiction Films* (Donald E. Palumbo, 2014)

49 *The Fantastic in Holocaust Literature and Film* (ed. Judith B. Kerman, John Edgar Browning, 2014)

50 *Star Wars in the Public Square* (Derek R. Sweet, 2016)

51 *An Asimov Companion* (Donald E. Palumbo, 2016)

52 *Michael Moorcock* (Mark Scroggins, 2016)

53 *The Last Midnight: Essays* (ed. Leisa A. Clark, Amanda Firestone, Mary F. Pharr, 2016)

54 *The Science Fiction Mythmakers: Religion, Science and Philosophy in Wells, Clarke, Dick and Herbert* (Jennifer Simkins, 2016)

55 *Gender and the Quest in British Science Fiction Television* (Tom Powers, 2016)

56 *Saving the World Through Science Fiction: James Gunn* (Michael R. Page, 2017)

57 *Wells Meets Deleuze* (Michael Starr, 2017)

58 *Science Fiction and Futurism: Their Terms and Ideas* (Ace G. Pilkington, 2017)

59 *Science Fiction in Classic Rock: Musical Explorations of Space, Technology and the Imagination, 1967–1982* (Robert McParland, 2017)

60 *Patricia A. McKillip and the Art of Fantasy World-Building* (Audrey Isabel Taylor, 2017)

61 *The Fabulous Journeys of Alice and Pinocchio: Exploring Their Parallel Worlds* (Laura Tosi with Peter Hunt, 2018)

62 *A Dune Companion: Characters, Places and Terms in Frank Herbert's Original Six Novels* (Donald E. Palumbo, 2018)

63 *Fantasy Literature and Christianity: A Study of the Mistborn, Coldfire, Fionavar Tapestry and Chronicles of Thomas Covenant Series* (Weronika Łaszkiewicz, 2018)

64 *The British Comic Invasion: Alan Moore, Warren Ellis, Grant Morrison and the Evolution of the American Style* (Jochen Ecke, 2019)

65 *The Archive Incarnate: The Embodiment and Transmission of Knowledge in Science Fiction* (Joseph Hurtgen, 2018)

66 *Women's Space: Essays on Female Characters in the 21st Century Science Fiction Western* (Edited by Melanie A. Marotta, 2019)

67 *"Hailing frequencies open": Communication in Star Trek: The Next Generation* (Thomas D. Parham III, 2019)

68 *The Global Vampire: Essays on the Undead in Popular Culture Around the World* (Edited by Cait Coker, 2019)

WOMEN'S SPACE

Essays on Female Characters
in the 21st Century
Science Fiction Western

EDITED BY MELANIE A. MAROTTA

CRITICAL EXPLORATIONS IN SCIENCE
FICTION AND FANTASY, 66

Series Editors Donald E. Palumbo and C.W. Sullivan III

McFarland & Company, Inc., Publishers
Jefferson, North Carolina

ISBN (print) 978-1-4766-7660-9
ISBN (ebook) 978-1-4766-3672-6

Library of Congress and British Library
Cataloguing data are available

Library of Congress Control Number: 2019943588

Front cover image by Jessica Truscott (Shutterstock)

Printed in the United States of America

McFarland & Company, Inc., Publishers
Box 611, Jefferson, North Carolina 28640
www.mcfarlandpub.com

For my mother, with gratitude

Acknowledgments

My love for science fiction began with the release of *Star Trek: The Next Generation*, but my fascination for popular culture, specifically American, has been life-long. My mother, a native Californian, passed on her interest in popular culture to me while my fascination with the Western came from both my mother and my grandfather. Studying the subgenre of the science fiction Western makes the best of both worlds for me.

As always, I thank my mother for my interest in American popular culture and for her support during the process of completing this collection. I am grateful to Donald Palumbo, C.W. Sullivan, and Layla Milholen at McFarland. My thanks to Nathaniel Fuller for his assistance with the copy editing. Finally, I was one of the participants in the National Endowment for the Humanities summer workshop, Westward Expansion and the Constitution in the Early American Republic, at the University of Oklahoma. The lectures and conversations with the workshop leaders, presenters, and participants were invaluable to this work.

Table of Contents

Introduction

Where Are We Going and Whence Have We Come?

MELANIE A. MAROTTA

"The psychosexual dynamic of a virginal paradise meant …
that real flesh-and-blood women—at least metaphorically—
were dispossessed of paradise" (Kolodny 3).

"To many, the term *Western* implies wild chases, distraught
maidens, and shoot-'em-up showdowns, just as to many
others, the term *science fiction* implies ray guns, distraught
maidens, and bug-eyed monsters" (Mogen 15).

Overview

Paul Green defines the Science Fiction Western as "A traditional Western setting with science fiction elements or themes, often involving future technology or extra-terrestrials" (2). He continues to document that "A science fiction story set in outer space that contains Western genre elements or themes" is considered to be what he terms a Space Western (2). If a reader looks closely at Green's definitions, the difference is a slight one, but one integral to the Western genre itself. In accordance with Green's definitions, the difference between the SF Western and the space Western is an environmental one: while the SF Western is set on land, the space Western occurs in, logically, outer space. Green adds a third definition, naming the subgenre of the weird Western and offering that Western and supernatural attributes have been combined to create texts in this area. This subgenre has been omitted from this collection other than a brief observation later in this introduction.

During the historical Westward expansion, women were responsible for

1

the home and family while men were to be providers, to be active in farming the land, and to protect the family. In twenty-first century SF Western contributions to the subgenre, public and private spheres, which actively controlled women's actions in the eighteenth and nineteenth centuries, have been transgressed. As Green indicates in his definitions, location is a key trait in the construction of the SF Western much as it is in the Western genre itself. The parameters for this collection are defined by this definition of the SF Western subgenre: a contribution which contains attributes of both the science fiction and Western genres set in a space representative of the frontier. What the pulp writers have done is to provide readers with an adaptation of the Western mythos. They created a subgenre of the Western (which predates science fiction) while still retaining its essential elements, namely humanity's journey into the new—the frontier. Regarding investigations of this subgenre, while representations of the frontier are integral to the study, whether the frontier is on land on Earth or another planet or in a ship in space is not. What is essential is the SF Western is based in the possible rather than the fantastic. Science fiction, while seemingly incredible, is feasible (see *Star Trek/Star Trek: The Next Generation* for the appearance of tablets, flat screen televisions, and Facetime). Ultimately, parameters must be set and the focus narrowed in order to create a cohesive yet viable collection.

The supernatural Western (Green's Weird Western), which may be contemporarily represented by *Wynonna Earp* (SyFy Channel 2016–present), has not been included here due to its implausibility.* I have also limited the collection's scope, thereby excluding cartoon/anime contributions to the subgenre (ex. *Cowboy BeBop*) and fan adaptations. While Linda Hutcheon observes that adaptations appear in many forms, I have elected to narrow the focus to literary contributions, live-action film and television, and video games. Upon publication of this collection, the largest contribution to the subgenre exists in these areas.

According to Nina Baym:

> In general terms, the West was seen to allow women to become capable, physically active, independent, honest, and forthright. Ideas of bigness and spaciousness, of freedom from convention, of physical development, contribute to a sense of the western heroine as a new kind of person. The West, with its supposed lack of class distinction, its acceptance of every person on his or her own merits, presumably allowed women without pedigrees to make something of themselves—but only if they also possessed and preserved the delicacy that is taken as foundationally female [9].

---

*_Wynonna Earp_, based on the comic book series, is female-centric, featuring women on screen and behind the scenes. The protagonist, alongside her sidekick sister, Waverly, fight revenants, which are the spirits of the criminals that Wyatt Earp killed. Even though the absence of *Wynonna Earp* and Stephen King's *Dark Tower* series may be questioned, I want to clarify that I have included the futuristic rather than the supernatural.

Baym's female Western conceptualization can be witnessed ideally in the immortal figure of Annie Oakley, one of the stars of Buffalo Bill's Wild West show. Notably, she was a crack shot, completing numerous marksman tricks without concealing her gender identity. There is a popular misconception that women were minor figures on the American frontier. Victoria Lamont observes that "As scholars recovered the western and argued for its significance in the late twentieth-century, a western canon emerged from which women writers were excluded" (126). As many Western historians, including Lamont, have shown, females were a part of the western expansion, but for an extensive period their contributions were omitted from the canon. Over time, theorists like Lamont have called attention to their contributions—Lamont discusses the inclusion of women writers in Western pulps—and, as a result, have claimed women's rightful place in the Western canon. I have compiled this collection so that adjustments to the subgenre's study may be made, namely to examine contributions to the SF Western subgenre featuring women.

This collection explores the SF Western and the changing roles of female characters in the twenty-first century within this subgenre. The purpose is to ascertain whether changing societal constructs regarding gender and ethnicity are reflected in contemporary multimedia sources or disregarded in favor of nostalgic typecasting. The reader must be aware that this collection focuses not on the frontier with ambiguous connections to the West, but on the appearance of the Western motifs in multimedia sources set on both land and in space. It is my hope that this collection will offer an inclusionary look at the SF Western by showing readers how female characters are reclaiming agency in this subgenre and that those characters included are not only cisgendered, white women. I have selected essays documenting the evolution of this character and those that feature transgender females and females of color.

Typically, the SF Western concentrates on the white male protagonist; in this introduction, I have offered readers a brief overview of the Western and the SF Western in order to highlight the progression of the SF Western since its inception. Regarding the collection's organization, I want to emphasize that I chose to begin with two essays that touch on the late-twentieth century (late 1980s to early 1990s) because this is when the focal point of the Western genre began to alter with this change also affecting the SF Western. As noted later in the introduction, this is approximately when the New West, the flawed (rather than idealized) version of the Western, received a great deal of cinematic and literary attention. I have chosen eleven essays for this collection, given in chronological order, so it may be shown that while the conceptualization of the female character may still be constructed in accordance with Western stereotypes, there is hope that female characters' objectified state is in the process of changing. As the twenty-first century progresses, SF

Western female characters advance in their construction and, crucially, become protagonists in major multimedia productions (see HBO's *Westworld*).

Case studies about the SF Western have been limited, tending to concentrate on male characters and their impact. In John Rieder's contemporary publication about the SF Western, "American Frontiers," he provides an overview of the genre, examining what he terms American exceptionalism. Offering one explanation as to how the westward expansion was accomplished—the frontier myth—Rieder cites "the frontier itself as the lynchpin for an exceptionalist account of American history that identified the rigors of the frontier as the catalyst of America's capacity for continual renewal and reinvention of itself" (168). Further, Rieder offers a detailed timeline beginning at the turn of the twentieth century with Edgar Rice Burroughs and the pulps, concluding with Afrofuturism and Indigenous SF. While Rieder's essay is more inclusive than others in this field, and he has addressed the application of American Western motifs to multimedia sources, the research about female characters is insufficient. Here, the reference that has been included is Richard Slotkin's analysis of Burroughs' Dejah Thoris (*A Princess of Mars*), notably as the sexualized Native American woman whose character contains traits that make her an acceptable love interest for John Carter. Rieder also references C.L. Moore's short story "Shambleau," but then the analysis of female characterization concludes. The remaining analysis touches on both female and male characters, but not on gender identity.

Joseph Maddrey's *The Quick, the Dead and the Revived: The Many Lives of the Western Film* (2016) offers readers an insightful look at Western films, beginning with 1939. Ensuring that his critical overview is comprehensive, Maddrey has included a portion of a chapter about cinematic SF Westerns. Starting in the 1970s and working his way through the 1980s, Maddrey discusses the effects of Ronald Reagan's election, in particular his revisiting of the Cold War political viewpoint, had on Western cinematic productions while lightly touching on television from that time. Included within his analysis are the iconic SF Westerns *Star Trek* and *Star Wars*, and Peter Hyams' film, *Outlander* (1981), which Maddrey deems "a nightmare vision of unregulated capitalism" (135). Maddrey then proceeds to discuss the dystopic anti-hero SF Western, *Escape from New York* (1981). This film, directed by John Carpenter, features the iconic Snake Plissken (Kurt Russell), who appeared in a later sequel, *Escape from L.A.* (1996). Unfortunately, while the book offers an excellent breakdown of Western films throughout the twentieth and early twenty-first century, the female SF Western characters are absent. When Maddrey examines *Firefly* in a later chapter as well as the subsequent film *Serenity*, the view is political rather than gender-based (there is no mention of the female characters).

Esteemed SF theorist and educator Gary Westfahl compiled and edited

Space and Beyond: The Frontier Theme in Science Fiction (2000), a collection stemming from the 1997 jointly held Science Fiction Research Association and J. Lloyd Eaton Conference. Westfahl concentrates his introduction to the collection on two poignant moments in American history and their connection to late twentieth century frontier SF multimedia sources. Frederick Jackson Turner's conceptualization of the American frontier in 1893 and John F. Kennedy's 1961 speech where "he described outer space as 'the New Frontier'" both impact works in the Western genre (1). According to Westfahl, Kennedy desired to connect the frontier to space in order to obtain support for America's new venture: the space race. As Westfahl documents, Kennedy's association was unsuccessful in his endeavor as "the frontier myth itself has become increasingly unappealing" and space has grown to appear most unhospitable to human life (3). It is the latter upon which Westfahl's collection of essays has been concentrated. While the collection's essays focus intriguingly on the New Frontier, the focal point is not primarily on female characters and Western motifs.

Carl Abbott's later monograph, *Frontiers Past and Future: Science Fiction and the American West* (2006), includes an increased concentration on female characters, which is appreciated, as is his inclusion of the mythic motifs. In particular, Abbott's chapter, "On the Urban Edge," includes an examination of the NoCal (San Francisco) and SoCal (Los Angeles) urban spaces depicted as representative of the New West. Beginning in the mid-twentieth century, the primary sources Abbott examines feature female protagonists—Thomas Pynchon's Mrs. Odeppa Mass from his postmodernist *The Crying of Lot 49* (1966)—and their interactions on the Californian frontier, which are more dystopic than utopic.

One of the finest monographs about the SF Western utilizing Western motifs is David Mogen's *Wilderness Visions: The Western Theme in Science Fiction Literature* (1982). Even though a revised edition of Mogen's monograph was released in 1993, the information is somewhat dated. Specifically, Mogen begins by discussing the SF Western and the space opera, noting that neither was considered to be a reputable genre. William H. Katerberg's monograph, *Future West: Utopia and Apocalypse in Frontier Science Fiction* (2008), is a noteworthy addition to the field but, like many writers, he primarily concentrates on the frontier instead of American Western motifs. Interestingly, Katerberg includes texts not traditionally thought of as SF, such as Leslie Marmon Silko's *Ceremony* (1977), an approach that does have merit. Katerberg examines the frontier as a utopic or dystopic space as do others, but the aspects in which the motifs are noted are limited. The goal of this collection is to not only consider how the roles of female characters have progressed, but also to investigate the continued perpetration of American Western motifs in multimedia primary sources. In this collection, I have included essays representative, not comprehensive, of the current offerings available about female characters in the subgenre of the SF Western.

Overview of the Frontier and Start of the SF Western

In 1890, with the incorporation of towns and an end to open spaces, the American frontier was deemed closed by the U.S. Census. This area was no longer considered to be lawless and uncivilized as governments were now in place. Once closed, land was no longer offered to settlers in such great quantities and at such a low cost. The popularity of the American West in the American imagination, however, did not diminish and, in fact, even today the frontier myth continues to increase desire for migration to this space. Buffalo Bill's Wild West show, which began in 1883, was famous in America and in Europe. In the late nineteenth century, Buffalo Bill's Wild West show came to England and was viewed by hundreds of thousands including Queen Victoria, thereby showing that both sexes and varied classes had an interest in the spectacle that is the American West. Notably, the late 1800s saw the precursors to the SF Western. In reference to what he terms "inventor fiction," Brian Stableford asserts that "Edward S. Ellis's pioneering account of *The Steam Man of the Prairies* (1868) was, in fact, a Western, as were many of the items in story series featuring inventors such as Frank Reade and Tom Edison, Jr." (22). Unfortunately, while women may have been attracted to the frontier myth concept, they are infrequently the primary focus of American Western stories. Adult males, however, prominently appear within literature in connection to this myth. As implied in Kolodny's quotation given at the start of this introduction, the desire to obtain all that the American West had to offer was a primarily male one with pioneer women begrudgingly coming along for the proverbial ride (Kolodny 3). Even after closure, the frontier continued to live on in various media, and Mogen explains why this happens in reference to SF: "The frontier metaphor, applied to the future, expresses both deeply-ingrained attitudes adopted toward the challenges the future represents—the stance of the indomitable pioneer—and, in many cases, fantasy of a particularly American kind, expressive of desire to recover a sense of heroic purpose identified with the frontier past, a sense of infinite possibilities" (26). The desire to locate, immerse oneself in, and conquer paradise is reflected in media representations of the American West, including those belonging to the subgenre. The Western as a literary genre had already appeared but grew in popularity with the publication of Owen Wister's adventure novel *The Virginian* (1902).

As time progressed, the American imagination was captured. The Western no longer appeared purely in literary form, but also in film and, subsequently, television. Stacy Peebles observes that *The Great Train Robbery* (1903) signals the commencement of the Western cinematic construction; Peebles then refers to the later film, *Stagecoach* (1939), as the "Western's 'classic of classics"' due to its capacity to offer depth of plot and characters (122). Richard Etulain also acknowledges that *The Great Train Robbery* is the starting point for the Western. According to Etulain, audiences thoroughly enjoyed the film because of its familiar romantic storyline, one which included the outlaw figure ("Broncho Billy" 1). The historian continues his examination, highlighting a new cinematic aspect brought to viewers via *The Great Train Robbery*: the creation of the "first Western star, Broncho Billy Anderson" (1). Anderson was the lead of the Broncho Billy silent Western film series (1). In reference to the silent films of the early 1920s, Etulain describes them as "heroic men on horseback, capturing thieves and other bad men"; he notes that the epic Westerns were also created during the 1920s (Introduction viii). Broncho Billy also gave viewers a male character type Etulain calls "the 'good, badman' character," one who "seemed a rascal but proved to be a man of true grit with a heart of gold" ("Broncho Billy" 6). This character type is often seen in the SF Western.

It is no coincidence that what may be considered the earliest SF Western on record, Burroughs' *A Princess of Mars* (1917), was released during this period. Focusing on the adventurer John Carter, Burroughs' story was first published in the pulps as *Under the Moons of Mars* (1912), later rereleased and rebranded under the aforementioned title. The hero, a Confederate soldier, goes west with another former soldier on a quest for gold. After battling with Native Americans (the cowboys and Indians motif appears here), Carter finds himself transported to Mars. Burroughs' fascinating tale contains the standard motifs of the Western, including those laid out by Mogen. In fact, the "fantasy" was so engaging that Disney produced the film *John Carter* (2012), which ultimately flopped (Mogen 26). Notably, both observations from Kolodny and Mogen apply to Burroughs' story: for women there is no utopic equality in space. When Carter meets Martian Sola, she resides among other female aliens in something resembling a harem, and it is the women that act as caregivers for the Thark hatchlings, thereby placing them in the traditional mother role. Accordingly, with the Western genre it is not Sola that Carter attempts a romantic relationship with, even though he admits his attraction to her, rather the biracial Dejah, the Heliumite princess Sola refers to as the "'red woman'" (Burroughs). Subsequently, Carter sets out with his companions in a daring mission to rescue Dejah from the symbolic "savages." The duo marry, but when Carter attempts to save the Heliumites from suffocating, he is transported from them before their fate is known. It is telling that the white man and the Other are ultimately separated (an interracial relationship not being permitted) with Carter surviving and longing for Dejah. It is also notable that when he finds himself once again in Arizona, his first thought is for the frontier, which is represented as Mars, rather than for Dejah.

While women did act in early Western films, viewers had to wait until after World War II to see cinematic constructions that were not primarily male-centered (Etulain, Introduction viii). Glenda Riley notes that starting in the 1930s, actor Barbara Stanwyck revised the female in Western films (121). "Stanwyck eschewed such traditional figures as the wife, the civilizer, the schoolteacher, and the soiled dove," preferring to take the roles that Riley calls "'tough broads'" (121). The women in the films of the 1930s and 1940s were endowed with strength of character without having to sacrifice their femininity (Riley 121). As Riley documents, "In Stanwyck's Westerns, women were not simply adjuncts or satellites. They could, and did, express their own wills and take action for themselves" (121–22). Unfortunately, Stanwyck's strong women roles were a rarity; female actors were primarily cast in non-realistic, passive positions.

Jeffrey Richardson examines early twentieth-century Western films, calling Gene Autry's twelve-part serial, *The Phantom Empire* (1935), the beginning of the SF Western subgenre; Ron Briley concurs with this assertion, documenting that the popularity of the film and the dime store texts at the time contributed to subsequent "acclaimed space operas *Flash Gordon* (1936) and *Buck Rogers* (1939)" (6). Regarding this film, which solidified Autry's place in Hollywood as an actor and as the singing cowboy, Miller states, "This novel hybrid intermingled the familiar with the strange, combining Western music popularized on radio and the much-loved Western serial format—already a mainstay of American film entertainment—with the novelty and innovation of other-worldly science fiction" (8–9). The film concentrates on the exploits of Gene Autry's character of the same name; because Autry discovers a secret underground society, Murania, Queen Tika has him kidnapped and brought to her. Unfortunately, whether it is a literary or cinematic construction, the primary focus remained on the male character and his contact with the West. In particular, the cowboy character often appeared as heroic, taming the frontier while rescuing the female character from its grasp. For example, beginning in the 1940s Roy Rogers and Dale Evans were featured in the singing Western films, but it was Rogers and his horse, Trigger, that were favored by the studios with Evans received inferior billing to the duo. By doing so, the studios placed the singing cowboy character in a position of prominence while the female character appears as inferior. So that he may save himself, Autry must trade the queen for safe passage out of Murania. At the film's conclusion, Autry successfully returns home while the queen, after contact with the surface-dweller, chooses to die rather than escape her collapsing society.

Eventually, the public's interest in the standard cinematic Western waned, and it needed to be reconstructed so as to retain its audience (Etulain, Introduction x). By the late 1960s and early 1970s, the public's attention started to shift from the classic Western, which resulted in film and television producers altering this genre's format. As Etulain notes:

If *High Noon* and *Shane* (1953) represented the classic Western before the mid–1960s, the Spaghetti Westerns of Clint Eastwood and director Sergio Leone and such films as *The Wild Bunch* (1969) and *Little Big Man* pointedly reminded viewers how much the Western was changing. Intense violence, explicit sexuality, and more significant roles for minority groups marked the new form of the genre [x].

The change in the Western was dictated by societal unrest, mainly in the 1960s, due to the alterations in societal values and occurrences of wars. During this time, a significant addition to the SF Western subgenre was made: Gene Roddenberry's *Star Trek*.* In reference to Roddenberry's most famed series, *Newsweek* observes that "When he launched *Star Trek* in 1966, its high concept (no one called it that) was 'Wagon Train to the Stars': a Western in space. Roddenberry's model, though, was *Gulliver's Travels*: social, political, even philosophical commentary disguised as adventure." By introducing each episode with Captain Kirk telling the viewer, "Space, the final frontier…," Roddenberry highlights the Western connection, the exploration of the unknown. In the episode "Errand of Mercy" (1967), Captain Kirk says to the Organian council, "I'm a soldier, not a diplomat." By making this statement Kirk highlights the violence associated with Western exploration. For a short period, only three seasons, the SF Western obtains some interest; while airing *Star Trek* did garner some popularity, it was not until after the series concluded, however, that it garnered its monumental fan base and became a cult classic.

Star Trek, Star Wars *and Cyberpunk:* The Continuation of the SF Western *into the Twenty-First Century*

Audiences in the late 1970s and early 1980s were fortunate to witness George Lucas' *Star Wars* films; their monumental popularity and Lucas' desire to continue the story prompted the production of more films in the twenty-first century. Western authority Slotkin identifies *Star Wars* and its massive acclaim upon release as the catalyst for "a boom in fantasy and science-fiction epics that were closely related in theme and visual style to the imperial epics of the 1930s" (634). While the male Jedi, Luke Skywalker, and the reformed criminal, Han Solo, are the focus of the initial release, so is Princess Leia. Even though the plot of *Star Wars: A New Hope* (1977) revolves around the proverbial rescue of the princess, in this case from the Empire and Darth Vader, Leia is a capable leader in her own right. It is she that attempts to save the

*Upon *Star Trek*'s fiftieth anniversary in 2016, *Newsweek* reprinted a version of its article published at the time of Gene Roddenberry's death in the 1990s.

Rebellion, but her role is later undercut by the scene where she is clad in only a bikini while being chained to Jabba the Hut in *Star Wars: Return of the Jedi* (1983). While *Star Wars* can be placed in the space opera subgenre, it may be also classified as a SF Western because of its exploration of the frontier and its inclusion of the outlaw character, Solo. In reference to what he terms "classic space opera," which appeared in the 1930s, Westfahl writes that "since space was a relatively new setting for fiction, a literary frontier as it were, writers sensibly used familiar storylines from genres dealing with frontiers, such as the ocean, criminal underworld and Wild West, to introduce the universe to readers in reassuring fashion and blaze a trail for works that would display more imagination" (199). In *A New Hope* and *The Empire Strikes Back* (1980), the Western attributes are in a position of prominence, especially Luke's (the Jedi's) desire for exploration and the Empire's for colonization. In "Mara Jade, Frontier Woman: Agency in *Star Wars* and Influencing the Transmedia Franchise," Monica Louzon offers an excellent exploration of Mara's character as one who defies binary gendered constructs. As Louzon explains, while the *Star Wars* universe was first introduced in 1977, readers first meet Mara in Timothy Zahn's novel from 1991. Over the course of the 1990s to the aughts, Louzon documents Mara's transition from assassin working for the Empire to mother, wife, and rebel fighter. Louzon shows us a twenty-first century female character that transgresses gendered roles.

The SF Western amassed renewed interest in the 1980s, with the introduction of cyberpunk, and the late 1980s, with the next installment in the *Star Trek* franchise, *Star Trek: The Next Generation*. The 1980s were, in fact, a SF Western treasure trove, but this is not overtly discernible. For SF, readers in the early 1980s witnessed the introduction of the monumental subgenre popularized by Bruce Sterling and William Gibson. Cyberpunk centered on the male console cowboy and his experiences traversing cyberspace. In the infamous *Mirrorshades* Preface, Sterling discusses the symbolism behind the iconic image of the mirrored sunglasses: "By hiding the eyes, mirrorshades prevent the forces of normalcy from realizing that one is crazed and possibly dangerous. They are the symbol of the sun-staring visionary, the biker, the rocker, the policeman, and similar outlaws" (xi). Sterling documents the commonalities in meaning and in structure from cyberpunk writers while simultaneously noting their refusal to conform to the norm. In "The Reformation of the 'Plastic Girl': Prostitute/Killer and Messenger Characters in Cyberpunk to Post-Cyberpunk," I discuss Walter Jon Williams' novel, *Hardwired* (1986), and a selection of cyberpunk and post-cyberpunk texts as SF Westerns. I highlight the presence of Western archetypes, which include the presence of the outlaw figure, and how the Western setting permits freedom for the female characters. Cyberpunk, which has a reputation for demeaning women in its visual depictions, has only one female writer, Pat Cadigan (*Syn-*

ners; "Pretty Boy Crossover"), and female characters tend to be depicted as prostitutes. The women, like Mara Jade, tend to be killers; however, as cyberpunk (late twentieth century) undergoes a transformation from the nineties to the aughts, like I show in my work, so do the female characters as they become more developed. As cyberpunk is based on the noir genre, the femme fatale is integral to its literary contributions; this character has more depth, is no longer only the sexualized object as the genre transitions to become post-cyberpunk. Late twentieth-century cyberpunk is not the only SF Western that catered to what writers believed was a primarily male audience, *TNG* did as well with its introduction of the Deanna Troi character.

In their sixth season, *TNG* writers paid tribute to the Western with the episode "A Fistful of Datas." Worf and his son, Alexander, venture into a holodeck staging of the Wild West. In this episode (6.8), Worf is the sheriff, Alexander the deputy, and Counselor Troi, the stranger turned lawman. While writers Robert Hewitt Wolfe and Brannon Braga clean up the West for television (Miss Annie is a dance hall girl rather than a prostitute), the most striking alteration is the addition of Troi as the stranger. Notably, in the creation of this episode, *TNG* writers have channeled Sergio Leone's famed spaghetti Western, *A Fistful of Dollars* (1964) starring Clint Eastwood. *TNG* writer Robert Hewitt Wolfe "flips the script" when he replaces Eastwood's character, The Man with No Name, with Troi. Taking the holodeck narrative seriously, Troi plays The Man flawlessly except for a few moments when she breaks character: once to chastise Worf's lack of immersion in the narrative and when Worf is shot. In this episode, the character's best for development I might add, Troi transgresses boundaries and departs from her stereotyped role. Symbolically, in order to do so she must become The Man. When the series begins, the Troi character is overly emotional, sporting a tight-fitting jumpsuit which shows an overabundance of cleavage; she is decidedly an amalgamation of female stereotypes and, decidedly, was created to draw the male viewer to the series. As the series progresses, Troi's character becomes more developed—she is promoted to lieutenant commander in the seventh season—and she is more confident in making command decisions.

The 1990s and the SF Western

It was not until 1990 with the release of Kevin Costner's *Dances with Wolves*, and later Clint Eastwood's *Unforgiven* (1992), that the Western genre experienced a significant increase in audience interest (Etulain x). Rather than portraying Native Americans as adversaries, novelist and screenwriter Michael Blake offers them as a community for Lt. Dunbar (Costner). It is with this film that viewers see significant alterations made to the standard Western construct. Richard Etulain refers to the film as "a revisionist-style Western sympathetic to Native Americans" (Introduction x). In his introduction to his collection, *The Hollywood West*, Etulain goes on to document the character construction of the white antagonist as flawed. In this Costner-directed film, no longer is the lone male a gunfighter character; rather, he is a seemingly courageous officer in the military. Out of loneliness, Dunbar acquaints himself with the local Sioux and, over time, he resides more so with them than at his military camp. The white woman, Stands with a Fist, lives with the Sioux and is there of her own volition, thereby refuting the image portrayed in the captivity narratives of the 1800s. Unfortunately, the alteration to the Western construct is temporary. While Dunbar protects and sides with the Sioux, at the conclusion of the film he and Stands with a Fist, the only white people in the community, go off on their own presumably to rejoin white society. They do so in order to protect the Sioux, but their coupling is problematic. By having the groups separate, the myth that white people and Native Americans cannot reside together in harmony continues to be perpetuated. Costner, an avid fan of Westerns, continues his foray with the speculative Western films *Waterworld* (1995) and *The Postman* (1997). In the former, Costner plays an unnamed loner that scavenges for items to trade; he comes across a young girl with a map to dry land tattooed on her back. In the latter, Costner again plays a loner character lacking a name; here, the character dressed in an old-fashioned postal worker's uniform becomes a one-man Pony Express, delivering mail to those in a post–American dystopic space. Unfortunately, the advancements made in *Dances with Wolves* wane in the aforementioned films, and audiences are left to wonder about the preponderance of white male leads and the lack of strong female characters in the SF Western.

The Fox network, ever-present in the SF television market, debuted *The X-Files* in 1993, introducing viewers to FBI agents Fox Mulder and Dana Scully. While the series is not a SF Western per say, the viewer does encounter the extraterrestrial frontier and the protagonists are often assisted by the aptly named Lone Gunmen. This trio of outsiders is comprised of conspiracy theorists (their name is based on the JFK lone gunman theory) that reveal themselves to Mulder throughout the series only when solving the case appears implausible. In the fifth season, "The Unusual Suspects" episode aired, offering viewers' insights into how the Lone Gunmen met and began to work for Mulder. In this flashback, it is ascertainable that the Lone Gunmen characters are outsiders, a parallel to the Western gunfighters, who find acceptance from one another and then later Agent Mulder. The aforementioned is a notably male-centric group with one exception: Agent Scully is billed as the rational scientist character to Mulder's often agitated dissenter. It is she who is often realistically the gunfighter character that bestows order on her chaotic societal interactions. This series is an appropriate lead-in to the twenty-first century for SF Western television.

The Twenty-First Century SF Western

From the seventeenth to the early twentieth century, the westward expansion was intended for patriotic, middle-class, white Americans. While the Westward expansion was heralded as a sign of great progress for America, it was an exclusionary practice dominated by the issues of the commodification of space and of ideologies concerning gendered behavior. The release of Joss Whedon's *Firefly* affirms that some modifications that have been undertaken with regards to the SF Western female character, notably that the future is racially inclusive. Unfortunately, even though some positive adjustments to SF Western female character are being made early in the twenty-first century, the unfavorable female frontier character construct does rear her head on occasion.

With the appearance of Whedon's groundbreaking (if short-lived) series *Firefly* (2002–2003), the viewers' attention is once again turned to the SF Western, a form popularized in the pulps of the 1920s. In fact, in the early twenty-first century, there has been a SF Western production boom. Starting with *Star Trek: TNG* and *The Adventures of Briscoe County, Jr.* (1993–1994) and then continuing with *Firefly*, the Fox network aids in sustaining the public's interest in this SF subgenre. With Whedon's series, the viewer witnesses both the stereotypical roles for Western women and the placement of women in roles traditionally occupied by men. On the one hand, Whedon's series objectifies women by including as one of his characters a female sex worker. Inara is a licensed "companion"; while sex work may be legal and accepted in the *Firefly* universe, by offering a woman in this role Whedon shows that the concept of the female as commodity is still a reality in early aughts' television. The commodification of Inara becomes more problematic than normal as she is also a person of color. While it may appear that the plan is to show Inara's position as a licensed companion garners her more freedom, this assertion falls flat due to her ultimate objectification by the same group. In "Shindig" (episode 4), Inara attends a ball escorted by Atherton Wing, who hired her for this occasion. While the pair is dancing, the jealous captain of Inara's ship, Captain Malcom (Mal) Reynolds, cuts in, and an argument ensues. Mal physically assaults Atherton after he informs Mal that Inara belongs to him because "money changed hands" ("Shindig"). Visibility theorist Thomson documents the freak show in Western culture, citing how people of color were often exoticized and placed on display for white Europeans and later American audiences (63). Thomson asserts that by exhibiting people of color, they become the spectacle, thereby normalizing white people's place in their respective societies. Sander Gilman has written an iconic essay about the sexualization of black women, noting in particular Sarah Bartmaan (also called the derogatory name of Hottentot Venus), an African woman put on display in nineteenth-century

London (213). Gilman recounts that there are two women labeled as the Hottentot Venus, one of which was exhibited to ball guests in Paris. According to Gilman, "Sarah Bartmaan's sexual parts, her genitalia and her buttocks, serve as the central image for the black female throughout the nineteenth century" and recounts how both were shown to viewers before and after death (215–6). In other words, the black woman was seen as overly sexual, a stereotype battled for centuries, one which Whedon continues to allege with the inclusion of a woman of color as the sex worker character.

If the reader is wondering why I did not include an essay about *Firefly* or the subsequent film, *Serenity*, in this collection, I want to clarify. Both series and film have been examined extensively in previous publications. In fact, I contributed an essay, "Domestic Space and Identity: Joss Whedon's Futuristic Frontier in Firefly," to Juliette C. Kitchens' collection, *At Home in the Whedonverse: Essays on Domestic Place, Space and Life*, which delineates the role of domestic space in Whedon's numerous series, including the infamous *Buffy the Vampire Slayer*. When selecting essays for this collection, I wanted to include examinations of media not often studied, and there is a plethora of *Firefly* examinations currently on the market. If further reading is desired, Michael Goodrum and Philip Smith's collection *Firefly Revisited: Essays on Joss Whedon's Classic Series* and Rhonda V. Wilcox and Tanya R. Cochran's *Investigating Firefly and Serenity: Science Fiction on the Frontier* are invaluable resources.

To continue, *Firefly* and the subsequent film, *Serenity* (2005), contain two characters that resists gender typecasting: Zoe and Kaylee. Zoe is the African American first officer of the Serenity, and Kaylee is the engineer. Together, the female crew members keep the ship and its community from coming apart in times of crisis. Even though the image of the two women (three when Inara is aboard) engaged in assuring the success of the crew's missions and the cohesiveness of the crew itself may appear to be a positive one, it is disconcerting that the women are placed in the roles of caregivers, thereby all but negating the progress made for women in this SF Western. At the close of the film, Zoe's husband, Wash, dies thereby leaving her alone. Zoe has acted as the hero throughout the series, supporting her captain (they were also soldiers together) in his illicit schemes and even battling her husband when he attempts to uphold constructed guidelines for the wife. For all of the problems with this series, Whedon does close it with affirmation of the womens' role in the future. Wash must die, leaving Zoe because he is not willing to accept that the sexes are equals either in marriage or otherwise. As the ship's crew symbolically rides into the sunset, it is River Tam who pilots the ship even though Mal is in the cockpit with her. In 2005 with the release of the film, *Serenity*, the woman in the SF Western looks promising to the viewer. The video game releases in this subgenre, however, are another story.

In the late twentieth century, there is some interest in the Western video game. For example, the TAD Corporation released the stereotypical "Cowboy and Indian" arcade game called *Blood Bros.* (1990), thereby showing that the Old West typecasting was alive and well. Later, in 2005, Capcom and Ubisoft released their take on a Western with *Darkwatch*; here, the vampire gunslinger protagonist, Jericho Cross, pursues his nemesis, a vampire by the name of Lazarus Malkoth. It is not until the initial release in a popular video game series two years later that gamers obtain an authentic SF Western game. In his essay, "'Shut up and get over here': Lovers and Cattle in *Mass Effect*," Adam Crowley examines a major video game series, *Mass Effect* (2007–present). Crowley documents the reliance on the passive female character construct favored in video games. In the series' introductory game, the main character, Commander Shepard, may be either played as male or female. As Crowley reveals through his examination, the positive evolution of the SF Western female character is stunted in the video game medium.

In 2008, the Fox network continues its foray into the SF Western with the series, *Fringe*. Teresa Forde examines the maturation of the female SF Western character through her examination of Olivia Dunham, the protagonist of the series in her essay, "Olivia Dunham and the New Frontier in *Fringe*." Forde envisions Olivia, the FBI agent investigating alternate realities, as a female gunslinger figure. In her essay, the writer shows that while Olivia is at the forefront of the series with a positive representation of a multi-faceted female character, the series follows a predictable path as it progresses and places its female character in the proverbial backseat of the plot. After *Fringe* concluded in 2013, so did Fox's reign over the SF Western, a crown that was passed on to the SyFy Channel.

Before the *Fringe* series concluded, a notable cinematic contribution to the SF Western genre was released. Directed by Jon Favreau, released by Dreamworks, and based on the 2006 graphic novel of the same name, the SF Western film *Cowboys and Aliens* (2011) stars Daniel Craig as Jake Lonergan, a cowboy who awakens with no memory of his past and a mysterious piece of metal encircling his arm. As the film progresses, the audience discovers that Jake is a criminal who has stolen alien gold, and his wife has been abducted by aliens. Jake has been on the alien spaceship and is the only survivor, the one who can tell the others how get aboard. Craig's character is to represent the black-hatted figure undergoing a transformation of redemption, which is why he wears the brown hat. According to Cynthia J. Miller, the fans of the two genres cite problems with the film's production while she observes that the film "successfully merges the two genres in a high-budget format designed for mainstream audiences" (9). The film did show viewers a striking female character, Ella Swenson, one who just happens to be an alien. Miller describes Ella as "One part Rancher's Daughter, one part Ancient Alien, and one part Mystic Ancestor, Swenson is, herself, a hybrid character who bridges the gap between self and Other, past and future, wisdom and instinct, faith and action" (9). While I do not necessarily agree with seeing Swenson as a "futuristic spiritual guide," she is characterized as the Other and does achieve acceptance by the Western community through her acts of strength and courage, such as when she saves the protagonist from certain death. The issue that viewers must question is her characterization as an alien. One could see this film as resembling Burroughs' novel, however, with some twenty-first-century twists. When the viewer first sees Ella, she wears the stereotypical Western muslin-flowered dress, but sports a gun belt. She later saves Jake from getting shot in a fight with the sheriff by hitting him on the head with her gun. It is also Ella's plan to save humanity, an act which unites the "cowboys" with the Native Americans. The fact that ultimately makes the film problematic is that Ella is the only female in the group of men who go to protect humanity, and she solely gets to join because she is the alien. Cinematic SF Western productions featuring women continue to be imperfect at this time; however, two years later great achievements are made in the medium of text-based video games.

In Joshua King's "A Fistful of Gender: Power and the Body in Text-Based Trans-Femme SF Western Video Games," the writer investigates two SF Western text-based video games: Anna Anthropy's *And the Robot Horse You Rode In On* (2013) and Porpentine's *Wild Wild Gender Mines* (2014). Anthropy and Porpentine are transwomen game designers who embrace the twenty-first century by offering their players an interactive experience, playing a character in a gender-fluid world. These designers' text-based games are among the few that deliver an immersive experience with women at the forefront, showing the advancements made to the SF Western female character.

In 2013, the SyFy Channel introduced its SF Western multimedia immersive experience with the television series, *Defiance*, and Trion World's MMO.* Hutcheon reveals that "in the last six years, what has become evident is that the new entertainment norm, not the exception, is 'transmedia' storytelling" (xxiii). Going on to analyze the desirability of transmedia storytelling to audiences, Hutcheon cites Christy Dena as stating "'not everyone wants to watch the movie and play the game'" (Hutcheon xxiii). While the series lasted for three seasons, it lagged in viewership after the first, leading to its cancellation. Interest in the MMO continued with the release of *Dark Metamorphosis*, Trion World's update to the game; notably, the company calls

---

*The MMO (massive multi-player online) video game that fans could play existed to offer *Defiance*'s audience a more in-depth look at the characters while also ensuring an interactive experience.

this update Season Four. In July 2018, the developer released *Defiance 2050*, a continuation of the *Defiance* saga. In reference to the television series, *Defiance*'s strongest resemblance to the SF Western occurred in the first season. The town of Defiance, built under the arch in former St. Louis, is a struggling community's chance at survival. Here, the Western frontier has been depicted true to its mythological form but with some contemporary updates. For example, the female characters no longer exist as secondary characters. Instead, the mayor is a woman, Amanda Rosewater, and the plot, while appearing to revolve around the "lawkeeper" character, Joshua Nolan, actually focuses on his adopted alien daughter, Irisa. Here, the cast of characters is decidedly familiar. We have representations of the law, Amanda and Nolan; the criminal element, Datak Tarr; the prostitute, Kenya Rosewater; and the wealthy landowner, Rafe McCawley. The notable changes to the Western construction pertain to the characters and their societal roles. Unlike *Dances with Wolves*, which separates white people and the Sioux (the Other), *Defiance*'s communal structure includes both those from Earth, the representation of whites, and the Other, the aliens. In the series, various alien races have warred with humans in an attempt to reside on Earth. Eventually, the war is declared a stalemate, and many that remain try to live together in a desperate effort to survive. Irisa, the focal point of the plot, is rescued by Nolan as a child and becomes one of his deputies; she is also an Irathient—an alien. While the series endeavors to alter Western gender constructs, racial divisions remain intact. While the city of Defiance has a diverse community, there is a lack of acceptance for those who would be considered non-white. Irisa has alien features, a red complexion, and a tendency to be violent. She exemplifies the Native American stereotype; in fact, her species is segregated from everyone else, and at one point in the series Irisa joins them.

During the eighteenth- to nineteenth-century westward expansion, those deemed Other were subjected to discriminatory practices, culminating in constant displacement. Native Americans were objectified in order to ensure compliance during the power and land grab that was the American West. As Brett H. Butler shows in his essay in this collection about *Guardians of the Galaxy*, inappropriate portrayals of Native Americans have continued in contemporary films. The year 2014 also brought audiences the CW's release of the series, *The 100*. In "Wanheda, Commander of Death, Healer: Hybrid Female Identities in the Post-Apocalyptic Wars of *The 100*," Lindsey Mantoan examines the series' female characters, both human and alien. Mantoan shows that traditional (constructed) gender lines have been blurred, that female characters in this series successfully navigate their respective society by taking non-gendered societal roles. Notably, this contribution from the CW also reflects the viewership and the times as *The 100* also offers positive LGBTQ characters to its viewers.

In 2014, Marvel Studios released their foray into the SF Western, *Guardians of the Galaxy*, which has continued with the sequel, *Guardians of the Galaxy Vol. 2* (2017), and the appearance of the characters in *The Avengers: Infinity War* (2018). Brett H. Butler, in "The Most Dangerous Woman in the Universe: Redefining Gamora as a Female Native American in *Guardians of the Galaxy*," delves into both the Marvel film and comic book versions of *Guardians of the Galaxy*. Butler explores the female character, Gamora, as a representation of the stereotypical Native American character construct. While Butler reveals that comic book characters and their formations in film do not show advancement for female characters, Laurie Ringer shows that there are more possibilities in literature. Becky Chambers' novel, *The Long Way to a Small, Angry Planet* (2014) offers the Other character acceptance whereas humanity receives rebukes for its exclusivity and self-oriented behavior. Humanity has had to leave Earth after it causes its own environmental disaster. The captain, Ashby Santoso, sums up humanity's migration to the frontier and their desire to reconstitute their lives there: "To some, Humans, the promise of a patch of land was worth any effort. It was an oddly predictable sort of behavior. Humans had a long, storied, history of forcing their way into places where they didn't belong" (203). Through the experiences of the crew, including the female human protagonist, Rosemary, who has a relationship with a female of another species, Chambers offers her readers an inclusive frontier where humans must live in harmony with others in order to ensure their survival. Ringer's "Accidents of Occidentalism: Women, Science Fiction and Westerliness in Becky Chambers and Nnedi Okorafor" offers the reader a refreshing look at both of Chambers' novels, *LWTSAP* and *A Closed and Common Orbit* (2017). So that Ringer may fully document changes made to female characters, she has included Nnedi Okorafor's Binti novella series in her examination. Importantly, Ringer shows that some contemporary female writers give readers inclusive Western environments rather than those only devoted to Caucasian heterosexual males. Ringer's essay is timely as Chambers and Okorafor have both been nominated for numerous awards stemming from their aforementioned publications, which include females of various ethnicities and sexual orientations.

The bonanza for the SF Western reader and viewer happened in 2015. During this year, the SyFy Channel and the Space Channel in Canada jointly released *Killjoys*, *Dark Matter*, and *The Expanse*, all television series that revolve around the concept of the frontier and the capable female character. With 2015 came televised productions and literary constructions bringing strong female leads to audiences, ones that defy the pioneer woman/prostitute woman constructions standard in representations of the West. For example, in *Killjoys* Dutch is the captain and the highest-ranking Reclamation Agent/Killjoy (bounty hunter) on her ship. Dutch and two brothers, D'avin and John Jaqobis, reside on the ship but have an affinity for Old Town, a frontier town inside the Quad. While a Killjoy is supposed to be neutral, Dutch and the Jaqobis brothers choose to side with the hard-working, underprivileged non-conformists in Old Town. For almost the entire series, although Dutch's background remains a mystery even to her, the protagonist's motivations are consistently clear. Dutch is loyal to her crew, her friends, her job, and her community. As the series progresses, Dutch is no longer wary of accepting a community, thereby abandoning her solitary lifestyle. The protagonist is physically capable of combat—she has been trained as an assassin—and is mentally astute. Dutch is the twenty-first-century version of the pioneer woman, but with some notable exceptions. First, a female of color is the series' lead. Second, it is Dutch who does the majority of the saving in the series rather than being saved.

The literary portion of the collection concludes with Selena Middleton's essay, "If He Can Break It In, She Can Break It Out: The Public Impact of Domestic Machines in Elizabeth Bear's *Karen Memory*," about Karen Memery's Seattle exploits. Here, Middleton reveals how the protagonist, who begins *Karen Memory* (2015) working for a madam, utilizes her agency to escape from the brothel and keep other women from harm. It should be noted that Bear has been the subject of some controversy. In 2009, Bear wrote a blog post in which she attempted to explain how she included in one of her novels a multicultural cast of characters and how she believed she was unsuccessful in this attempt. Bear's blog post was problematic and offensive, and is now referred to as "RaceFail." Significantly, Middleton observes that while the lead of *Karen Memory* is white, there are women of color and trans characters in Bear's novel. She shows that for one of her latest works, Bear has created an inclusive community of women who support and encourage one another. The reader should observe that while Bear may create a diverse cast and a dynamic character in Karen, she also places an adolescent female protagonist in a brothel. With some exceptions, this collection shows that writers of twentieth-first-century literary contributions to the SF Western subgenre create confident female characters that are definitely an improvement over past incarnations but are not ideal just yet.

As Middleton identifies and is reflected in Canadian Madeline Ashby's novel *Company Town* (2016), women's bodies are still for sale in twenty-first-century literary contributions. In her transhumanist novel Ashby creates a new frontier, which exists in Eastern Canada as a human-made oil platform comprised of towers. Go Jung-hwa (Hwa) is Ashby's biracial protagonist, a female bodyguard who identifies as Korean and works for Mistress Séverine. At the start of the novel, Hwa ensures the safety of the unionized sex workers employed by Séverine, showing that once again in the mythologized West, a woman is primarily valued for her body first then her intelligence. Ashby's biopunk/SF Western novel fits the contemporary mold due to Ashby's attempt at diversity: Hwa is Asian and in her New Arcadia community she is considered disabled—she is organic, thereby having an unaugmented body. When selling her services as a bodyguard to Zachariah Lynch, the head of the corporation that has taken over New Arcadia, Daniel Síofra refers to Hwa as "Pure" (39). Daniel, who works for Urban Tactics, recruits Hwa to safeguard the heir to the Lynch corporation. Near the novel's conclusion, the time-traveling megalomaniacal villain, Branch, discusses how Joel Lynch and his generational ship are the future of the Lynch corporation. In order to en- sure that humanity ventures into space, Branch tells Hwa he is going to force Joel's metamorphosis into the leader that his group desires, that "'All you need are some images of nebulae and some swelling violins and suddenly every- one believes in manifest destiny again'" (268). So that humanity may conquer space, Branch indicates that colonization is a part of humanity's destiny. The farcical nature of space as utopic is indicated as is the human-made environ- mentally destructive oil platforms. Ultimately, Ashby presents readers with a SF Western/biopunk novel that in some ways is progressive, but in others is regressive. Offering a biracial female lead who is differently abled (disabled in her society due to her seizure disorder and physical "stain") and has phys- ically acuity is promising. It is disappointing for readers that an invisible per- son saves Hwa from death and her medical ailment, including her physical manifestation of it, is "cured" in the conclusion. The female character saves her charge but is unable to help herself, thereby channeling the mother/child positioning in which the mother sacrifices herself for her child. In reference to differently abled people and how others look at them, Rosemarie Gar- land Thomson states that "When we ourselves develop disabilities, we often hide them as well, sometimes through semantic slights-of-hand, sometimes through normalizing medical procedures that erase disability, and sometimes through closeting our conditions" (*Staring*). It is troubling that Ashby's Hwa does these things while feeling inferior to others because she appears phys- ically different. She concludes the novel with an idealized physical body, a male partner, Daniel, who is also perfect, and their child, Joel. The nuclear family symbolically exists once more and the inclusive New Arcadian society with gender-fluid characters is destroyed. Ashby's progressive text is undone by its close, leaving readers to wonder at the hopelessness of Ashby's ending and poor choices that she made.

Westworld: *The SF Western of the Future*

Of late, the SF Western film *Westworld* (1973) has been adapted as a television series on HBO (2016–present). The film, starring Yul Brynner, was billed as a science fiction remake of *The Magnificent Seven*. Michael Crichton,

Westworld's director and screenwriter, called it "a fantasy about robots." To further the futuristic appearance of the film, Crichton created "the first feature film to process imagery by computer," which contributed to it becoming a money-making hit. The subsequent series has received rave reviews, garnering a significant fan base in a short period of time. The series has been so popular that HBO contracted for a second season, released in April 2018, and launched a merchandising campaign on its website. In fact, Audi is marketing its A6 utilizing a set reminiscent of that belonging to *Westworld*. As with the myth of the American West, the series concentrates on the perception of space. In Crichton's film, the Delos amusement park is divided into three sections: Western, Roman, and Medieval, with human gratification being the constant. Now, the series has a decidedly contemporary feel to it as the female host, Dolores Abernathy (Evan Rachel Wood), is the protagonist with Maeve Millay (Thandie Newton) in the secondary storyline. As the episodes progress, the audience is treated to a decidedly stereotypical American Western mythological story but with a twist previously witnessed in *Defiance*. In both SF and the American Western mythology, a primary theme is that of exploration. The visitors to the park are engaged in pushing their personal boundaries as are the female hosts, Dolores and Maeve. Rather than concentrating the plot on what may be considered the Western norm—the black-hatted gunslinger (Man in Black, played by Ed Harris), or the proverbial white-hat (the younger incarnation of William), the writers have chosen the pioneer woman and her journey to awareness as the focal point. The pioneer woman construct decidedly takes on a new meaning. Both Dolores, the homesteader, and Maeve, the madam, are pioneer women in their own right as both have exceeded their programming in order to become human. In "A Host of Questions: Women's Artificial Agency in *Westworld*," Maria Elena Torres-Quevedo argues that the primary female characters—Dolores and Maeve—in the series take on the roles of the virgin and the whore. The virgin and whore binary (Mother Mary and Mary Magdalene) is common in works connected to Christianity and is reflected in traditional female Western character constructions. Torres-Quevedo examines Dolores and Maeve as being both innocent and worldly. In "Triggered: The Post-Traumatic Woman and Narrative Agency in HBO's *Westworld*," writing team Keith Clavin and Christopher J. La Casse envision Dolores as suffering from trauma stemming from her transition as a static android to a self-aware female being. *Westworld*'s production and its positive female roles point to the continuation of advancement in the creation of the SF Western. As *Westworld* has continued past its initial season into the second (renewed for a third) with Dolores and Maeve at the helm of the latest episodes, viewers can be hopeful that the representations of females in the SF Western will continue to develop in the future.

WORKS CITED

Abbott, Carl. *Frontiers Past and Future: Science Fiction and the American West*. UP of Kansas, 2006.

Ashby, Madeline. *Company Town*. Tom Doherty, 2016.

Baym, Nina. *Women Writers of the American West, 1833–1927*. U of Illinois P, 2011.

Briley, Ron. "Gene Autry and the *Phantom Empire*: the Cowboy in the Wired West of the Future." *Journal of Texas Music History*, vol. 10, no. 1, 2010, pp. 1–11. http://gato-docs. its.txstate.edu/jcr:877ef6b0-2968-462f-afac-13b6cff31c0d/.

Burroughs, Edgar Rice. *A Princess of Mars*. 1917. Open Road. Kindle.

Chambers, Becky. *The Long Way to a Small, Angry Planet*. Harper Voyager, 2015.

Crichton, Michael. "Westworld." *The Official Site of Michael Crichton*, http://www. michaelcrichton.com/westworld/.

"Errand of Mercy." *Star Trek*, created by Gene Roddenberry, performance by William Shatner, season 1, episode 26, Desilu Studios, 1967.

Etulain, Richard. "Broncho Billy, William S. Hart, and Tom Mix: the Rise of the Hollywood Western." *The Hollywood West: Lives of Film Legends Who Shaped It*, edited by Richard W. Etulain and Glenda Riley, Fulcrum Publishing, 2001, pp. 1–19.

_____. Introduction. *The Hollywood West: Lives of Film Legends Who Shaped It*, edited by Richard W. Etulain and Glenda Riley, Fulcrum Publishing, 2001, pp. viii–xiii.

"A Fistful of Datas." *Star Trek: the Next Generation*, created by Gene Roddenberry, performance by Patrick Stewart, season 6, episode 8, Paramount Studios, 1992.

"Gene Roddenberry's Wagon Train to 'Star Trek.'" *Newsweek*, 3 Jan. 2016, http://www. newsweek.com/wagon-train-stars-410030/.

Gilman, Sander L. "Black Bodies, White Bodies: Toward an Iconography of Female Sexuality in Late Nineteenth-Century Art, Medicine, and Literature." *Critical Inquiry*, vol. 12, no. 1, 1985, pp. 204–42.

Green, Paul. Preface. *Encyclopedia of Weird Westerns*. 2nd edition. McFarland, 2016, pp. 1–3.

Hutcheon, Linda. *A Theory of Adaptation*. 2006. 2nd edition. Routledge, 2013.

Katerberg, William H. *Future West: Utopia and Apocalypse in Frontier Science Fiction*. UP of Kansas, 2008.

Kolodny, Annette. *The Land Before Her: Fantasy and Experience of the American Frontiers, 1630–1860*. U of North Carolina P, 1984.

Lamont, Victoria. *Westerns: a Woman's History*. U of Nebraska P, 2016.

Maddrey, Joseph. *The Quick, the Dead and the Revived: the Many Lives of the Western Film*. McFarland, 2016.

Miller, Cynthia J. Introduction. *Encyclopedia of Weird Westerns*. 2nd edition. McFarland, 2016, pp. 4–13.

Mogen, David. *Wilderness Visions: Then Western Theme in Science Fiction Literature*. 1982. Edited by Daryl F. Mallett, Borgo Press/Wildside Press, 1993.

Peebles, Stacey. "The Western and Film." *The Cambridge Companion To The Literature of the American West*, edited by Steven Frye, Cambridge UP, 2016, pp. 119–135.

Richardson, Jeffrey. "'Cowboys and Robots: the Birth of the Science Fiction Western.'" *Crossed Genres*, crossedgenres.com/archives/006/cowboys-and-robots-by-jeffrey-richardson/.

Rieder, John. "American Frontiers." *The Cambridge Companion to American Science Fiction*, edited by Eric Carl Link and Gerry Canavan. Cambridge UP, 2015, pp. 167–178.

Riley, Glenda. "Barbara Stanwyck: Feminizing the Western Film." *The Hollywood West: Lives of Film Legends Who Shaped It*, edited by Richard W. Etulain and Glenda Riley, Fulcrum Publishing, 2001, pp. 121–140.

"Shindig." *Firefly*, created by Joss Whedon, performances by Nathan Fillion and Gina Torres, season 1, episode 4, Mutant Enemy, 2002.

Slotkin, Richard. *Gunfighter Nation: the Myth of the Frontier in Twentieth-Century America*. U of Oklahoma P, 1998.

Stableford, Brian. "Science Fiction Before the Genre." *The Cambridge Companion to Science Fiction*, edited by Farah Mendlesohn and Edward James, Cambridge UP, 2009, pp. 15–31.

Sterling, Bruce. Preface. *Mirrorshades: the Cyberpunk Anthology*, edited by Bruce Sterling, Ace Books, 1998, pp. ix–xvi.

Thomson, Rosemarie Garland. *Extraordinary Bodies: Figuring Physical Disability in American Culture and Literature.* Columbia UP, 1997.
_____. *Staring: How We Look.* Oxford UP, 2009. Kindle.
Westfahl, Gary. "Introduction: Frontiers Old and New." *Space and Beyond: the Frontier Theme in Science Fiction,* edited by Gary Westfahl, Greenwood, 2000, pp. 1–5.
_____. "Space Opera." *The Cambridge Companion To Science Fiction,* edited by Edward James and Farah Mendlesohn, Cambridge UP, 2003, pp. 197–208.
Westfahl, Gary, editor. *Space and Beyond: the Frontier Theme in Science Fiction.* Greenwood, 2000.

Mara Jade, Frontier Woman

Agency in Star Wars *and Influencing the Transmedia Franchise*

Monica Louzon

Since the release of *Star Wars: A New Hope* in 1977, the *Star Wars* franchise has evolved into a global transmedia phenomenon that includes films, books, graphic novels, video games, radio shows, television series, and toys. Set in a galaxy rife with untamed frontiers, the *Star Wars* film saga presents viewers with the classic struggle of good against evil in a space backdrop reminiscent of the American West. The widespread appeal of *Star Wars'* broad, relatable themes, the galactic scope of its fictional universe, and the mystical Force powers accessible to its Jedi and other Force-users created demand among fans for more *Star Wars* stories and paved the way for the franchise's expansion into other media. One of the key off-screen characters the *Star Wars* expanded universe explored was that of Mara Jade: assassin, spy, pilot, smuggler, Jedi, mentor, wife, and mother. This essay explores the degree of Jade's agency in the *Star Wars* universe, compares the extent of Mara's agency in the Science Fiction Western *Star Wars* universe with that of historical women of the American West, and underscores her importance as arguably the first dynamic female character with true agency in the *Star Wars* transmedia franchise.

This essay primarily focuses upon the plot arc set forth in the original and prequel *Star Wars* trilogies (1977–1983 and 1999–2005, respectively), and the original *Star Wars* Expanded Universe from the release of Timothy Zahn's Thrawn Trilogy in the early 1990s through the early 2010s. For the purposes of this essay, the American West refers to the western frontiers of the United States as it expanded from the Appalachian Mountains to the Pacific Coast between the late eighteenth and mid-twentieth centuries.

Star Wars, *a Science Fiction Western*

Star Wars shares many elements and tropes with Western-themed films and pulp Western fiction. In "Pulp Science Fiction," Jess Nevins asserts that pulp fiction across all genres emphasizes adventure, drama, and the avoidance of the mundane; pulp fiction exploits the exotic, emphasizes plot events and exaggerated emotions over character growth, and features a defined moral binary in which good typically defeats evil (93). The *Star Wars* films feature the characteristics Nevins names. For example, in the Original Trilogy (OT), Luke Skywalker abandons the boredom of moisture farming on a backwater planet to seek out adventure on a new frontier. Richard Slotkin argues that "both the *Star Wars* trilogy and the *Star Trek* series project a myth of historical progress similar to that in the progressive Westerns and 'empire' movies of the 30s and 40s" (635). In his analysis of the *Star Wars* landscape, "Design for Screen SF," Piers D. Britton states that "*Star Wars*'s aesthetic evokes the mixture of flyblown shabbiness and dustily expansive natural grandeur which John Ford, Sergio Leone, and Henry Hathaway has rendered so picturesque in their Technicolor westerns" (343). Additionally, both the Prequel Trilogy (PT) and the OT visually highlight the exotic, as Nevins notes, by regularly presenting viewers with new planets, aliens, ships, and costumes. In the classic battle of good versus evil, the light side always defeats the dark side of the Force in the end. In his concluding chapter to *Gunfighter Nation*, Slotkin emphasizes the Western elements in *Star Wars*:

> The worlds of *Star Wars*, and of films similarly set either in fantasy-worlds or galaxies "far far away," are presented to us as alternatives to the historicized spaces of the Western and pseudo-documentary or "journalistic" space of the crime film. Like fairy tales, they allegorize the condition and etiology of the present world, but they purchase imaginative freedom—the power to imagine the most magical or utopian possibilities—by keeping real historical referents at a distance [636].

Other more overt tropes specific to Western pulps and films also appear in the *Star Wars* films. Yvonne Tasker notes that Western tropes in cinema include the celebration of white masculinity and violence: the hero's violence is required to create a safe community in which he will forever remain an outsider, finding more harmony in the natural landscape than mingling with other people (112–3). One could interpret the actions of Anakin Skywalker, misguided as they are, as demonstrating this white masculinity found in Western heroes. In *Revenge of the Sith*, Anakin commits atrocities, including killing a cadre of Jedi students, because he believes he is creating a safer galaxy in which he will be able to save his wife from death and become one of only two living Sith lords. In the OT, Luke is a more typical Western hero: he helps destroy two massive battle stations and tries to kill Emperor Palpatine.

Similar to his father, Luke wants to create a safer galaxy, but he will be the only surviving Jedi until he can train more Force-sensitives in the Jedi way. Both Anakin and Luke, who are portrayed by white male actors, are willing to employ violence to safeguard the galaxy for posterity and, in the process, create for themselves unique outsider positions that place them outside the communities they are trying to help: Anakin, as the only extant Sith apprentice, and Luke, the only surviving Jedi. These tropes of pulp science fiction and Western films are integral to the *Star Wars* films and their ubiquitous nature fosters nostalgia toward the *Star Wars* characters and universe.

It should be no surprise, then, that fans clamored for more *Star Wars* upon the release of the first film, which prompted the creation of books and comic series that explored the adventures of Luke, Leia Organa, Han Solo, and other characters off-screen both before and after the OT. In "Military Culture," Steffen Hantke refers to *Star Wars* as "an intertextual behemoth," writing that "it is *Star Wars* that has come to define, for better or worse, the genre as it appears to average consumers" (331). The PT carried viewers to new frontiers as adventures on-screen unfolded on new planets not previously depicted in the OT. The galactic scope of the *Star Wars* films creates an unbounded imaginary frontier, much like the physical frontier encountered by historical American pioneers who explored and settled the United States' West. The boundaries of the American West shifted over time as the United States expanded during the late eighteenth to twentieth centuries; initially limited by the Appalachian Mountains, it edged further and further west until the frontier's westernmost limitation was the Pacific Ocean (Dixon 180–1). Carl Abbott noted the importance of physical setting in both fictional Western and science fiction media, observing that it serves as an active element in both genres and that "science fiction extends Western openness to infinity, from cold desert surfaces of the moon or Mars to wide-open spaces of entire galaxies" (12). The fact that the events of *Star Wars* are set "a long time ago in a galaxy far, far away" only further expands the imaginary and physical boundaries of the in-franchise universe. This generous physical setting means creators and consumers alike could explore new worlds, discover new characters, and experience new adventures without ever encountering the physical limitations of historic frontiers like that of the American West.

Female Agency in Star Wars

Previous academic studies and analyses of female characters' agency in *Star Wars* (Simpson, McDowell, Liedi and Reagin, Liedi, Hilck, and Wood) have almost exclusively focused on women represented in the *Star Wars* films and television series. Though women have been an intrinsic part of *Star Wars* since Princess Leia first appeared on-screen in *A New Hope* (ANH), their degree of agency has varied widely. The OT features three named women—Leia, Beru Lars, and Mon Mothma—but only two have significant roles. Although the PT includes more named women who deliver lines than the OT, the majority still "lack screen time and story-telling power" (Wood 64). Most named on-screen women in the OT and PT are relatively flat characters that can be easily categorized as good or evil because they are either presented as rebels, senators, and rulers trying to save the galaxy and protect their people, or they are more amoral and mercenary (Flotmann 230). According to Christina Flotmann, "the majority of the women depicted [in *Star Wars* are] not of decisive importance for the stories"; in other words, most women depicted in the plots of the OT and PT have little agency over their outcomes (231). Their lack of agency parallels that of women in films and fiction about the American West, of which Laura Woodworth-Ney observes "white women appear as supporting characters, but they lack real decision-making authority, and ethnic or racial women appear as prostitutes or as bad influences, if they appear at all" (1). This congruence between representations of women in the cinematic West and in the first six *Star Wars* films further supports categorizing the latter as a Science Fiction Western.

Since the release of the OT and PT trilogies, however, Lucasfilm, Ltd., the company that owns the copyright to *Star Wars*, has worked to address this lack of female agency in its animated television series *The Clone Wars* (2008–2014) and *Rebels* (2014–2018). Critics, such as Philip L. Simpson, note the irony in *Star Wars*: although both the PT and OT each feature women in positions of power (Padmé Amidala and Leia, respectively) who challenge the political status quo of their eras, the narrative that features such strong female characters then attempts to contain and even dissemble their power. Simpson argues this deconstruction takes place "first by coding their exercise of autonomy as *frigidity* and then placing both women in relationships that demand not just *thawing* but melting of their icy feminine royalty" (Simpson 115–6). At the beginning of the PT, Padmé is a queen with planetary authority and the bravery to challenge the decisions made by the Galactic Supreme Chancellor but, by the end of the trilogy, she occupies a minor, domestic, maternal role with no significant political or emotional influence over her husband, Anakin, or her own fate. Similarly, although Leia is initially presented in the OT as a spunky, strong-minded female lead, by the end of the trilogy, she arguably is also relegated to a passive, domestic role defined by her romantic relationship with Han and her fraternal relationship with Luke. *The Clone Wars* (2008–2014) and *Rebels* (2014–present), however, portray female characters with more agency and driving force than found in either the OT or PT. By increasing the number of females with agency in the *Star Wars* universe, these television shows help "redefine *Star Wars* as a franchise that welcomes women and strives to make them visible in a number of roles" (Wood 74). The new *Star Wars* sequel trilogy, which continues the saga of the Skywalker family, and the *Star Wars* anthology film *Rogue One* (2016) have also portrayed female leads as women with decision-making power, independence, and the ability to take control of their fates. Although this shift toward intentional female empowerment in *Star Wars* occurred on-screen in the late 2000s and the 2010s, strong female characters with agency are not a new phenomenon in the *Star Wars* universe—they have existed off-screen since at least the early 1990s.

Star Wars *as a Transmedia Franchise*

The *Star Wars* novels, comics, video games, television series, and radio shows created between 1977 and 2012 all constitute an original Expanded Universe (EU) of in-universe history and lore set within the same transmedia franchise. Colin Harvey defines transmedia as relational storytelling that transcends any one medium, is typically governed by legal parameters, and relies on collective memory (1–2). According to Harvey, transmedia storytelling "tends to be characterized as telling *new* stories in different media but set within a consistent diagetic world" (3). The *Star Wars* franchise certainly satisfies Harvey's parameters: the stories of the EU feature timelines extending well beyond the story arcs of the *Star Wars* films themselves, exploring frontiers and introducing off-screen protagonists. Lucasfilm, Ltd. loosely oversaw and maintained some consistency across EU narratives through its official licensing process for decades until its acquisition by Disney in 2012. During this pre–Disney period, creators and fans arguably maintained the lore and "canon" of *Star Wars* through a collective memory-based hierarchy capped by the *Star Wars* films themselves.

In 2014, because Disney planned to begin producing new *Star Wars* films, it announced a new Lucasfilm story group would closely oversee and coordinate all aspects of *Star Wars* storytelling from that point forward to ensure consistency across future films and EU tales ("The Legendary Star Wars"). To further this narrative consistency and create a new creative frontier for the upcoming *Star Wars* films, Disney also announced the original EU would remain in print but sport a Legends banner on their covers to distinguish them from the new, coordinated *Star Wars* transmedia canon ("The Legendary Star Wars"). By creating an entirely new canon under Disney's Lucasfilm, the company enabled itself to produce cinematic sequels to the OT and even stand-alone anthology films without the constraints imposed by more than three decades of loosely-managed transmedia publishing in the *Star Wars* universe. Even more importantly, viewers of new *Star Wars* films would be able to immerse themselves in the new cinematic releases without needing to catch up on the extensive adventures and backstories published in the newly rebranded *Star Wars Legends*.

In academic circles, however, the *Star Wars* transmedia behemoth encounters the negative connotation still associated with popular culture franchises. Peter W. Lee describes this obstacle, noting that although transmedia franchises are "generally accepted as a legitimate source of scholarly attention," they still contain "a stigma of low-brow, disposable junk—merely fads for the masses, and surely not on equal footing as 'high' culture" (1). Because the desire to generate money from fans willing to consume any franchise tie-in products tends to be the driving force behind multimedia franchises like *Star Wars*, stories published within these shared universes are notorious for sacrificing quality in favor of expediency. The quantity-over-quality mindset that typifies transmedia franchise publishing has led academics to let these works fall by the wayside. *Star Wars Legends* does feature subpar writing—fans commonly cite Vonda McIntyre's *The Crystal Star* (1994) and Barbara Hambly's *Children of the Jedi* (1995) as the worst books in the original EU—but it also includes "classics" that marked turning points for the *Star Wars* franchise. The most notable of these *Star Wars* "classics" is Timothy Zahn's landmark Thrawn Trilogy, which introduces readers to former Imperial assassin Mara Jade and reinvigorated interest in the franchise just as popular demand flagged in the early 1990s.

Mara Jade, Emperor's Hand

Mara Jade, arguably the most iconic female character of *Star Wars Legends*, plays various roles throughout its narrative arcs and repeatedly exhibits agency as she refuses to let others dictate her fate. Between the early 1990s and early 2010s, readers of the original EU learned about Mara's service to the evil Emperor Palpatine as his personal assassin and spy, her struggles after his death in *Return of the Jedi* (RTJ) to find a place in the galaxy, her journey to become a Jedi, and her role as Luke Skywalker's wife and mother of their child, Ben. Mara defies SF Western tropes; in fact, the agency she demonstrates would not have been out of place on the frontiers of the actual American West.

Zahn's first *Star Wars* novel, *Heir to the Empire* (1991), introduces readers to Mara Jade several years after Palpatine's death. She has just been called to meet with Talon Karrde, the leader of the smuggling group with which she has worked for a few months:

The door slid open, and with her usual catlike grace Mara Jade walked into the room. "You didn't say what—" her green eyes flicked to the elaborately set table "—this was all about," she finished, her tone just noticeably different. The green eyes came back to him [Karrde], cool and measuring.

"No, it's not what you're thinking," Karrde assured her ... "This is a business meal—no more, no less" [29].

With this quick exchange, Zahn establishes Mara as a self-assured, intelligent woman who knows her own physical beauty but still prefers to achieve her goals through merit and skill, not shortcuts and seduction. As the dialogue continues, Karrde reveals he appreciates Mara's talents and wants to make Mara his second-in-command but makes clear this promotion is not motivated by romantic or sexual reasons; he finds her a valuable asset because she is a talented pilot, able to deliver and accept orders, and is flexible in unexpected situations. Although she remains wary throughout the conversation, once she ultimately accepts his offer events prove his intentions are, indeed, business-based. Through the exchange between Karrde and Mara, Zahn underscores Mara as a character respected by her male supervisor; unlike many women of pulp Westerns, Mara is invited to assume a decision-making role based on her skills alone.

One might argue Mara's wariness with Karrde reflects her desire to throw off the trope-filled role of a SF Western woman thrust upon her during her tenure as Emperor's Hand; many of Mara's disguises have her play the sexy yet dull-witted female who swoons over her male targets in order to accomplish Palpatine's goals. Taken by the Emperor from her parents at a young age due to her nascent Force sensitivity, Mara is raised on Palpatine's estate and becomes an expert combatant, spy, assassin, and duelist (Wallace 161). Her Force sensitivity enables her to telepathically communicate with the Emperor across the galaxy as she performs high-risk jobs in his name: including exposing traitors, eliminating enemies, and helping the Emperor maintain control over the planetary bureaucracies. In one instance early in her career as the Emperor's Hand—Palpatine's personal spy and assassin—Mara masquerades as a wealthy young countess to gain access to an Imperial commander's private offices and determine whether he has been embezzling funds from the Empire. In this instance, which is documented in Zahn's *Star Wars: Allegiance* (2008) amongst other sources, Mara relies on her physical attractiveness and disguises to elicit information from corrupt Imperials; she is Nevins' exotic female playing the seductress in a manner reminiscent of non-white women in pulp Western fiction (Nevins 93; Woodworth-Ney 1). During her time as Emperor's Hand, Mara does, to a certain extent, fit the trope of a SF Western woman who does not think critically and remains oblivious to the extent of the Empire's cruelty. For example, Mara believes the Emperor would never sanction the slaughter of innocent civilians even though such Imperial massacres are commonplace and, as a result, is perceived as "awfully naïve" by the soldiers with which she works (Zahn, *Allegiance*, 395).

Unlike the typical SF Western woman, however, Mara learns the value of acting judiciously and thinking critically during her tenure as Palpatine's Hand. Her role gives her the authority to use special code phrases to commandeer personnel and resources but doing so requires her to prove her identity to someone in the Imperial hierarchy and makes her vulnerable (see *Allegiance* and *Star Wars: Choices of One*). The need to protect her cover limits the frequency with which Mara can justify using her special authorities, forcing her to think through scenarios and evaluate whether revealing herself would ultimately compromise her mission. While working on missions for the Emperor, Mara also sometimes chooses to wait until she can uncover the facts before meting out Imperial justice. On one mission in Zahn's *Choices of One*, Mara opts not to immediately execute a bureaucrat for treason because she learns a local warlord kidnapped his family and could be manipulating him; instead, she decides she must first gather the evidence and assess whether his allegations of coercion are true. Although Mara is not willing to accept that the Empire is a flawed institution until after Palpatine's death, as Emperor's Hand, she values individuals who object to corruption, embezzlement, and other abuses of power and believes an institution capable of producing such people remains an institution that merits her energy, her life, and her allegiance. While operating under Palpatine's command, Mara may not be fully informed, but she demonstrates a capacity for analytic thinking uncharacteristic of women presented in SF Westerns. Her experiences as Emperor's Hand make her all the more attuned in a post–Palpatine galaxy to instances of potential favoritism based on her sex rather than her hard work and skills that readers might describe as "men's work."

One can draw parallels between Mara in her role as Emperor's Hand and the historic figure of Annie Oakley both women were highly skilled in their professions and relied on a certain amount of deception to execute their performances. Like Phoebe Ann Mosey (1860–1926), who was more commonly known as Annie Oakley, Mara relied on a certain degree of deception to execute the roles she assumed as she performed so-called "men's work." Oakley is best known for her performances as an ambidextrous sharpshooter in Buffalo Bill's Wild West Show, a touring exhibition about the American West that traveled throughout the United States and Europe. Similar to Mara, who traversed the galaxy in various disguises while on assignment for the Emperor, Oakley traveled great distances and performed for several European monarchs. In her examination of Oakley's performances and disruption of Victorian-era gender roles, Lisa Bernd notes that Oakley "often deliberately tripped over her own feet during a run of shots to make the trick look harder than it was" (44). If needed, Mara, too, feigned vapidity or weakness while operating in disguise to lull her targets into complacency and mitigate suspicion. Bernd continues to observe that Oakley's "dress, actions and associations resulted from the freedoms she experienced as a performer, especially as a woman doing a 'man's' work" (40).

Mara's duties as an assassin can be considered a "man's work" in Palpatine's Empire. The Emperor's closest associates on-screen in the PT and OT films are almost exclusively male and, even in the *Star Wars Legends* narratives, Palpatine has few close female associates and considers none of them his equals. The upper echelons of the Imperial military are primarily male, including all thirteen Grand Admirals of the Imperial Navy (Wallace and Peña 44–9). Less than a handful of Imperial women besides Mara prominently feature across plot arcs in *Star Wars Legends*, namely Natasi Daala, the first female Admiral in the Imperial Navy; Ysanne Isard, the Director of Imperial Intelligence; and Shira Brie, the Emperor's Hand, later known as the Dark Lady Lumiya (Wallace 33, 48–9, 83–5). Considering the paucity of named Imperial women in Legends who hold leading military roles and the number of named on-screen male Imperial leaders in the PT, the OT, and Legends, it is reasonable to declare that in her role as Imperial assassin and spy, Mara is—as Annie Oakley was—performing a "man's work" as the Emperor's Hand.

Like the female leads of the *Alien* (1979–2017) and *Terminator* (1984–2015) franchises, both of which were ongoing when Zahn wrote his Thrawn trilogy, Mara's character is not primarily a sex object or a helpless victim; like them, her heroism initially consists of personal survival (Faithful 349). Mara's desire to advance through life based on her own individual achievements and "men's work" after the Emperor's death is a tacit rejection of SF Western female tropes and falls far more in line with the determined independence demonstrated by American frontier women.

Mara Jade, a Journey of Self-Discovery

Mara's first true exercise in independence occurs after the death of Emperor Palpatine, a pivotal event that thrust her into a new, unpredictable life, much like that experienced by female settlers of the American frontier. Just before Palpatine's death, Mara receives a final telepathic command from the Emperor through the Force—to kill Luke. The command tests both her fealty and her agency as she tries to create a new life for herself. With Palpatine's death, Mara finds herself without a place in the galaxy because she worked outside the traditional Imperial hierarchy as the Emperor's Hand and no records were kept of her activities, leaving her without resources or contacts. The loss of the Emperor also means Mara loses her identity because she has defined herself for most of her life as his tool and servant. Now, she has no place in the post–Palpatine Empire—or, more accurately, the Imperial Remnant—because, for all intents and purposes, she never existed in the original

Empire. Thus, the Emperor's last command to her is one of her first tests of agency because only she would know whether she has fulfilled her final duty as his Hand.

The questions Mara faced about her own future after the Emperor's death echo some of the uncertainties encountered by the women of the American frontier as they grappled with new, unfamiliar responsibilities and increased agency. In her analysis of the westward migration of American women and their families in the late eighteenth century, Elizabeth J. Clapp observes that this journey was a testing ground because "the unpredictability of the trip itself and the perils faced along the way meant that women were unable to adhere to any rigid interpretation of what their role should be" (66). Mara's role as Emperor's Hand repeatedly places her in peril, and the role itself has no rigid guidelines; no two missions are identical, and there are no societal or administrative guidelines beyond how Palpatine's will shapes her duties. As with the female settlers who found themselves confronted with danger, unpredictability, and less well-defined gender roles, so, too, is Mara in service to the Emperor. For Mara, life becomes only more unstable and uncertain after Palpatine's death because she could no longer rely on Emperor-assigned missions to structure her life, rendering her future and role in society fluid like those of frontier women moving westward and fighting to survive.

Mara finds some structure in her work with Karrde's group of smugglers after the Emperor's death but finds her fealty to Palpatine tested and her destiny in flux after she first encounters Luke. Mara meets Luke during a galactic crisis: Imperial Grand Admiral Mitth'raw'nuruodo ("Thrawn"), forgotten in the wild Unknown Regions at the edge of the mapped galaxy, has returned to seize command of the Imperial Remnant and sends the fledgling New Republic into chaos. During Mara and Luke's duel with the clones of Joruus C'baoth, an insane clone of a dead Jedi, and Luke himself, C'baoth tries to force Mara to become his apprentice, arguing, "It is the destiny that is demanded of her by the Force" (Zahn, *The Last Command*, 330). Mara, however, has no interest in serving C'baoth and rejects his claims of predestination, asserting her agency and control over her own future rather than allying herself blindly to a new master. During the fight, Mara kills the clone Luke to save the real Luke; in doing so, she also fulfills the Emperor's last command by killing *a* Luke Skywalker. By opting to kill the clone and save the real Luke, Mara both proves her fealty to Palpatine and demonstrates creative control over her own future. Mara again rejects the choice to ally herself with a new master by electing to remain a member of Karrde's smuggling organization rather than follow Luke to become a student at his Jedi Academy. Although Mara visits the Academy periodically, she feels she "deserved at least a little special consideration" after saving Luke's life and cannot commit to becoming a Jedi Knight (Zahn, *Vision of the Future*, 25; 111). Rather than place herself in a position of dependency upon Luke by staying at the Jedi Academy, Mara picks the future that best empowers her and returns to her work as Karrde's second-in-command. In this role, she enjoys the freedom to run missions for the smuggling organization and explore the galaxy, taking on the role of the male Western hero exploring the American frontier.

In her refusal to apprentice herself to C'baoth and to attend Luke's Jedi Academy, Mara rejects the SF Western trope of dependent females while revealing her desire for an existence not defined by her allegiance to other Force-users. Mara's rejection of taking on a new master is similar to the stubborn independence asserted by some women of the American West when their husbands deserted them or died. Casey Ryan Kelly describes the factors that led female settlers to take control of their households:

> In the nineteenth century American West … particularly during the settlement of California and the Pacific Northwest, women who lost their husbands to the hardships of the overland journey, the seductions of gold mining, or who migrated west on their own to seek a richer life were able to choose independence by refusing to relinquish control over their household affairs to a new husband [204].

Once given a taste of independence, these women were not necessarily ready to take on a new husband and give up their newfound agency simply because they had a new spouse who could perform a "man's work" around the homestead. They developed an appreciation for their own gender role-defying aptitudes, just as Mara does for her own capabilities as she learns more about herself and what she wants for her own life after Palpatine dies.

Mara Jade, the Guardian

In Zahn's *Vision of the Future* (1998), once Mara understands her own capabilities and the implications of taking agency over her own fate, she can move forward and assume new roles. These roles overlap with frontier women's roles and those belonging to the trope of the pulp Western mother figure. Mara becomes a Jedi Knight, takes on the role of instructor at Luke's Jedi Academy, and marries Luke after realizing her attempts to cut herself from emotional attachments have stunted her own development as a Jedi and a person. Mara's decision to marry Luke stems from a near-death experience they share while attempting to uncover the truth behind a plot to destabilize the New Republic and restore the Imperial Remnant to its former glory, as recounted in Zahn's *Hand of Thrawn* duology. As death by drowning draws near, the pair connects telepathically through the Force. In that moment, Mara realizes how badly she has wanted to be close to another person "who understood her as intimately as she understood him" and how, after so many years, "her determination to lock herself away from others had ended up hurting her [,] had stunted her own growth and life just as her stubborn refusal to accept the responsibility of her Jedi abilities had limited their growth" (Zahn, *Vision of the Future*, 476). Although Mara telepathically connects to Palpatine during her service as Emperor's Hand, she is simply a tool to him; while bonding with Luke, Mara realizes that he sees her as an equal and cares deeply for her. By choosing to open her mind and heart to Luke through the Force and in marriage, Mara also opens herself to a new, more domestic role—that of wife and mother—that echoes the frontier mother's experience.

In *The New Jedi Order* series, which is set several years after Mara marries Luke, she contracts a mysterious, lethal illness and discovers she is pregnant with Luke's child. These challenges parallel experiences of some pregnant women of the American West as Mara's agency over her own fate is tested. Mara's pregnancy is fraught with insecurity: her illness relapses then returns, and she obsesses over the potential harm it might do her unborn son, Ben Skywalker. Even worse, she fears she will be unable to protect her son after his birth and questions whether the role of mother will come as easily to her as her prior roles have. Because Mara is slowly wasting away, she finds herself more physically limited than she ever has before in her life. Mara's experiences during pregnancy mirror those of pregnant women living on the frontier and parallel some of those had by frontier missionary women. In the nineteenth century, pregnant women were considered infirmed, and "during pregnancy, women stayed inside, visited only with close family and friends" because "[f]ertility and childbirth were often viewed as akin to illness" (Woodworth-Ney 107). During her pregnancy, Mara is isolated—cut off from her customary freedom to roam the galaxy because her body cannot handle the same stressors. She interacts primarily with close family, friends, and her medic—as pregnant women of the West were. Unlike her real-life Western counterparts, however, Mara's isolation is due to a physical illness, not the societal misconceptions held by those around her.

When Mara's illness begins gaining ground, she tries to hold it off by pouring all her energy into a Force barrier protecting her womb and son from the disease. During one of her visits with a Jedi healer, Mara admits, "I already knew it [the illness] was coming back. I thought if I was alone, in total concentration and without distraction, I might be able to control it like I did before" by putting all her energy into the Force barrier (Keyes, *Edge of Victory II: Rebirth* 155). In her steadfast unwillingness to allow the disease to afflict her unborn son, Mara resembles Mother Amadeus, a missionary nun in Montana who refused to yield to societal biases, illness, or infirmity in the pursuit of her mission and whose self-discipline and fiery spirit inspired the nuns she supervised (Butler 102). Like Mother Amadeus, Mara holds out against the disease and ultimately triumphs, surviving and safely delivering her son, exhibiting the same willfulness that allowed women like Mother Amadeus to succeed in the harsh physical environment of the American West. Mara's ferocity and willingness to sacrifice her own life force to protect her son exemplifies her desire to have some control over the future, and she succeeds, giving birth to Ben and sending the illness into a permanent remission.

More than a decade later, in the *Legacy of the Force* series, Mara finds herself exercising a different kind of agency over her fate: choosing her death, and, in doing so, utterly challenging the science fiction trope of the absent mother. By this time, Ben has become a Jedi apprentice to Jacen Solo and commander of a special counterterrorism force for the Galactic Alliance ruling the galaxy. Mara, however, suspects Jacen may have fallen to the dark side and could be leading her son down the same path. When Ben reveals Jacen is voluntarily aiding Luke's former nemesis Lumiya, however, Mara justifies using the skills she developed as Emperor's Hand to protect her child and sets out to kill Jacen after assessing her nephew has fallen too far into self-obsession and the dark side to redeem. In Karen Traviss' *Sacrifice* (2008), Mara tracks Jacen down and duels him in melee combat but, ultimately, falls victim to a Force illusion he uses to project Ben's face over his own, allowing Jacen to fell her with a poison dart. Even as the poison's lethal paralytic effects set in, Mara remains lucid and defiant to the end, telling Jacen, that although he thinks he has beaten her, she refuses to let him destroy her son's future.

Mara was always been a present, engaged parent before and after Ben's birth up until her death during his late adolescence. Although the absent mother trope exists in *Star Wars* (i.e., Padmé died giving birth to Luke and Leia) and is common in science fiction, Mara's presence in her son's life is more in keeping with the mother figure of pulp Westerns. While she is not passive and domestic, Mara does play an active role in raising Ben and tries to guide him out of trouble, which, in this case, is the dark side. When she sets out on her hunt for Jacen, Mara knows that she is risking her life trying to kill a Sith as she has worked for one for most of her youth. In choosing to pursue Jacen, Mara chooses to sacrifice herself to safeguarding her son's future and rid the galaxy of another evil Force-wielder who aspired to be a galactic despot and, in doing so, she demonstrates the same determination in the face of adversity demonstrated by mothers of the fictional and actual American frontier.

Mara's fierce, single-minded desire to keep Ben safe is reminiscent of the same protective instinct demonstrated by female settlers of the American West toward their own children. For example, settlers of Appalachia in the mid- and late eighteenth century lived under constant threat of violence because of white settlers' encroachment on Indian hunting grounds, inter-colonial conflicts, and colonial power struggles with Great Britain (Clapp 66). This persistent threat of violence meant that the female settlers performing their duties on the homestead needed "to remain watchful and ready to protect their families in the event of a raid. The nature of settler women's work might leave them isolated and unprotected" because they had to "spend a great deal of time at their homestead either alone or with small children" and they "had to be inventive and use their own initiative in order to defend themselves" in the event of an attack by Native Americans (69–70). Like the women of the Appalachian frontier, Mara lives with what was essentially a constant threat of violence: her husband Luke and her in-laws Leia and Han are prominent figures on the galactic stage. Mara's closest living relatives are prime targets for assassination, as are the Solo's Force-wielding children. This meant that, from the moment he is conceived, Ben is in danger. Mara needs to remain watchful and alert to best keep Ben safe—to protect him first from the disease that almost killed her, and later, from Lumiya and Jacen. Just as frontier mothers had to be inventive, so does Mara; she draws upon her own life force to keep Ben safe while she is pregnant, and then has to think unconventionally as she investigates the potential threat Jacen poses to Ben's wellbeing. Like the women of back-country Appalachia, Mara even needs "to be careful not to undermine men's sense of themselves as protectors" (Clapp 74). When Mara leaves to hunt Lumiya and Jacen in *Sacrifice*, she avoids waking Luke because she knows he would try to stop her from killing their nephew and risking her life for their son's safety. By slipping out without telling Luke her plans, Mara takes initiative to defend her family and son without directly challenging Luke's self-identification as her husband and protector and subverts SF Western tropes of passive, dependent wives. Mara's initiative, inventiveness, and self-sacrifice would not have been uncharacteristic of a woman who wanted to defend her family on the Appalachian frontier.

Conclusion

Mara's strong-willed, independent character more closely parallels the actual women of the historical American West than it does the women of SF Westerns. Women of the American West demonstrated agency and adaptability, and Laura Woodworth-Ney argues that the history of women of the American West features most prominently the theme of "the fluidity, complexity, and interconnectedness of women's lives. Women's lives are not compartmentalized, and neither is the history of their experiences" (xvi). Like actual women of the American West, Mara Jade's story is one of flexibility, which is one of the very traits Karrde praises her for when offering her the chance to be his second-in-command; of complexity, for Mara is a character with a complex backstory and emotions who consistently attempts to seize control of her fate; and of interconnectedness, because Mara falls back on her experiences and past roles to address and overcome new challenges. In the same way that real women of the historical American West assumed diverse and adaptive roles and played critical roles in the real-world drama of the West (Jones and Wills 122), so too is Mara a critical player in *Star Wars Legends* as a female character with agency participating in pivotal galactic events. She directly serves the Emperor during his reign, conducting investigations and enforcing Palpatine's will throughout the galaxy. As a smuggler and pilot, Mara participates in the fledgling New Republic's battles against the Imperial Remnant resurgent and helps defeat a crazed clone Jedi Master who, together, threatened the return of democracy to the galaxy. As a Jedi and mother, Mara investigates and hunts her power-hungry nephew who turns to the dark side and is on the path to becoming a galactic dictator, as he believes only he can bring stability to the galaxy and sacrifices herself to protect her son's future. Contrary to the domestic women found in some SF Westerns, Mara is not limited by gender roles and more closely parallels the lives of historical women of the West. In the American West, "Gender roles as dictated by popular culture translated into 'men's' jobs and 'women's' jobs on the homestead.... However, the dictates of the frontier economy frequently saw this system break down" (Jones and Wills 133). In the *Star Wars* galaxy, societal gender roles certainly exist, but these roles vary widely across cultures and planets. As there are more genders in the *Star Wars* galaxy than social binaries of male/female gender roles allow for, it would be unfeasible to confine a specific set of roles to one gender galaxy-wide, and the frontier-like environment of the *Star Wars* galaxy further makes it impossible for a restrictive, defined social gender hierarchy to exist. Instead, the *Star Wars* galaxy created for Mara a realm of opportunities for personal advancement, particularly after Emperor Palpatine's death, in a manner similar to how the West "volunteered an intense and colorful theater for female advancement" for women who chose to resist contemporary social gender conventions (Jones and Wills 141).

Mara Jade, though no longer a "canon" character in the ongoing *Star Wars* Expanded Universe, remains one of the most influential characters in the history of the *Star Wars* transmedia franchise and, perhaps, in its future, too. Mara's life, as explored in *Star Wars Legends*, encompasses a narrative trajectory that the Lucasfilm story group and new *Star Wars* EU writers must still consider when plotting out the future of the Skywalker family and other characters within the *Star Wars* universe. Because the *Star Wars Legends* narratives in which Mara appears would create too many limitations upon the storylines for the *Star Wars* sequel trilogy films, Mara will almost certainly not appear in the new *Star Wars* canon as Luke's wife. Nevertheless, she could still be included in this new EU as a character—perhaps with the same name, perhaps not—who possesses the same personality, independent streak, complex toolbox of skills, and perhaps even some of the same early back story as the Mara of *Star Wars Legends*. Indeed, each of the sequel trilogy films has been surrounded by rumors during filming that an incarnation of Mara Jade might appear on-screen, particularly the last of the three sequel trilogy films (Hood). Ignoring Mara's story within *Star Wars Legends* would place limitations on the possibilities for the future of the *Star Wars* universe and, in the real world, upon the future of scholarly analysis of the *Star Wars* transmedia franchise. The *Star Wars* narrative universe is a great science fiction frontier, featuring adventures, worlds, and characters yet to be explored. Mara is a key figure in the original *Star Wars Legends* with agency reminiscent of that demonstrated by women of the American West and uncharacteristic of women in SF Westerns. As new *Star Wars* stories emerge and the franchise expands its frontiers, Mara Jade remains an iconic character who deserves to be remembered and memorialized by science fiction scholars for her role as a pioneering woman who lived in the *Star Wars* galaxy a long, long time ago.

WORKS CITED

Abbott, Carl. *Frontiers Past and Future: Science Fiction and the American West.* UP of Kansas, 2006.

Bernd, Lisa. "Annie Oakley and the Disruption of Victorian Expectations." *Theatre Symposium*, vol. 20, 2012, pp. 39–48.

Britton, Piers D. "Design for Screen Sf." *The Routledge Companion to Science Fiction*, edited by Mark Bould et al., Routledge, 2009, pp. 341–349.

Butler, Anne M. "We Had No Assistance from Anyone-Happier to Do It Alone: Montana, the Missions, and Mother Amadeus." *Portraits of Women in the American West*, edited by Dee Garceau-Hagen, Taylor & Francis, 2005, pp. 91–120.

Clapp, Elizabeth J. "'Where I First Learned the Nature of Care': Women and Violence on the Late Eighteenth-Century Frontier." *American Nineteenth Century History*, vol. 16, no. 1, 2015, pp. 59–81.

Dixon, Kelly J. "Historical Archaeologies of the American West." *Journal of Archaeological Research*, vol. 22, 2014, pp. 177–228.

Faithful, George. "Survivor, Warrior, Mother, Savior: the Evolution of the Female Hero in Apocalyptic Science Fiction Film of the Late Cold War." *Implicit Religion*, vol. 19, no. 3, 2016, pp. 347–370.

Flotmann, Christina. *Ambiguity in* Star Wars *and* Harry Potter: *a (Post-)Structuralist Reading of Two Popular Myths.* Transcript-Verlag, 2013.

Hantke, Steffen. "Military Culture." *The Oxford Handbook of Science Fiction*, edited by Rob Latham, Oxford UP, 2014, pp. 329–339.

Harvey, Colin. *Fantastic Transmedia: Narrative, Play and Memory Across Science Fiction and Fantasy Storyworlds.* Palgrave Macmillan, 2015.

Hilck, Karin. "The Space Community and the Princess: Reworking the American Space Program's Public Image from 'Miss Nasa' to Princess Leia." *A Galaxy Here and Now: Historical and Cultural Readings of* Star Wars, edited by Peter W. Lee, McFarland, 2016, pp. 33–61.

Hood, Cooper. "Star Wars 9 Possibly Casting Expanded Universe Character." *Screenrant. com*, 20 Apr. 2018. https://screenrant.com/star-wars-9-cast-female-legends-mara-jade/.

Jones, Karen R. and John Wills. *The American West: Competing Visions.* Edinburgh UP, 2009.

Kelly, Casey Ryan. "Women's Rhetorical Agency in the American West: the *New Penelope*." *Women's Studies in Communication*, vol. 32, no. 2, 2009, pp. 203–231.

Keyes, Greg. *Star Wars: the New Jedi Order: Edge of Victory II: Rebirth.* Del Rey, 2001.

Lee, Peter W. "Preface: Galactic Graffiti." *A Galaxy Here and Now: Historical and Cultural Readings of* Star Wars, edited by Peter W. Lee, McFarland, 2016, pp. 1–6.

"The Legendary Star Wars Expanded Universe Turns a New Page." *StarWars.com*, 25 Apr. 2014, http://www.starwars.com/news/the-legendary-star-wars-expanded-universe-turns-a-new-page.

Liedi, Janice. "Teen Queen: Padmé Amidala and the Power of Royal Women." *Star Wars and History*, edited by Nancy R. Reagin and Janice Liedi, Wiley, 2013, pp. 151–175.

Liedi, Janice, and Nancy R. Reagin. "Part of the Rebel Alliance and a Traitor: Women in War and Resistance." *Star Wars and History*, edited by Nancy R. Reagin and Janice Liedi, Wiley, 2013, pp. 41–65.

McDowell, John C. *Identity Politics in George Lucas' Star Wars.* McFarland, 2016.

Nevins, Jess. "Pulp Science Fiction." *The Oxford Handbook of Science Fiction*, edited by Robert Latham, Oxford UP, 2014, pp. 93–103.

Rogue One: a Star Wars Story. Directed by Gareth Edwards, Walt Disney Studios Motion Pictures, 2016.

Simpson, Philip L. "Chapter 7: Thawing an Ice Princess." *Finding the Force of the* Star Wars *Franchise: Fans, Merchandise, & Critics*, edited by Matthew Wilhelm Kapell and John Shelton Lawrence, Peter Lang, 2006, pp. 115–130.

Slotkin, Richard. *Gunfighter Nation: the Myth of the Frontier in Twentieth-Century America.* U of Oklahoma P, 1998.

Star Wars: Episode III: Revenge of the Sith. Directed by George Lucas, 20th Century–Fox, 2005. DVD.

Star Wars: Episode Iv: a New Hope. Directed by George Lucas, 20th Century–Fox, 1977. DVD.

Star Wars: Episode VI: Return of the Jedi. Directed by Richard Marquand. 20th Century–Fox, 1983. DVD.

Star Wars: Rebels. Television Series. Disney–ABC Domestic Television, 2014–2018.

Star Wars: the Clone Wars. Television Series. Disney–ABC Domestic Television, 2008–2014.

Tasker, Yvonne. "Contested Masculinities: the Action Film, the War Film, and the Western." *The Routledge Companion to Cinema and Gender*, edited by Kristin Lené Hole et al., Routledge, 2017, pp. 111–120.

Traviss, Karen. *Star Wars: Legacy of the Force: Sacrifice.* 2007. Del Rey, 2008.

Wallace, Daniel. *Star Wars: the New Essential Guide to Characters.* Revised Edition. Del Rey, 2002.

Wallace, Daniel, and Abel Peña. "Who's Who: Imperial Grand Admirals." *Star Wars Insider*, vol. 66, 2003, pp. 44–49.

Wood, Mara. "Feminist Icons Wanted: Damsels in Distress Need Not Apply." *A Galaxy Here and Now: Historical and Cultural Readings of* Star Wars, edited by Peter W. Lee, McFarland, 2016, pp. 62–83.

Woodworth-Ney, Laura. *Women in the American West.* ABC-CLIO, 2008.

Zahn, Timothy. *Star Wars: Allegiance.* 2007. Del Rey, 2008.

_____. *Star Wars: Choices of One.* 2011. Del Rey, 2012.

_____. *Star Wars: Heir to the Empire.* 1991. Del Rey, 1992.

_____. *Star Wars: the Last Command.* Bantam, 1993.

_____. *Star Wars: Vision of the Future.* Bantam, 1998.

The Reformation of the "Plastic Girl"

Prostitute/Killer and Messenger Characters in Cyberpunk to Post-Cyberpunk

Melanie A. Marotta

Introduction

In traditional high-tech, low-life cyberpunk fashion, two of the primary characters in Walter Jon Williams' *Hardwired* (1986) and William Gibson's *Neuromancer* (1984) are loner rebels that take on their adverse environments in favor of improved living conditions. Significantly, these characters are female—most famously Sarah and Molly Millions—not male. It is the male character who is usually considered the standard focus for the cyberpunk text. In early cyberpunk narratives, the female cyberpunk character construct is created and repeated often: these characters tend to be highly sexualized and commodified, even appearing as prostitutes. Interestingly, cyberpunk is littered with references to the American West, authors going so far as to refer to hackers as console cowboys (see William Gibson), thereby invoking the famed frontier loner hero image. In historical and literary sources, American frontier women tended to be regarded as existing within the domestic sphere: they were responsible for the home and family. By extension, they also took it upon themselves to care for those considered vulnerable (i.e. Native Americans) and were often found to include them in their communities, thereby extending their protection to them. Robert V. Hine and John Mack Faragher document the experiences of pioneer women, in particular their feelings towards their solitary existence and their desire for community. The historians report that "The struggle to make and sustain connections between isolated western households—the work of constructing a community—was perhaps the most difficult of all pioneer tasks" (148). While the community is necessary on the frontier, Hine and Faragher observe that the sexes tended to be divided as were activities in accordance with gender.

In cyberpunk, the female characters' actions are not traditionally domestic in nature, but they are protector figures. On the surface, these women appear like arm candy for the hackers, but beneath their sexualized exterior they have the ability to make choices much like their male counterparts do. They are only empowered to a certain degree as the male characters also are. While Sarah and Molly are reminiscent of the American Western prostitute character, they are, in fact, much more like the frontier pioneer woman who dared to choose to protect her community and herself in the face of unforeseen dangers. This act by the pioneer women and these newer characters is not one of self-sacrifice, but one of self-preservation. As writers modify the genre's construction (post-cyberpunk) to reflect more contemporary issues, the female characters once again take on the role of the Western pioneer woman. In discussing gendered communal responsibilities, Hine and Faragher show that the women take on the responsibility of education. Like these women, many of the post-cyberpunk female characters are teachers, those responsible for passing on knowledge to others. Characters like Y.T. in Neal Stephenson's *Snow Crash* (1992) and Twinkle in Jeff Noon's *Vurt* (1993) are presented as the classic female messenger character central to early cyberpunk. This character type is so integral to cyberpunk, she has been extensively repeated, emulated in media such as James Cameron's television series, *Dark Angel* (2000–2002) and, most recently, Gerald Brandt's Young Adult novel, *The Courier* (2016). While a male protagonist may still feature prominently in post-cyberpunk's literary contributions, women are now more conspicuous, but it is not due to the overt sexualization of the characters or their violent acts. Female characters are shown as teachers capable of asserting themselves in their respective societies in order to enact change and to create communities.

Cyberpunk and Noir

As has often been documented, the cyberpunk literary construction has similarities to that of noir. In particular, cyberpunk texts prominently feature the femme fatale character reminiscent of those from classic film noir; however, this character has been modified to suit the society in which cybernetics play a significant role in the empowerment of the characters. The main issue with this female character is that she has been constructed, as Christine Gledhill has stated, as a "male fantasy" (qtd. in Crewe 17). Images of the cyberpunk female as the "male fantasy" have overrun the internet, including various social media discussion boards and deviantart.com. She appears multiple times in these spaces barely clothed in sexually suggestive poses with wires emanating from various ports placed strategically on her body. The femme fatale user becomes the used in these images; this conceptualization is contrary to that of the traditional cyberpunk female as portrayed in literature.

Walter Jon Williams' Hardwired and William Gibson's Neuromancer and "Johnny Mnemonic"

As William's *Hardwired* begins, the protagonist, Cowboy, shows that his "fantasy" centers on his image and his adventures as a panzer driver (Williams ch. 1). Here, Cowboy envisions what it would have been like if he had insisted on monochromatic ocular implants: he could see events like "a black-and-white fantasy, an old moving picture starring the likes of Gary Cooper or John Wayne" (Williams). As this novel is the cyberpunk Western, the console cowboy begins the text with his foray into the technologically-centered world. Williams, however, alters the traditional cyberpunk construction, preferring instead to immerse Cowboy and Sarah in a frontier society dominated by real world politics rather than to primarily situate the plot in the virtual world. While Cowboy, the proverbial gun for hire, romanticizes his identity, he does not inflate his societal importance. For example, Cowboy is chased by Missouri privateers while in the panzer on a drug run; he has to hide the panzer in a barn while repairing the damage and waiting for nightfall. In the barn, Cowboy encounter two adolescents from Buffalo, whom he attempts to pay not to reveal his location. They take the food supplements he offers, leaving the check behind because they see Cowboy as a hero. The male verbally refuses to take the payoff from Cowboy, citing the illegal delivery of drugs as a lifesaving act in the East.

By beginning the novel with the male character's endeavors, specifically those of a criminal nature, Williams appears to construct his text much like that of his fellow writers. For example, Gibson's short story, "Johnny Mnemonic" (1981), starts with the character of the same name readying himself for a meeting with his contractor, Ralfi Face. Both Cowboy and Johnny as well as Gibson's Case have had their bodies technologically modified in order for them to do business in their respective societies. As it is for Johnny, it is the thrill not materialism that drives Cowboy to be a panzer driver, to fly drug shipments in his plane, the Pony Express. For him, income is secondary but is still motivation for his physical acts. For example, when Cowboy is first witnessed by the reader, he is driving his Maserati through the use of the neural interface, noting "It's almost like flying" (Williams ch. 1). Cowboy is alone while speeding into Custer County and, once the black-and-white world recedes, the narrator strikingly observes, "Cowboy has friends here" (ch. 1). While he is immersed in a technologically-driven society, as standard, he appears alone, Williams' construction of Cowboy breaks the mold for this character construct by immediately making him a part of a community. In reference to the public and private spheres of the nineteenth-century, Amy Kaplan asserts, "When we contrast the domestic sphere with the market or political realm, men and women inhabit a divided social terrain, but when we oppose the domestic to the foreign, men and women become national allies against the alien…" (Kaplan 582). Cowboy may begin the novel by behaving in typical console cowboy fashion by actively seeking the next thrill, but by merging SF and the Western, Williams creates a character that is more accepting of change; this includes accepting a partnership with a woman who refuses passivity and actively asserts herself as his protector. It must be understood, however, that there is a substantial difference between the American West myth and the actual American West.

In his documentation of SF's historical background, specifically discussing what he terms "inventor fiction," Brian Stableford writes, "The hybridization of inventor fiction and westerns emphasized the importance of the myth of the frontier to American attitudes to technological development" (22). Stableford continues to highlight the influence not of the authentic American West on the aforementioned inventor fiction, but rather the concept of the West, hence the myth and its centralization on "the West as a place where the future was to be found and made" (22). While Stableford argues that this concept is inherent to the myth, the ownership of land is truthfully an integral piece of American western expansion. When dealing with SF rather than the actual West, expansionists tend to be focused on conquering that which exists in space over the now defunct Earth. In *Hardwired*, Williams's Earth is no longer a desirable space to reside, so those of means depart for the Orbital blocs. As with the standard cyberpunk plot construction, the private corporations tend to act as ruling bodies, and there is a certain amount of elitism exuded. What that leaves is a commodified society made up of those that exist safely outside of it and those that have no other choice but to be immersed within it: Williams' mudboys and dirtgirls. Historian Paul Gilje, in his discussion of capitalism in the Early American Republic, notes in reference to banking institutions that "Corporations originally were special grants of privilege (often a monopoly) to private individuals to pursue an activity for the general welfare. [Robert] Morris, [Alexander] Hamilton, and the other men who organized the first banks argued that their institutions would pursue the public good" (4). Williams's Orbitals, which focus their enterprises on the production of pharmaceuticals, appear on the surface to be sympathetic to those that reside on Earth—are for "the public good"; this perception quickly alters once it becomes known that viral Huntington's, a disease causing violent deaths on Earth, has been created in order for the Orbitals to offer a cure, thereby making an excessive profit based on the suffering of others. Gilje continues his discussion of the banking institutions, noting that this phase passed after a few years: "Privilege might have survived if it did not have to rely on elected officials from a broadening electorate of white adult males" (4). Once again there is an aura of elitism associated with the West as there is in cyberpunk. Sarah's desires for her brother and herself to no longer exist on the lowest rung of the hierarchal ladder but rather to be part of this exclusive society.

Sarah is more realistic about her place in the hierarchy than Cowboy who resents being associated with the mudboys. The hackers believe that they exist between hierarchal groups: they are not part of the corporations although they may work for them by choice or by force, nor do they consider themselves to be part of the masses. They are elitist, although they do not consider themselves as such. The female killers are aware that they are different from the dirtgirls, the norm, because of their skills and technological enhancements but simultaneously understand that, like everyone else, the corporation may destroy them on a whim. According to Katherine Harrison, "Cyberpunk explicitly sets out to upset preconceived notions of identity and 'a good life' by proffering values which highlight alternative ways of being, coupled with an anarchic disrespect for authority associated with the punk ethos" (212). After Cowboy finishes his discussion with the adolescents in the barn, he goes through his post-run routine. While lying in his bunk in the panzer, Cowboy contemplates his existence, calling attention to his perceived freedom. Cowboy asserts:

> It was enough to be a free jock on a free road, doing battle with those who would restrict him, keeping him bound to the Earth as if he were nothing more than a mudboy. It hadn't mattered what he was carrying. It was enough to know that, whatever the state of the rest of the country, the blue sky over his own head was the air of freedom [Williams ch. 3].

Like Johnny, Cowboy takes any work as long as it offers the notion of personal freedom. Case is willing to undergo highly dangerous surgery in order to repair his damaged nervous system, so that he may, once again, be capable of entering the matrix, thereby regaining his position in society. By doing so, Case loses his freedom because he now owes Armitage and the corporation that employs him. Case becomes an indentured servant instead of the free hacker that he envisions himself to be. Unfortunately for Cowboy, Johnny, and Case they only have an idea of freedom instead of the real thing. Unbeknownst to him, the console cowboy tends to be trapped in a system run by corporations until he meets the female protector figure, and she saves him from his fate. While the female killer/prostitute character is often thought of as inferior to the hacker, they actually have similar character development paths. The difference, however, is that the female characters are charged with caring for other characters. For Sarah, this desire to protect her brother, Daud, is used as a method by which to ensure her services to Cunningham and the corporation. By the conclusion of the novel, the male protagonists and the "razorgirls" come to learn that they are not separate from the masses. They belong to a community that subsequently vies for freedom for those in disadvantaged areas since they are also in need of saving. They must no longer be objectified by those in power.

Kaplan discusses both spheres, noting how the white middle class is portrayed in nineteenth-century women's texts. Kaplan reveals that "the private feminized space of the home both infused and bolstered the public male arena of the market..." (581). Here and throughout her article, Kaplan documents how women, many times fearful of losing their position in the West because they will no longer be needed in the same manner in this space, elected to write, thereby defending their political points of view; they are anonymous activists. Continuing her previous point, Kaplan remarks "that the sentimental values attached to maternal influence were used to sanction women's entry into the wider civic realm from which those same values theoretically excluded them" (581). In cyberpunk, men have a clear societal role—they appear as the hackers, the heads of industry—but where are the women? In this genre, women appear to not belong, thereby living on the fringes of society as prostitutes or as killers, utilizing these roles to immerse themselves in a society that does not seem to want them except as possessions. The killer characters do not fall into traditional Western gendered positions and are shown as taking on what I would consider for 1980s fiction to be a gender-neutral role. They modify their status, taking on roles that during the 1980s were reserved for male characters and, as a result, they become subjects rather than objects. As it does for pioneer women, the frontier (when included in cyberpunk fiction) tends to offer choices, a new life for the killer characters—they have the ability to take agency in their lives and those of their community. Unfortunately, the female characters are objectified first before they make take control of their lives. When she appears in many cyberpunk texts, the primary female character is shown as a sexualized body. For the hackers, the body is shown as secondary to the technology. As Case sits with Linda, a former lover, in a bar the following moment occurs: "All the meat, he thought, and all it wants" (Gibson, *Neuromancer* 9). For women, the body and mind may appear as separate entities in some cases (Sarah and the weasel), but in others they must work in unison in order for the characters to be successful in their activities. In other words, there is conscious thought with regard to the female's actions. As Sarah enters the Aujourd'Oui bar in order to meet her target, the writhing dancers' bodies and their immersion in club technology is first witnessed by readers as is violence and chaos. Notably, this is the reader's initial introduction to Earth's urban space and to Sarah. Previously, Williams plunges the reader into Cowboy's world; however, his space drastically differs from Sarah's. It is isolated, rural, and privileged. Cowboy's space appears cut-off from the rest of dirt society, limited to Cowboy and his crew. His space and his behavior towards his opinions and vice versa denote Cowboy's elite status in the hierarchy.

Sarah, however, is one of the masses, and spends her time attempting to flee Earth for the West's proverbial Eden. She sees the most desirable space as that which exists off-world; in *Hardwired*, for Sarah and many others the Orbital blocs exist as the Edenic space whereas Earth is the post-apocalyptic frontier. For many pioneering women who migrated to the West, they did so for the sake of their families. For Sarah, saving her brother from her fate is her priority, but her motivations are in flux. She approaches her brother's life both as a non-optional task she must complete (she has to save him in order to give him the life that she cannot have); she also sees herself as a parent to Daud. For much of the text, however, Daud is a job and she treats him much like the dancers in the bar—as just another thing. As Sarah walks into the bar she, like Case, refers to the body as "meat," but her demeanor towards the dancers is cold and calculating rather than just coming off as distasteful (Williams ch. 2). She describes them as "a twitching mass of dying flesh, bloody, insensate, mortal. Bound by the mud of the earth" (ch. 2). Interestingly, both Sarah and Case are introduced to the reader in a bar setting. The space is known for its social atmosphere; however, both Sarah and Case prefer to keep to themselves. They choose to separate themselves from the masses while simultaneously appearing as the spectacle. One of the primary differences between the two characters is the fact that the male hacker is not literally considered to be a prostitute while the female character is.

As Sarah seeks her target in the Aujourd'Oui, one of the many advertisements that Williams has strategically placed throughout his novel appears; it is selling a new body to those parties interested. After the advertisement, which acts as a symbolic break in the plot, Williams has the reader witness a previous planning session between Sarah, Firebud, and Cunningham. Firebud, the body designer, and Cunningham, the man who hired her for the assassination, discuss Sarah's appearance and the changes that are going to be made in order for her to successfully lure her target to her death. While the Western pioneer woman lived in the private sphere, Mary Murphy in her discussion of prostitutes in nineteenth-century Butte, Montana, documents that because of their profession, prostitutes are always in the public eye. Sex, something that the Victorians considered private, is now out in the open, thereby violating societal guidelines regarding female behavior (Murphy 195). Because of this societal breach of conduct, prostitutes are offered very little by way of protection from violence. In her examination, Murphy breaks prostitution down into three categories: women that work in parlor houses (for madams), in brothels, and on their own. "Madams hired attractive women, usually white, who dressed well, acted like ladies, and played the parts of companions as well as sexual partners," writes Murphy (194). While Williams alters the construction of the 1980s cyberpunk femme fatale by making Sarah bi-racial rather than white, unfortunately, he then prostitutes her by having Sarah sell her body for two tickets off planet to the Orbital bloc. As she enters the Aujourd'Oui, Sarah resembles the high-end prostitutes that worked for the madams rather than the lower-class prostitute she was in her past. In fact, at sixteen years old Sarah had "bought her way out of her first contract" and then had gone to work at another brothel, a place that she had taken drug-addicted Daud to in order to save him from their father (Williams ch. 2). Before delving further into the assassination plot, Williams offers the readers glimpses into Sarah's past as a child in post-war America and into life with Daud. Whereas Gibson tends to concentrate his efforts on male character development and gender specific societal roles, Williams gives Sarah depth and makes Daud a homosexual prostitute, a position males very rarely hold. After she completes a job for the thirdmen, Sarah goes to the apartment she shares with Daud and takes a dose of endorphins in order to mask her physical and mental pain. The reader witnesses Sarah's relationship with her abusive father, her and Daud's escape into a drug-induced state, and her worry that Daud may fall into the same trap as she and become involved with a thatch (a John willing to kill a prostitute). While Daud is assaulted by a thatch, it is Sarah's involvement with Cunningham and an Orbital bloc that almost gets them both killed.

Unlike Gibson, Williams allows for maturation, a transformation of his female character throughout the novel and, ultimately, it concludes with Sarah looking as if she is headed towards becoming a functional member of the frontier community. Many nineteenth-century prostitutes were not offered the opportunity for redemption and, instead, their short lives ended in violence. When many cyberpunk texts open, several major female characters have taken steps to move away from an objectified state—that of the prostitute. Before she reaches the stage of transformation, she must take control of her body; when many texts begin this character has removed herself from the realm of prostitution and has now become the assassin. After Sarah leaves her apartment but not her worry for Daud behind, she goes to the Plastic Girl to meet Cunningham and contract for work. Continuing his discussion of the femme fatale (a cyberpunk staple character), Crewe states that "Her sexuality builds on that from an earlier era of cinema—the 'vamps' of silent cinema … but is enriched with an ambiguity, an unknowability, a sense of impossible

distance" (17). When Sarah is first witnessed in the Aujourd'Oui she is "hunting," engaged in a chain of events previously set in motion with Cunningham
at the Plastic Girl (Williams ch. 2). Out of necessity, Sarah behaves much as
Crewe has observed; she has distanced herself from her target and her body
has been remade by Firebud for her task at hand. She uses her body which retains her dirtgirl scars to entice Princess, the member of the Orbitals, so that
she may be brought back to Princess' home in order to murder her. Once she
has sex with Princess, she uses the weasel to violently kill her; subsequently,
she retrieves the requested data and then goes home. Anne M. Butler, a Western historian, documents the misperceptions regarding nineteenth-century
prostitutes in the West, noting the disservice that has been done to them by
Hollywood. Specifically, in the mid-twentieth century, Western prostitutes
have been remade into women who were portrayed as "hav[ing] no sexuality"
(88). Historically, prostitutes existed much in the frontier as they do in cyberpunk societies. Butler elaborates on the reality of being a nineteenth-century
Western prostitute, noting amongst other things the inherent dangers associated with the position. They are marginalized within their communities,
likely to succumb to death due to drug addiction, alcoholism, or violence
(death by prostitute or by patron). These women have barely enough money
on which to survive. Sarah routinely uses drugs and receives payment for her
jobs in drugs, subsequently trading them for goods and services. She shows
that she is capable of completing any act which may ensure passage off-world
for Daud and herself. Even though Sarah comprehends the elitism that exists
in her society and that the Orbitals see mudboys and dirtgirls as trivial, she
refuses to acknowledge the possibility of Orbital bloc betrayal. Sarah asserts
her belief that she has advanced in the societal hierarchy, but once she becomes involved with Cunningham, the Orbital bloc, and Cowboy, she comes
to understand the disposable nature of the people that remain on Earth.

Butler continues her discussion of issues facing prostitutes in the
nineteenth-century West:

> customers soliciting western prostitutes were not particularly interested in helping the
> women advance to a higher economic realm, looking to establish long-term meaning-
> ful friendships, or seeking a sophisticated brothel world akin to a seventeenth-century
> European salon. The men wanted a sexual encounter, and they went to those western
> locations where they could buy it [84–5].

Once she arrives home after Princess' death, Sarah's apartment is blown up,
and Daud is seriously injured. She then comes to the realization that she is
inconsequential, that her death had always been a part of the plan. Interestingly, Sarah is never actually seen as a prostitute in the novel, nor is Molly,
who describes herself as a "working girl" (Gibson, *Neuromancer* 13). Both
of them talk about this period in their lives as something that has transpired
in the past. While she is no longer a prostitute, the members of the Orbital

blocs treat her as such, but Sarah refuses to permit their perversion and degradation of the dirtgirl identity, so she rebels. These women have moved on to positions which enable them to actively make choices about their futures, and as assassins, they refuse to be victimized by anyone. Sarah chooses to take Cunningham's job because she truly believes that by doing so she can get Daud and herself away from Earth to Eden. Betrayal and the threat of death lead to Sarah taking Michael Hetman's job to protect Cowboy. Instead of permitting the Orbital bloc to have her killed, she takes a dangerous job with Cowboy. While she has her own agenda, thereby protecting Daud and herself over anyone else including her lover, Cowboy, Sarah comes to the understanding that she, Cowboy, and the other panzer drivers/crew members must form an alliance, a community, in order to protect themselves from the orbitals. In reference to the cyberpunk genre, Helen Merrick comments that "Despite the potentially liberating promises of an escape from the body (and thus modernist notions of gendered subjectivity), and the presence of strong female characters, the dominance of the mind/body dualism in cyberpunk serves to reinforce the associated gender binaries" (250). In cyberpunk, many texts begin with female characters being associated with the body and hackers associated with the mind. Sarah and Molly are hired for their bodies, while Case is for his mind. Those that defer from the norm are Johnny Mnemonic, whose brain (body only, no thought) is used to transport stolen data and Pat Cadigan's Allie, who illegally utilizes hardware and is arrested by the Brain Police. In *Mindplayers* (1987), a representative from the Brain Police offers her the following choices: go to jail for her crime or become a mindplayer and complete community service. When Sarah becomes more than just a body, once she recognizes her contribution to society as part of the panzer uprising, she becomes an effective societal member. It is she who ensures the success of the panzer rebellion: she saves Cowboy repeatedly, puts together the team of flyers, and reports Daud's betrayal, therefore defending her community. Once the female characters move past being only killers for hire, they actively accept the male protagonists as their communities and work towards improving their respective societies.

William Gibson's Virtual Light

In post-cyberpunk, the female character appears more often as a messenger rather than as a prostitute or killer. In cyberpunk, the most memorable appearance of this archetype is in Gibson's *Virtual Light* (1993) with the introduction of Chevette Washington. Gibson's novel revolves around Chevette, a bicycle messenger that traverses post-apocalyptic San Francisco delivering packages. After she steals a pair of virtual reality glasses, Chevette spends the remainder of the plot desperately avoiding those sent to kill her and retrieve the glasses. Hine and Faragher document the late-nineteenth-century migration of women from Western rural areas to urban, noting that their desire to do so stemmed from the need to increase their prospects (170–1). Like these women, Chevette's need for relocation is great; however, this only occurs once she leaves the bridge. According to Hine and Faragher, more women than men left their rural homes for the cities; they state that many critical sources believe "young women were pushed out of the countryside by constricted opportunities and the lingering legacy of patriarchy" (170–1). In Gibson's dystopic novel, the San Francisco Bay Bridge has been transformed from a means of transport to and from the city, to a residence for outsiders. Chevette is safe as long as she remains within her community on the bridge; once she departs, she is subjected to the patriarchal ideals regarding women as are those that remain in rural areas. For example, after Chevette delivers a package to a lawyer in a Tenderloin hotel, she decides to attend a party uninvited. Throughout this essay, Chevette repeatedly emphasizes her outsider status. In fact, while at the party an attendee, Maria, questions Chevette about residing on the bridge, an inquiry to which Chevette expects the usual reaction of disbelief and even revulsion to her response. The partygoer, instead, sees Chevette as a spectacle, observing that she would like to see the bridge "'but there are no tours'" (Gibson, *VL* 47). To a certain degree, Chevette appears as a teacher, educating others about the bridge community, but in this novel the character has not fully matured as evidenced by her theft and subsequent move from the bridge community towards one that offers fame. The narrator reveals, "Chevette never stole things, or anyway not from other people, and definitely not when she was pulling tags. Except this one bad Monday when she took this total asshole's sunglasses, but that was because she just didn't like him" (41). She attempts to educate Maria about the bridge area, that it is a freeing space rather than one that is hazardous. This event occurs after she goes to the party and is accosted by the man with the glasses. As Chevette enters, she surveys the room, noting the lavish surroundings and the guests' attire. She separates them into two groups: those that belong and locals, prostitutes included. Unfortunately, Chevette is confronted by the glasses courier, and he verbally intimates that she is a prostitute as well. Here, Chevette becomes angry and asserts her position as a messenger, thereby showing that she separates herself from the others and holds a position of importance. While outside of the bridge, her home, Chevette tries to teach others about her community, but societal constructs and her maturity get in the way of her success. At the close of the novel, Chevette is arrested for her part in the theft and subsequent events, but this act is a performance of sorts. Her participation in the theft and subsequent arrest lead her to an offer to be famous; in order to obtain this fame, she must sign a contract and leave the bridge community.

William Gibson's All Tomorrow's Parties

In Gibson's post-cyberpunk novel, *All Tomorrow's Parties* (1999), the third novel in the Bridge Trilogy, Chevette continues her journey as the messenger character. Post-apocalyptic San Francisco remains the primary locale for this novel; however, it exists as a place to which Chevette must return in order to obtain self-acceptance. Upon reintroduction in this series, Chevette does not appear in concrete form but rather is spoken about by her ex-boyfriend, Berry Rydell. In a conversation between Rydell and Buell Creedmore, Creedmore asserts that Chevette has dissolved their relationship so that she may date a documentary production coordinator named Carson. When Creedmore declares that Chevette has treated Rydell badly, Rydell responds that leaving her is a choice that she made: "'Well,' Rydell said, 'I figured it's her call'" (Gibson, *ATP* 20). Rydell reveals Chevette's ability to take agency over her life as she chooses to end their relationship, thereby preferring Carson over Rydell. Unfortunately, now that Chevette has left the bridge community—her home—her life loses its stability.

After ending both relationships (Carson is abusive), Chevette moves into a sharehouse in Malibu. This space is transitional, not a home. In reference to the American West, Annette Kolodny states that "Once arrived on a new frontier, women would have settled in permanently, unimpressed by appeals to an El Dorado further west and generally uncomfortable with the nomadic existence of successive removes" (11). Regarding Western migration, Kolodny contends that men desired the move West, not women. Chevette's move to Malibu is propelled by the desire to escape Carson's controlling behavior. In fact, her departure from the sharehouse back to the bridge is partially caused by Carson's harassment of Chevette. Tessa, one of the USC media students living in the house, is desperate to film Chevette and the bridge community. Tessa urges Chevette to flee for the bridge, taking her recording equipment and herself as well. Like many pioneer women, Chevette's displacement from her home makes her vulnerable. The impending danger from Carson and Tessa's verbal persuasions push Chevette towards her former community, one she is in need of desperately. Chevette proclaims that she lives in the sharehouse because she lost her job and her income. While Chevette may no longer be employed as a messenger she, once again, becomes the educator upon her return to the bridge. Before leaving the sharehouse, Chevette is unsure of herself and permits Tessa to influence her manner of thinking. Once she retrieves the jacket of her friend and father-figure, Skinner, from the sharehouse before leaving and once she nears the bridge, Chevette regains her voice. She instructs Tessa about how to behave in order to protect her property and herself from harm. As Kolodny states, pioneer women prefer stability over perpetual movement and reject isolation (11). Chevette moves back to the bridge, rejoining her community and teaching those considered to be outsiders to the bridge community how to form a functional community and to accept those that are marginalized.

Neal Stephenson's Snow Crash

As in Gibson's *Bridge Trilogy*, Stephenson creates a character, Y.T. that, like Chevette, is employed as a messenger. In this case, Y.T. is an adolescent Kourier that rides a skateboard and uses Hiro Protagonist's Deliverator vehicle to hitch a ride to her next destination. Unfortunately, due to Hiro's lateness in obtaining the pizza for delivery and also his fear of death for delivering that pizza late, he takes a shortcut and crashes his vehicle into a pool. It is here that the duo meets and where Y.T. saves Hiro from death at the hands of the Mafia. She delivers the pizza, and then they become a team desirous of saving the lives of many from a Metaverse virus and a destructive cult; first, however, they deal in information together. As with Williams' novel, Stephenson's narrators, Y.T. and Hiro, switch throughout. As this is a post-cyberpunk text, the body is no longer separated from the mind. So that Y.T. may be a successful messenger, she utilizes both in her effort to ensure the future of a commercialized California. Kolodny examines writer Margaret Fuller's experiences on the frontier, noting that "The dream of a domestic Eden had become a nightmare of domestic captivity" as men were outdoors while women were to remain inside caring for the children (9). Y.T. refuses to remain indoors at the Blooming Greens burbclave, preferring instead to act as a Kourier without her mother's knowledge. When kidnapped by the cult and the Mafia, it is Y.T. that rescues herself with the help of her Kourier community after informing another of the Kouriers that she is in danger. He calls in a Code and once she poons out of a helicopter, she escapes in time to watch Fido, the Rat Thing cyberdog, destroy the head of the cult, L. Bob Rife, and his virus. Previously, as she is saving Hiro again from death, she also rescues the Rat Thing, a cyberdog that no one else offers any care. Y.T. makes sure that her community is protected and functioning as do Cerise and Twinkle.

Melissa Scott's Trouble and Her Friends

In Melissa Scott's post-cyberpunk *Trouble and Her Friends* (1994), Cerise, one of the protagonists, was also a prostitute of sorts but is so before the novel begins and before she takes the cybersecurity job that leads her to altering the discriminatory nature of her society. As she walks by a group of female students at the "secretarial so-called college" observing their attire and behavior, Cerise reveals that they are "kids who had indentured themselves to the school and its placement service to get the implants, dollie-box and dollie-slot, that could eventually win them a decent job with a corporation" (Scott 24). Cerise shows that females in her society, including herself, have very few options, so many sell their bodies in an effort to enhance their minds. For Cerise the frontier is not an Eden but a harsh reality which must be reformed. Kolodny examines what she calls the frontier fantasy, noting that it was created by writers in order to ensure that women would be desirous of this "enticing image of a flowered prairie paradise, generously supporting an extended human family, at the center of which stood a reunited Adam and Eve" (9). In Cerise's society, the real world and its structure must be altered in order to make the fantasy a reality. Both Cerise and her partner, Trouble, repeatedly escape to the virtual plane as both work as hackers and are lesbians, a relationship not accepted in their society. Seahaven, the virtual reality space, is depicted much like that of a seaside frontier town; it is initially created as a refuge for those refusing to conform to what is considered by society to be acceptable. It is Eden, albeit a false one; once the brainworm, a hacker's tool utilized by the marginalized, is outlawed, Cerise must take steps to reunite with her partner and reform her prejudiced society into one that resembles the frontier fantasy.

Jeff Noon's Vurt

Unlike in Stephenson's novel, Noon has elected to include the prostitute character in his post-cyberpunk novel, *Vurt*. Noon has some of his female characters prostitute themselves for Vurt feathers (drugs), which enable them to enter a different plane of existence. The protagonist in this novel is Scribble, who is desperate to remove his sister, Desdemona, from the alternate world of Vurt. Scribble and his friends, the Stash Riders, take many Vurt feathers throughout the plot in an effort to conform to the norm of their society and also to escape post-apocalyptic Manchester. Unlike the Stash Riders, Scribble, Beetle, Mandy, Bridget, and the Thing, the character of Twinkle is a young female who Noon shows as the voice of reason to Scribble. Twinkle first appears outside of the Stash Riders' apartment seeking acceptance from the group, but mainly Scribble. Throughout the text she refers to the protagonist as Mister Scribble, thereby revealing her youth. Her age also shows in her tenacious attitude: even though she is repeatedly rejected by the group and Scribble, she refuses to give up. In fact, it is Twinkle that asserts to Scribble that he must "'keep the faith'" (315) even though it appears as if getting Desdemona back is an impossible task. She remains his supporter through the ploy, enabling him to finally enter the Vurt verse alone and sacrifice himself for his sister. The messenger characters allow for the maturation of the male protagonists and for the alteration of their respective societies.

Conclusion

Brian Attebery documents the appearance of Molly in Gibson's "Johnny Mnemonic," noting that while she has superior physical capabilities for fighting, she "plays a surprisingly small part in determining the course of the stories. She serves more as ornament and as backup for the hero than as a motivating force in her own right" (86). Molly, who is present in both "Johnny Mnemonic" and *Neuromancer*, represents the iconic female character for the cyberpunk genre. Whereas Molly may appear as secondary to Case, as Attebery has noted, she is arguably the most memorable of Gibson's characters. Gibson depicts Molly as having razor blade implants for fingernails and mirrored technologically-advanced lenses in place of eyes. According to Bruce Sterling, one of the fathers of cyberpunk, "Mirrored sunglasses have been a Movement totem since the early days of '82.... By hiding the eyes, mirrorshades prevent the forces of normalcy from realizing that one is crazed and possibly dangerous" (xi). When the reader meets Molly in Gibson's short story she, like Sarah and Case, is in a bar. Contrary to the hackers, Molly is engaged in looking for work instead of already being contracted to complete a job. She is over-eager and is willing to sacrifice the lives of others in pursuit of her own desires. According to Crewe in his definition of the femme fatale, "the women of film noir prove more important to the plot than the putative protagonist" (19). Like Gibson, Williams has the male hacker start his novel and be its protagonist; Williams also has the female character enter the hacker's life later in the text. Williams' work then differs in construction from the norm. Sarah is not part of his story at first because she has her own story. In fact, Williams begins by alternating the focus of his novel, first introducing Cowboy and then Sarah, thereby giving the female character her own timeline. This is not to say that the male hacker is not the center of attention; rather, the reader's attention is equally placed on both male and female points of view throughout the novel. By doing so, Williams indicates that the female character's contribution to the reconstruction of Earth's society is as relevant as that of the hacker's. In both the cyberpunk and post-cyberpunk novel, the female characters encounter versions of the nineteenth-century Western frontier. As in fictionalized literary interpretations of the frontier, the men in the cyberpunk novels are shown as if the space is for males to conquer and the women are to remain in the background tending only to the domestic space. While post-cyberpunk novels generally still retain a male protagonist as do their predecessors, as the genre alters so does its focus. It is the female characters in both incarnations of the genre that ensure the stability of the community within each text. While it may be thought that these characters are secondary to the males, this observation is false. The female characters are at the forefront in these science fiction westerns, therefore stabilizing the frontier for their communities and for future generations. It is recommended that readers be watchful of alterations to the cyberpunk genre as the movement permeates other genres of literature, namely Young Adult. Writers Brandt of the San Angeles series and Dan Wells of the Mirador series have released female-centric Anthropocene novels. Brandt creates Kris Merrill, the Courier, and Wells that of Marisa Carnesca, the female gamer. Both of these characters offer readers the positive experience of a female-led text. What is painfully obvious is the lack of Western elements. There is no visible frontier and no new spaces to explore. Instead, the writers are proclaiming that the setting is not the space upon which readers would focus, but rather the literary media itself is the frontier that has been conquered by female characters.

WORKS CITED

Attebery, Brian. *Decoding Gender in Science Fiction*. Routledge, 2002.

Brandt, Gerald. *The Courier*, DAW, 2016.

Butler, Anne M. "Mattie, Katie, and Ida: Western Women at Risk." *Wild Women of the Old West*, edited by Glenda Riley and Richard W. Etulain, Fulcrum Publishing, 2003, pp. 70–93.

Cadigan, Pat. *Mindplayers*. Bantam, 1987.

Crewe, David. "Cherchez la Femme: the Evolution of the Femme Fatale." *Screen Education*, vol. 80, 2016, pp. 16–25.

Gibson, William. *All Tomorrow's Parties*. 1999. Ace, 2000.

_____. "Johnny Mnemonic." 1981. *Burning Chrome*. Eos, 2003, pp. 1–23.

_____. *Neuromancer*. Ace, 1984.

_____. *Virtual Light*. 1993. Bantam, 1994.

Gilje, Paul. "The Rise of Capitalism in the Early Republic." *Wages of Independence: Capitalism in the Early American Republic*, edited by Paul Gilje, Madison House Publishers, 1997, pp. 1–22.

Harrison, Katherine. "Gender Resistance: Interrogating the 'Punk' in Cyberpunk." *At the Interface/Probing the Boundaries*, vol. 85, 2012, pp. 209–227. http://web.b.ebscohost.com/.

Hine, Robert V. and John Mack Faragher. *Frontiers: a Short History of the American West*. Yale UP, 2007.

Kaplan, Amy. "Manifest Domesticity." *American Literature* vol. 70, iss. 3, 1998, pp. 581–606. http://www.jstor.org/stable/pdf/2902710.pdf.

Kolodny, Annette. *The Land Before Her: Fantasy and Experience of the American Frontiers, 1630–1860*. U of North Carolina P, 1984.

Merrick, Helen. "Gender in Science Fiction." *The Cambridge Companion to Science Fiction*. 2003. Edited by Farah Mendlesohn and Edward James, Cambridge UP, 2009, pp. 241–252.

Murphy, Mary. "The Private Lives of Public Women: Prostitution in Butte, Montana, 1878–1917." *The Women's West*, edited by Susan Armitage and Elizabeth Jameson, U of Oklahoma P, 1987, pp. 193–205.

Noon, Jeff. *Vurt*. St. Martin's Griffin, 1993.

Scott, Melissa. *Trouble and Her Friends.* Tor, 1994.

Stableford, Brian. "Science Fiction Before the Genre." *The Cambridge Companion to Science Fiction.* 2003. Edited by Farah Mendlesohn and Edward James, Cambridge UP, 2009, pp. 15–31.

Stephenson, Neal. *Snow Crash.* 1992. Bantam, 2008.

Sterling, Bruce. "Preface." *Mirrorshades: the Cyberpunk Anthology.* 1986. Edited by Bruce Sterling, Ace, 1988, pp. ix–xvi.

Williams, Walter Jon. *Hardwired.* 1986. N.p., 2011. Kindle file.

"Shut up and get over here"

Lovers and Cattle in Mass Effect

ADAM CROWLEY

Published shortly after the release of BioWare's innovative, science fiction role-playing game *Mass Effect* (2007), John Wills' "Pixel Cowboys and Silicone Gold Mines: Videogames of the American West" (2008) explores the development of the "videogame Western" from the late 1970s to 2006 (275). The document is remarkable in terms of the author's awareness that a "new West" is emerging for players, one that promises to expand gamers' access to tropes and clichés from literary and cinematic Westerns (276). For Wills, the chief features of this new frontier are expanded "transportation" options between madcap landscapes (297), increased opportunities for the player to exercise "directorial control" over the plotting (299), and a related "postmodern" experience of fashioning diverse characters for and through gameplay (297). While Wills does not make direct reference to *Mass Effect*, the gameplay features he associates with the rapidly developing digital frontier are significant to the title and its scholarship. Such relevance takes on special and as-of-yet unexplored meaning in the context of the title's period of production, which happens to coincide with the emergence of the "new West." Consequently, it is reasonable to ask if *Mass Effect* is relevant to Wills' observations.

Inquiries into this and related matters can begin with the sobering realization that while Wills does mention a few science fiction videogames (e.g., *Computer Space* [1971] and *E.T.: The Extra-Terrestrial* [1982]), he does not address these titles with an appreciable level of specificity. This is, of course, not a shortcoming of his argument, which takes the Western itself as its prime object of interest. Fortunately, it is possible to associate Wills' fundamental notions with the work of Jane Tompkins, who establishes a framework for considering works of science fiction in the context of the literary and cinematic Western in *West of Everything: The Inner Life of Westerns*. With regards to the special topic of women and their representation in the Science Fiction

Western, an association of Wills with Tompkins is quite exciting, as the subject of women and their representation in Westerns is one of Tompkins' key
concerns. In this study, I establish Wills and Tompkins' essential, compatible
positions; identify a program for the analysis of videogames that draws from
these positions; and apply that program to *Mass Effect*. The analysis affirms
Wills' contention that the "new West" does indeed bring an expanded cata-
logue of Western clichés to gamers. Unfortunately, in terms of *Mass Effect*,
one such cliché pertains to the representation of women as heroes prone to
silencing themselves to affirm a sexual partner's masculinity.

To begin, Wills attends to what he calls the "story content" of the videogame Western and the significance of a theme of violence to such content
and, finally, to the relevance of this theme to the New West in video gaming
(275–76). Beginning with the notion that storytelling—such as it is—in early
videogame Westerns deviates little from an established set of genre-defining
clichés from twentieth-century film and television, Wills goes on to argue
that the realization of violence in such titles relies "on the palpable myth of
the lone gunfighter as its pivotal narrative" (287). Wills' attention to the generic conventions of arcade and videogame Westerns is interesting in that it
invites the reader to consider the much broader genre of the Western itself,
a notion that is made plain in the author's association of games like *Boot
Hill* (1975), *Desperados* (2001), and *Gun Fight* (2005) with television and film
projects such as *Deadwood* (2004–2006), *Open Range* (2003), and *Brokeback
Mountain* (2005). However, these appreciable associations—and even the
author's comments on individual videogame Westerns—are ultimately compromised by related assertions that these and other titles can be aligned not
only with a Western genre but with multiple other genres, none of which
are fleshed out in any detail. For example, the term genre emerges some ten
times and always without appreciable explanation or elaboration. There is a
"gun-shooting, or Western shooter, genre," a "new digital genre" (275, 276).
There are "entertainment genres," as well as a "genre of interactivity," to say
nothing of "gaming genres," and even "genres" for "law-enforcement, alien
takeover [and] zombie infestations" narratives (279, 291, 295). As a result,
the reader is very hard pressed to determine what it is that Wills means to
convey with "genre" or "genres," though—importantly—this confusion does
not undermine the notion that the videogame Western "genre" conveys, at a
minimum, specific storytelling concerns, most notably the theme of violence
and its relation to a lone gunfighter. Moreover, there is nothing essentially
wrong with this basic understanding of the term, but Wills' grand postula-
tions about the re-visioning of the Western in the "ever-reconstructing digital
domain" do lead to as-of-yet unaddressed questions of the Western genre as
it might be applied in that setting, to say nothing of how it might be related to
the numerous, essentially superficial so-called "genres" identified in the argu-

ment (303). Fortunately, significant work on genres emerged at the end of the twentieth century that is well-suited for framing and potentially expanding upon the term as it emerges in Wills' argument so that it can be associated with the work of other scholars, like Tompkins.

For example, in *The Architext* (1992), the famous French narratologist Gérard Genette argues against dogmatic conceptions of genre—e.g., the kind of conceptions that are tacitly affirmed but never actually explored by Wills. Genette suggests that critics should essentially eschew that concept of genre altogether and re-direct their attention to "thematic, modal and formal determinations" that are "constant and transhistorical" (78). The consideration of same, he contends, reveals "the landscape in which the evolution of the field of literature is set" and exposes "something like the reservoir of generic potentialities from which that evolution makes its selections." For Genette, the revelation of this reservoir—of its curves, contours, and content—is valuable because it illuminates the narrative potentialities that precede and exceed the birth, development, and inevitable decline of human civilizations. The notion shares more than a passing resemblance to Northrop Frye's comments in *The Secular Scripture: The Study of the Structure of Romance* on biological "imaginative structures," the assumedly fundamental patterns of mind that underlie human belief and understanding (13). Unlike Frye, Genette is not opposed to the notion that this landscape can and does change over time. However, he asserts that any potential "rhythm of variation" is perceptibly slower than the "rhythms of [human] History" (78).

As is evident by Genette's differentiation between thematic, modal, and formal determinations, the concept of "determination" is the lynchpin notion in *The Architext*'s consideration of genre. While Genette does not define the term *per se*, it is—as presented there and in other texts by Genette such as *Fiction and Diction* and *Narrative Discourse: An Essay in Method*—understood to stand in anticipation of a specific rhetorical value that is relevant to the critical enterprise at hand: e.g., one that is possibly thematic, modal, or formal but necessarily reflective of some critical standard. Consequently, and precisely because Genette urges the critic to consider constant and transhistorical values, the consideration of a given determination—however construed—generates questions of whether the concept has relevance not only to a select group of works but also to and between many works stretching across centuries. Indeed, the aims of such inquiry are so broad as to be impossible to satisfy in any single investigation or series of investigations. Nevertheless, and at a minimum, they are valued to the extent that they encourage further consideration of a bonded analytical scheme.

These notions are relevant to Tompkins' remarkable *West of Everything: The Inner Life of Westerns* (1992). There, Tompkins identifies what she examines as the common, formal features that have defined the Western for American audiences in the nineteenth and twentieth centuries. These features include the following determinations, which she calls "the elements of the typical Western plot" (38), all of which have special connotations in Tompkins' argument: "women, language, landscape, horses, [and] cattle" (6). In keeping with the logic of Genette's suppositions, the argument does not require an individual narrative to address all these elements or to address them in a specific combination or to a certain effect. Rather, their presence is simply regarded as likely and is assumedly constructive to the general field from which individual Westerns derive what Genette describes as the "occasional surprises, repetitions, capricious decisions, sudden mutations, or unpredictable creations" of literature (78). Considering Wills' interesting but essentially mysterious comments on genre, Tompkins comments on the formal elements of the Western are quite useful. The author uses these elements to rationalize a connection between the Western and science fiction genres (and several other genres) and reveals patterns for the representation of women across related literary traditions.

Tompkins' argument begins with the useful notion that the Western finds its origins in a larger cultural movement against nineteenth century "sentimental domestic novels" (219) as produced by authors such as Harriet Beecher Stowe, Susan Warner, Maria Susanna Cummins, and others "whose novels spoke to the deepest beliefs and highest ideals of middle-class America" (27). Tompkins writes, "Culturally and politically, the effect of these novels is to establish women at the center of the world's most important work (saving souls) and to assert that in the end spiritual power is always superior to worldly might" (38). It is, she explains, the tendency of the Western to illustrate the "pattern" of such novels "in reverse" (39). That is, its formal features work in concert to "push women out of the picture completely or assign them roles in which they exist only to serve the needs of men." In her scheme, she links this tendency of ignoring or diminishing the roles of women with a larger, multi-genre thematic concern—shared, as she notes, with the literary genres of police narratives and science fiction—with "numbness" or, more specifically, with the hero's "need for numbness" (218). She associates this need with the Western hero's efforts to deny his emotions in the service of a larger aim. She writes, "over and over again in countless Westerns we watch the hero swallow his feelings in order to carry out his difficult and distasteful tasks" (218).

Moreover, Tompkins argues that the numbing process has acquired grand cultural currency since the emergence of the Western, and that it gains "momentum in post–Western cop narratives like the Dirty Harry series … and it ends in robotization in science fiction extensions of this line of development such as *The Terminator*, *RoboCop* and *Total Recall*" (218). While this is a limited and highly particular connection between traditions, it illuminates enough ground to stand on and ask an essential question about certain hybrid narratives, e.g., the science fiction Western. Namely, to what extent might such work either affirm the need for numbness in ways that are in keeping with Tompkins' observations or—and with an eye toward Genette—to what extent might it invert such narrative expectations in ways that potentially delight the audience with "occasional surprises … capricious decisions, sudden mutations, or unpredictable creations" (78).

This question has special relevance to BioWare's *Mass Effect* franchise. The franchise's initial trilogy, composed of *Mass Effect*, *Mass Effect 2* (2012), and *Mass Effect 3* (2013), concerns the desperate adventures of Commander Shepard to spread awareness of the "Reapers," an ancient race of intelligent machines that has returned to humanity's new "frontier"—the Milky Way galaxy—with an intent to exterminate all organic life. One of the definitive features of the series is the numerous instances it provides for the player to choose between one of several options for immediate as well as long-term possibilities for plotting, several of which are framed as moral or ethical conundrums. There are indeed many difficult and distasteful tasks Commander Shepard, the game's protagonist, must undertake in pursuit of the larger goal of raising galactic awareness about the encroaching existential threat that is posed by the Reaper invasion. For example, Shepard is put in the position of determining the life or death of not only individuals but also entire races and, indeed, worlds themselves. In his or her rationalizations (the game allows the player to choose Shepard's gender identity), Shepard must necessarily become numb to the horror of individual decisions in the service of a larger ethical concern (or to reject a larger ethical concern).

When Tompkins writes of numbness and its relation to the plot elements of the typical Western, she is not commenting on space aliens or sentient machines. Rather, she is attending to other matters, most notably the element of cattle and the Western hero's larger struggles to engage, manage, or somehow overcome frontier economies. Writing in the context of films like *A Man Called Horse* (1970) and *Red River* (1948), she notes that the Western hero must "take pain silently" and learn that the "habitual numbing of himself makes it easier for him to inflict pain on others" and to even "kill when necessary" (119). Perhaps most notably, Tompkins makes the appreciable observation that such numbness in a story like *Red River* "is most evident where it is least able to be apprehended—in the treatment of the cattle" (120). While it would be reductive to carry this logic without modification into the *Mass Effect* franchise, it is the case that the "Western hero" in these titles literally has the name Shepard. Additionally, Shepard is, at least metaphorically, working in the service of herd management, insofar as she or he is trying to move the galactic races away from a danger they are too slow to see and appreciate on their own. Moreover, it is rational to argue that Shepard's own numbness is most evident where it too is least able to be apprehended—in his or her treatment of lovers.

While this rather broad interpretation of the original *Mass Effect* trilogy's plot may establish some ground for anticipating, if not considering, the general impact of the Western on a science fiction franchise, a far more overt and specific association with the Western was made by the BioWare corporation itself at the Electronic Entertainment Expo in Los Angeles, California, in mid–2015. The first trailer for *Mass Effect: Andromeda* was presented at that expo, and the trailer's inclusion of Stan Jones' 1948 Western classic "(Ghost) Riders in the Sky," as performed by Johnny Cash, drew immediate ire as well as admiration from franchise enthusiasts. For example, David Griner offers a same-day, frothy refutation of the "soundtrack selection" under the logic that it is a "dumb pick" and somehow a "crunchy bit of rootin' and tootin'" that promises a supposedly novel direction for the series: namely, a concern with gunfighters and gunfights, as opposed to the assumedly heady-by-comparison experience of saving entire worlds (Griner). The fact that neither gunfights or gunfighters are mentioned in the song appears to be of no consequence to Griner (nor does the fact that the actual trailer provides explicit details of the game's anticipated characters literally battling their way across a range of worlds—presumably as saviors of one kind or another). Elsewhere on the internet, there were glowing affirmations for the song and its inclusion. For instance, an anonymous *Reddit* poster, Incendivus, praised the choice as a "perfect fit thematically," under the assertion that the game's "new N7 crew" are "elite special agents"—assumedly "Specter" class agents, in the well-established nomenclature of the *Mass Effect* narrative—and are thus quite literally "ghosts" in the sky (Incendivus). The association is useful, as it draws attention to the relevance of the song's lyrics—which concern the need for a cowboy to make correct choices or risk a damnation of riding "on a range up in the sky" forever chasing "the devil's herd." The concept of choice with consequences is, of course, the central connection to the Western in this argument, insofar as such choices with consequences bear on the theme of numbness.

Because there is rational ground for investigating the theme of numbness in the *Mass Effect* franchise, it is reasonable to ask if that theme takes any of the anticipated curves or has any of the anticipated contours that are expected under Tompkins' argument in the game: how does it bear on the representation of women? While the author does not provide many details on the kinds of narrative steps that might be associated with the need to numbness, she does write about the traditionally male Western hero's experience of "numbing," which "requires the sacrifice of his own heart, a sacrifice kept hidden under his toughness, which is inseparable from his heroic character" (219). She asserts that this is "one of the underlying continuities that link Westerns to the sentimental domestic novel."

With regards to women, such sacrifice—on the part of the male hero—occurs in the anticipated context of what Tompkins identifies as the formal elements of "Women and the Language of Men" (46–67). Beginning with the notion that "Westerns distrust language" (48), Tompkins introduces the idea that Westerns present a world where language is often utilized most effectively by individuals with "class, privilege, political clout, [and] financial strength" (51). While these qualities do not fully encapsulate the broader matters of the heart that the Western hero must numb him or herself against, they certainly bear on and are descriptive of such matters.

Tompkins elaborates by noting that this distrust tends to be dramatized through an active association of loquacity with "women, religion, and culture" (55), which the Western hero is often required to overthrow or rescue. Regarding women, Tompkins identifies a long tradition of Western women appearing "strong and resilient" (61) through their language. However, the illusion is generally undone in this genre by fortune or circumstance, with the women either abandoning speech for masculine action—or crumbling into the arms of a silent but powerful masculine hero. It is at this point that certain questions can be raised about the relevance of Tompkins' argument to the concept of women in the Science Fiction Western. For example, to what extent are individual characters regarded as threatening because of their loquacity? When, where, and why do such characters compel through speech or some other verbal communication the hero to numbness, precisely so that the hero can go on to endure that which must be accomplished? And when and where do these characters fall helplessly into the arms of masculine action?

These questions take on special significance given certain observations that have been made about *Mass Effect* in the popular press. For example, and as critic Christopher J. Ferguson points out, one of the more interesting controversies at the time of *Mass Effect*'s initial release concerned the title's so-called sex scenes ("The School Shooting"). There are several such scenes in the game, divided by gender and partner species. For example, a male version of Shepard can have a romantic encounter with a female human, Ashley Williams, as well as with alien, Asari characters, Liara and Sha'ira. The female version of Shepard can have a romantic encounter with a human, Kaidan Alenko, or the same Ansari characters. Except for the Sha'ira instances, these encounters share at least two significant qualities. First, they occur at the end of long narrative progressions in the game, with the player choosing to "woo" his or her desired partner at multiple points, through dialogue choices before their potential romantic interaction. Second, regardless of the pairing, these encounters arrive at a common and specific point in the game: immediately before the title's rising action leads to the climax, a sequence that radically limits the player's opportunities for play in the run-up to the final encounter with the villain, Saren, an encounter for which Shepard must "steel" him or herself.

These shared features are important to the early controversy some identified in *Mass Effect*. As Ferguson explains, while speaking to Fox News, "the psychologist Cooper Lawrence discussed the video game … and compared some scenes in the game to pornography" (32). Lawrence would later recant this observation with another claim that helps to specify what it is she was trying to suggest. She says, "Before the [interview] I had asked someone about what they had heard, and they said it's like pornography…. But it's not like pornography. I've seen episodes of *Lost* that are more sexually explicit" (Schiesel). For Lawrence, then, the accusation that *Mass Effect* contained pornographic material initially rested on the assumption that it contained exceptionally sexually explicit content. While the charge alone managed to generate a lot of interest in the title, there has been little attention paid to the essential if not broader purpose of these scenes to the game itself. Tompkins' theory of the need for numbness as well as for the diminution of women in the Western can be applied productively to these scenes to reveal the extent to which they individually and collectively meet or exceed formal Western expectations.

However, before investigating any of these scenes, it is important to note that none of them are required of the player during the act of play. Each emerges as one possible outcome for a series of decisions that the player can make at various points in the game. Consequently, the scenes and their potential significance for the representation of women (as well as men) should be understood as a component of play, but as an optional component. This distinction is important because it underscores the contingency of these instances to the plot and highlights the relevance of Tompkins' arguments to the title, insofar as her conception of the Western appears to be relevant to *Mass Effect* even at the level of its most extraneous features: the so-called sex scenes. To put it another way, and in keeping with Tompkins' commentary on *Red River*, the significance of examining these scenes for their relevance to the need for numbness is that it stands to determine if such need is evident where it is least able to be apprehended—quite literally in the game's discretionary scenarios.

Of the six possible encounters in the game, the earliest is with the mysterious Ansari consort Sha'ira. Shepard encounters Sha'ira at a moment when the consort is having difficulties with the character, Septimus, who is spreading lies about her and her clients. When Shepard completes the Septimus plot line, Sha'ira confronts Shepard with a promise of words, "A gift of words, an affirmation of who you are and who you will become" (*Mass Effect*). Importantly, the sex scene between the two characters is dependent upon Shepard expressing disdain for these words that, once expressed, initiates the sexual encounter. The broad outlines of this exchange are in keeping with Tompkins' theory of the role of women and the language of men in the Western. Sha'ira is literally presented as a paragon of class, privilege, political clout, and financial strength in the Citadel, the title's strategic center for the Milky Way's many civilizations. She is known and discussed by many people on the station, and her chambers evince a relative refinement that is missing from other offices, common spaces, and abodes in the game. Her political clout is underscored by not only her long waiting list of connected clients but also by her financial prowess. The player is told that a single visit to the Consort can cost as much as half a year's pay. All of this is established before Shepard has a chance to dismiss her speech. These associations are not trivial, insofar as they reveal the very—to use Genette's term—"selections" that have been made to frame and contextualize the exchange. If the player is surprised by the outcome, such surprise can be traced to the hypothetical reservoir of narrative possibilities that Tompkins associates with the rise of the Western within a constellation of other literary traditions: e.g., the sentimental domestic novel, post–Western police narratives, and science fiction.

In addition to these qualities, both the character and her plotline are intimately connected with the concept of language. More to the point, the language issues surrounding Sha'ira bear on notions of women, religion, and culture. Her essential situation is that her cultural status in the Citadel has been imperiled by the lies Septimus is spreading about her, a scenario Shepard must correct for Sha'ira by spreading awareness of Septimus' actions to an alien diplomat. The essential peril of the scenario underscores the notion that language—and specifically language concerning a powerful female figure—is not to be trusted. The notion is relevant to Shepard's opportunity to dismiss the Consort's language when she offers Shepard a "gift of words" at the completion of his quest. While her powerful insights into Shepard's past and potential future should (and do) identify her as a strong if not resilient figure, he pushes her away, with the curious consequence of the Consort's quite literal abandonment of speech at the same moment that she falls into his arms.

While it is perhaps not as significant to the encounter as the role of words, it is interesting to note that the sexual act itself is presented with an allusion to the union of Jack and Rose in *Titanic* (1997). A single Ansari hand rises into an otherwise empty shot and slaps against what is presumably a window, in a gesture that calls to mind Rose's similar movement in the film, when she and Jack are entangled in an automobile. While the broader context of *Titanic* is not a major concern of this essay, Slavoj Žižek has already identified the intense class and gender implications of that union, and the significance of a powerful woman abandoning notions of class and breeding as she subjects herself—momentarily—to less refined masculine desire (*Pervert's Guide*). The association is made even more interesting, perhaps, by *Titanic's* own strong narrative ties to the sentimental domestic novel, as described by Tompkins. However, to be sure, the correlation is challenged by the relevant distinction that the Ansari is, at a minimum, a sex worker of some renown, while Rose, of course, is not.

But to return to *Mass Effect*, in the instance of Sha'ira, it should be noted that her romantic encounter with Shepard plays out the same way regardless of Shepard's gender. Consequently, it is reasonable to conclude that, in this instance, *Mass Effect*'s representation of women as lovers affirms Tompkins' comments on the element of women and the language of men in such a way that the gender choice that the player has made for Shepard has no bearing on the sexual politics of the Sha'ira encounter: Western distrust of language and women meets formal expectations regardless of the player's selection of Shepard's gender. Indeed, the Sha'ira encounter stands as useful context for the remainder of the title's romantic scenarios, which collectively indicate that the Western tropes for representing women trump specific gender choices that the player makes in the game.

Each of the remaining possible encounters contains important details that bear on Tompkins' theory in specific ways. However, it is important to note from the outset that every encounter that involves a male participant (three out of the four possibilities) contains a specific shot that affirms male domination over an involved female participant, whoever the participant may be. For example, in male Shepard's encounter with Liara and Ashley, the romance concludes with Shepard's mounting of either character, in a traditional sexual gesture of masculine domination, literally coupled with female submission as represented by a backwards head roll, with the involved woman's eyes closed and mouth just barely open. This is—and despite Lawrence's abdication of her reasonable if too general argument—quite easily associated with the visual history of pornography. Significantly, this same gesture is included in the encounter between female Shepard and Kaidan Alenko (a man)—where it is most notable because it inexplicably places the ever and always-dominant Shepard in a momentarily subordinate (to her literal subordinate, no less!) position. Interestingly (and tellingly), the gesture also appears in female Shepard's encounter with Liara. There, female Shepard is put in the position of the dominant body, which is a male body in every other permutation of this scene. In the context of the scene itself, the positioning is perhaps more emblematic of the game designer's male gaze (or simple lack of imagination) than anything else. However, in the larger context of all four scenes, and especially considering the Kaidan episode, the gesture conveys a similar sense of masculine dominance. At the very least, it does not appear to stand in defiance of those gestures in the service of some other articulated sexual agenda.

The context and content of these exchanges is informative of their commentary on notions of numbness and its significance to women and language. Liara approaches Shepard out of a stated desire to be "completely honest" and to seize on one "last chance to show each other how we feel" (*Mass Effect*). While Liara does not have the status or prestige of the consort Sha'ira, she is literally an expert on culture. Indeed, she is an explicitly identified expert on the very culture that is of most significance to events at the moment of her conversation with Shepard: the culture of the mysterious, alien Prothean race. Moreover, she is also associated with notions of wealth and extraordinary political power through her mother, the twisted Matriarch Benezia. While there is no explicit rejection of language in this union, it is notable that Liara asserts that the path to true "honesty" is to dispense with language altogether and instead engage in a physical and mental melding, a notion that Shepard affirms instantly. While the significance of this act is perhaps best understood in the context of Ashley Williams' potential encounter with a male Shepard at this same point in the game, the implication is clear enough: a female figure who has long been associated with "strong and resilient" language (and especially resilient, as Liara must speak her way through the necessary murder of her mother!) drops all pretense of using language to explain herself at the same moment that she surrenders to the male hero and his dominant embrace.

The Ashley Williams encounter with the male Shepard is perhaps the most clearly in line with Tompkins' theory, as it involves Williams' own, explicit disavowal of language—in this case the language of poetry, as she forcibly subjugates herself to Shepard. It begins with William's assertion that Shepard will always occupy a dominate position in her mind. She identifies him as "Skipper" and asserts that he "will always be the Skipper to me" (*Mass Effect*). This shameless notion of subservience is affirmed a moment later when she begins to recite Walt Whitman's "Oh, Captain! My Captain!" (1865) as a love poem to Shepard, which she—confusingly—claims is a better expression of sexual desire than she can state herself. The rest of the scenario essentially involves William's faux-feisty resistance to and then eventual submission to Shepard's sexual demands: e.g., he literally says, "Shut up and get over here" (*Mass Effect*). She does and thus subordinates herself to Shepard under the collective notions that, first and foremost, her own words are not fit for the task at hand, that she has no idea how to draw from culture to express her romantic desires for Shepard's masculinity, and that Shepard's unrefined "manly" speech is ideal—or at least preferable to her own—for initiating sexual submission. In these ways, the players see a woman submitting to sexual desire under concepts that are in keeping with Tompkins' argument on women and the language of men in the Western.

The female Shepard's optional encounter with Kaidan is also quite telling. The least verbose of the potential partners, Kaidan, a human, woos Shepard with the most stripped-down language, virtually none of which details his feelings for the Commander, other than the hardly descriptive "you make me feel human" (*Mass Effect*). For her part, Shepard is far from verbose, simply stating that Kaidan is a "sweetheart." However, and precisely because Kaidan speaks as a male figure can be expected to speak under Tompkins' theory, it is interesting that Shepard essentially succumbs to him wordlessly and is then represented in a position of contextual submission to him. This role reversal may surprise the player, but it is in keeping with the thematic expectations of the Western, as connected with the need for numbness as identify by Tompkins. Moreover, it is—precisely because of the individuals involved and the optional nature of all the sexual episodes—an excellent example of how the game's overarching commentary on women and language is most evident where it is least able to be apprehended: masculine desire is affirmed even when the affirmation would seem to short-circuit the logic of the plot.

An implication in each of these scenes is that the sexual encounter is occurring because the participants are uncertain about their future, and that the time to act on their romantic, or strictly sexual, interests is looming and fleeting. While the notion of sacrifice is relevant to these scenes to the extent that the involved characters are literarily about to sacrifice their safety to ensure the continuation of organic life in the galaxy, it would be hard to argue that these characters are sacrificing their "hearts" so that they can become numb to the dangers ahead. Rather, they are entertaining their desires so that they do not miss a final opportunity to do so, considering their fears of the future. Whether such storytelling decisions are informative of thematic, modal, or formal determinations that are, according to Genette, constant and transhistorical is an open question. Moreover, the question of whether the framing of such encounters to the same or similar ends is relevant to other titles with gameplay features that correspond with Wills' conception of the new digital West is also unknown at the time of this writing. However, and regardless, what these moments do establish is the relevance of Tompkins' conception of the Western to a work of science fiction that shares in the same novel gameplay features that Wills associates with the future of the videogame Western. As such, they establish common ground between not only specific literary traditions, but also between critical approaches to these same traditions.

While this common ground indicates one path forward for future criticism, it also comes with the necessary awareness that, at least in this instance, the notion that women should abdicate their learning and loquacity in the face of masculine desire is significant to the early gameplay conditions of the New West. Certainly, neither Wills nor Tompkins consider the Western for its efforts to establish parity between genders, nor do they regard the Western for its potential, progressive sexual politics at the level of cliché. Importantly, there is no reason to deny or overlook the possibility that such storytelling traditions exist and may themselves be constant and transhistorical; rather, that possibility must be explored. Future work could consider such matters and, through such considerations, bring added texture to Wills' digital frontier.

WORKS CITED

Cash, Johnny. "Ghost Riders in the Sky." *Silver*. Columbia Records, 1979.
Ferguson, Christopher J. "The School Shooting/Video Game Link: Casual Relationship or Moral Panic?" *Journal of Investigative Psychology and Offender Profiling*, no. 5, 2008, pp. 25–37.
Frye, Northrop. *The Secular Scripture: a Study of the Structure of Romance*. Harvard UP, 1976.
Genette, Gérard. *The Architext: an Introduction*. Translated by Jane E. Lewin, U of California P, 1992.
_____. *Fiction and Diction*. Translated by Catherine Porter, Cornell UP, 1993.
_____. *Narrative Discourse: an Essay on Method*. Translated by Jane E. Lewin, Cornell UP, 1980.
Griner, David. "Why Johnny Cash Was a Terrible Choice for the New Mass Effect Trailer." *Adweek*, 15 Jun. 2015, http://www.adweek.com/adfreak/why-johnny-cash-was-terrible-choice-new-mass-effect-trailer-165359.
Incendivus. "I Really Liked the Johnny Cash Song…. Here's Why." *Reddit*, https://www.reddit.com/r/masseffect/comments/3a2cym/i_really_liked_the_johnny_cash_song_heres_why/.
Mass Effect. BioWare, 2007.
Mass Effect 2. BioWare, 2010.
Mass Effect 3. BioWare, 2012.
Mass Effect: Andromeda. BioWare, 2017.
The Pervert's Guide to Cinema. Directed by Sophie Fiennes, Amoeba Film, 2009.
Schiesel, Seth. "Author Faults a Game, and Gamers Flame Back." *New York Times*, 26 Jan. 2008, http://www.nytimes.com/2008/01/26/arts/television/26mass.html.
Titanic. Directed by James Cameron, Twentieth Century–Fox, 1997.
Tompkins, Jane. *West of Everything: the Inner Life of Westerns*. Oxford UP, 1992.
Wills, John. "Pixel Cowboys and Silicon Gold Mines: Videogames of the American West." *Pacific Historical Review*, vol. 77, no. 2, 2008, pp. 273–303.

Olivia Dunham and the New Frontier in *Fringe*

Teresa Forde

Introduction

This analysis explores the frontier within *Fringe* (Fox 2008–2013). The Science Fiction Western explores the boundaries and frontiers of science, physics, and human development. Drawing upon a heritage of television shows such as *The X-Files* (1993–2002, 2016–2018) and *Lost* (2004–2010), *Fringe* encapsulates a consideration of weird scientific phenomena, the frontiers of the universe, and the implications for human and social boundaries. *Fringe* presents a multiverse scenario where many universes exist independently. FBI agent Olivia Dunham (Anna Torv) is a key character within the Fringe division, a part of the FBI that investigates unusual scientific and paranormal activity. Episodes oscillate between the investigation of paranormal and unusual scientific phenomena and the progression of the overarching story arc concerning Massive Dynamic and its trajectory of global domination. *Fringe* depicts the work of Dunham with her colleagues, Walter Bishop, a scientist; his FBI consultant son, Peter; and Olivia's assistant, Astrid Farnsworth. Olivia also has a close relationship with agent Lincoln Lee and a staunch ally in Special Agent Phillip Broyles. The series focuses on Olivia's discovery of her abilities against a backdrop of scientific development that breaks new ground and challenges existing knowledge. Olivia's abilities and memories are constantly pushing at boundaries regarding what constitutes the known world, and the series encapsulates fringe theories that challenge both scientific and geographical frontiers, establishing both a traditional and contemporary set of frontiers to "conquer" and explore. Different versions of history and the future are explored within the alternative universes that are all implicated by scientific knowledge.

As well as the exploration of weird science frontiers, *Fringe* depicts alternative universes (alt-verse) and alternative timelines. This story arc involves a parallel universe that is investigated, explored, exploited, and saved. The main alternate universe they encounter seems very similar to their own with corresponding characters in the alternative world and recognizable cityscapes. The notion of a fate or prophecy, sometimes viewed as fatalistic, is usually due to a causality loop, or a self-fulfilling prophecy that, rather than causing events to happen, either facilitates or enables them to occur. As Jan Johnson-Smith recognizes, this trope of "repeated explorations of these adjusted, amended and renovated journeys" is significant within American science fiction (5). Initially, the alt-verse seems to be technologically more sophisticated, more militaristic, and more idealistic than the original universe. It has not experienced the assassinations of President John Kennedy, Martin Luther King, Jr., and John Lennon whilst still experiencing a version of 9/11. The alt-verse's intrinsic structure, however, is affected by the characters crossing universes, which appears to have led to this militaristic approach. Markedly, it is the scarcity of coffee in the alt-verse that instantly differentiates it from the original universe where drinking coffee has become emblematic since the expansion of the Western frontier.

Fringe explores many Western motifs, such as the lone hero fighting for justice. This character traverses physical and psychological frontiers, defends communities, and explores the hero's moral code. Within the *Fringe* series, even the cow, Gene, who Astrid looks after and lives in the Walter's lab, evokes the Western past of cattle ranching and farming. In addition, the importance of history in influencing the future is repeated within *Fringe* to illustrate the ways in which actions can have significant effect. The new frontier is both spatial and temporal, and Olivia is depicted exploring the boundaries of her own mind, so she may affect change. Eventually, viewers learn that the Outsiders have come to Earth threatening the future of humanity, which is where the codes of morality and survival ultimately emerge. Olivia's path develops as she attempts to both save the universe and her own family.

As the initial hero in the series, Olivia travels physically and mentally across universes. In consideration of the television series *Stargate SG-1* (Showtime 1997–2007), Johnson-Smith notes how this kind of scenario "makes a connection between the epic journeys that blend together to form what we recognize as ancient mytho-history and the more recent dominant mytho-history of the USA—the story of the frontier, the 'Wild West' ... of epic journeys, part genuine exploration and part flamboyant speculation" (5–6). Such an account highlights the significant role the Western and the Wild West frontier have within broader histories and reasserts the protagonist as a negotiator of problematic and nation-building motivation. As David Mogen identifies, "Much of the expressive power of American science fiction results from the metaphorical and symbolic potency of the frontier myths it evokes"

(34). Olivia is able to traverse universes via her enhanced mental powers that enable her to cross over to the other side. Subsequent sojourns to the alternative universe, however, have further undermined its structure, which has become increasingly unstable. With Olivia's help, a bridge is established between the two universes in order to enhance travel to try to save both. This action illustrates that exploration (including potential exploration) reflects both physical frontiers and psychological boundaries to be crossed.

Both science fiction and Westerns have traditionally encountered borderlines, boundaries, and frontiers, with many SF Westerns translating the fight for supremacy in the American West into space travel and alien encounters that are depicted in terms of either dominance or conciliation. Traditionally, women in science fiction films, such as the 1950s invasion narratives, tended to play scientists or supportive figures in the lab as well as domestic types. Over time, these roles have developed as female characters became scientific experts in franchises such as *Jurassic Park*. Many critiques of traditional Westerns often show female characters as part of the "cult of true womanhood" (Manuel 25), which defined white women's role as homemaker and child-bearer. In many of John Ford's most iconic films, these women function as a representation of the domestic sphere, often configured as "home," and as exemplified in the homestead and the porch as a domestic boundary within films like *The Searchers* (1956). However, films such as Ford's *High Noon* (1952) seem to problematize these definitions and highlight the potential for the frontier as a place of critique and progress in the dichotomy of "outsider" female characters who challenge the status quo. There is also a strand of Westerns where glamour and humor are blended; film stars such as Mae West or Doris Day in *Calamity Jane* (1953) use comedy to play with existing conventions in classic era Hollywood films. As the form continues to diversify and adapt to both different genre and social influences, the concentration upon individual female characters emerges within narratives that further challenge women's roles. Feminist post–Westerns, including *Desert Hearts* (1985) and *Shame* (1988), have focused on breaking down both physical and psychological barriers to women's development. These films have brought female characters and their relationships with other women to the forefront of the action.

Within the evolution of the *Star Trek* Universe, there has been more space for complex female characters to emerge as part of ensemble casts. This is most obvious within the *Star Trek* television franchise, in which later series depict lead female characters and action heroines, such as Captain Janeway and B'Elanna Torres in *Star Trek: Voyager* (1995–2001). Contemporary hybrid Westerns often draw upon the notion of the frontier in complex ways and illustrate a move away from the traditional civilized/uncivilized dichotomy of the American West. As Paul Cantor argues in relation to television, "the Western did not die; it merely migrated and mutated. As the "Have Gun-*Star*

Trek" connection suggests, the Western was reborn in science fiction" (94). Characters boldly go into a scientific adventure, as the television reboot of *Westworld* (2016–present) portrays in the dystopian trajectory technology and exploitation amidst the setting of the American West.

Fringe: *Exploring Universal Laws*

Long-form television series such as *Fringe* offer the possibility for an ensemble cast and a community of characters to develop within complex timelines. They also offer the possibility of a larger range of characters and for female protagonists to emerge at the forefront of storylines. Within *Fringe*, events in each timeline are undergoing surveillance by the Observers, and multiple timelines offer additional dimensions to the story world. William H. Katerberg argues that the frontiers of science have become America's new frontiers and a focus on future technology illustrates that "it matters less and less whether the stories are set in the West itself. 'New World' hopes have moved on to the frontiers of the body and mind" (185). Olivia must negotiate her own inner turmoil whilst dealing with the effects of technology and the disconcerting effects of time travel in equal measure. Furthermore, she has been experimented on, so her mind has become a symbolic frontier that has been violated and needs to be defended.

Additionally, Olivia is fighting against capitalists with ambitious and exploitative science projects, and she has personally suffered numerous side-effects from their experiments.

The mutation of the Western enables a range of innovative developments that focus on the frontier motif within a science fictional world. The Western and science fiction also offer the possibility of social critique and an effective hybrid form as both contend with literal and metaphorical frontiers within their story worlds. Within *Fringe*, these frontiers are depicted in the Fringe Division consistently facing unexplained phenomena and negotiating the gateway to the alt-verse. In addition, the main protagonists must negotiate both spatial and mental frontiers as a consequence of this experimentation. The iconographic arc of the series begins in season one with Olivia as an FBI investigator and develops the scientific dimension of the plot. Each season of *Fringe* establishes its own "character" in terms of plot, setting, iconography and mise-en-scène. Prior to the timeline's development, the promotional material for the first two seasons depicts Olivia, Peter, and Walter outside at night in the countryside with a flashlight as if looking for clues. The backdrop is rural and looks like the American West whilst their clothing reflects the contemporary twenty-first century. It is only as the plot becomes more complicated and the timelines begin to shift that the iconography of the DVDs and posters for later series becomes more noirish in tone with darker images focusing on the significance of time and technology.

Fringe is complicated by a number of possible timelines emanating from different timelines and characters who may be "over here" and "over there." Alongside the attempt to control lawlessness and exploitation, there is great interest in the otherness of strange phenomena emerging from the technology of this alternative world. There is also a fascination with its inhabitants who are dopplegängers or alternatives of the characters within the prime universe and an initial assumption that these may be "villains" who must be defeated, echoing the "bad guy" construction of Westerns.

There's a New Sheriff in Town: "Olivia. In the Lab. With the Revolver"

As an FBI agent working with Walter, Peter, and Astrid, Olivia encounters strange phenomena which emerge as the result of previous experiences encountered in her life when she was younger. Eventually, it is revealed that Olivia was experimented on as a child—the cortexiphan experiments—which were conducted by Walter and his co-researcher, William Bell. These experiments cause Olivia to develop supernatural abilities but lead to her being haunted by their effects, thereby becoming socially withdrawn. Although socially she is somewhat a "loner," Olivia is passionate about fighting for justice and defending her team. These characteristics show her as the righteous Western lawman, sheriff, or territorial marshal. This character type is familiar from Hollywood Westerns as one who stands for justice in the face of opposition. It also emulates the prominent female figures of television who must challenge accepted procedures in order to save their crew. As Judith Butler argues, gender is enacted in the process of performativity "meaning is performed and acted" via "specific corporeal acts." The nature of this performativity enables the possibility of "cultural transformation" through the contestation of fixed boundaries (Butler 155). By challenging and pushing outside of accepted boundaries, these characters expand the potential to make changes. In the opening episodes, although undertaking a clandestine relationship with co-worker John Scott, Olivia is still depicted as somewhat socially isolated but is encouraged out of her protective world as she seeks Walter's help treating Scott's life-threatening condition. Olivia also begins to identify with others who have been affected by cortexiphan experiments, and she seeks justice for them, negotiating the responsibility for family with the need to save the world. Initially, Olivia is depicted as emotionally disengaged yet immensely moral in her role as a lawgiver, as a variation of the Western story of a lone hero protecting and defending a small town. It should be recognized that the sheriff in traditional Westerns is not always as isolated as he might first appear and that his alliances are fundamental to success. Although Olivia does have a single-minded approach, she does work with colleagues in order to achieve her end goals. The difference is in her own experiences and abilities that enable her to stand alone in the face of adversity and believe that she is correct in her acts.

Olivia's paranormal abilities, including pyrokinesis and telekinesis, are exploited by Bell and Walter as both a conduit to and protector from the alternative universe. As she comes to understand her "fate," Olivia is even more determined to use her powers to benefit humanity and to work towards a sense of good. She does so with a sense of duty that is informed by both her job and a personal code of honor, although by necessity this work can take on a "maverick" quality (Dirks). In her demeanor, Olivia emulates Western heroes who are a "maverick or rogue, often a loner, fiercely loyal, intelligent, resourceful and capable" who also "possess a strong moral code" (Keeble 143). Further, Olivia's actions illustrate the move from Frontier Law to law that is more regulated. Her extraordinary powers are drawn upon significantly in the final two episodes of the series when she doses herself with cortex-iphan so that she may go to the other side to rescue the empathetic Observer, Michael. In "Liberty," Olivia kills an Observer who has stalked her daughter before he disappears through time to kill others. The archetype of the hero working single-handedly conveys the significance of individuality and independence, even when working as part of a team. This sense of isolation is often established due to a strong sense of morality. Yvonne Tasker describes this experience in reference to the superhero narrative:

> Superhero fictions are frequently concerned not only with origins but with the psychic and emotional struggles faced by central characters in terms of coming to terms with their abilities, powers and bodies. The physical changes they experience involve them in new and different relationships to loved ones and to the wider society [*Hollywood Action* 180].

Olivia's transformation is influenced by her ability to control her powers and to trust others without losing her inner resolve.

Olivia's attire throughout the series reflects her identity. Olivia performs her role as FBI officer dressed in practical almost colorless outfits, consisting of black and grey trouser suits, white shirts, and black footwear. The monochrome wardrobe implies that she sees the world in a particular way and tries to simplify it. Her attire also acts as a mechanism by which she shields herself from being undermined by others, so she can focus on the job she needs to do and also maintain control. Olivia initially protects herself from her memories via this control over her persona and daily activities. Her wardrobe is scaled down to a small number of each set of garments. This choice of outfit serves as an iconic and reassuring uniform in which she can carry out her daily work and also establishes a sense of control and simplicity in her life. The uniform of her wardrobe includes one suit, one white shirt, one black leather jacket, and a G19 and a 57 pistol, as she is often depicted holding either one gun or two. Her dress and manner evoke the Western trope of the mysterious gunman with a secret past who is a highly moralistic upholder of the law. Her action figure is rarely seen without a gun as it is integral to her role. In one timeline, Olivia feels a great sense of justice and the desire to uphold the law: she shoots her stepfather with a sense of justified retribution due to his violence towards her family. As Kathleen McDonough recognizes, "The classic Western glorifies the individual. The hero is an outsider who often protects the community while remaining apart from it. One of the key questions in the Western is, will the hero join the community and be assimilated into the domestic sphere?" (102). She establishes her status as a hero in the series, although she positions herself outside of the wider community. As she develops a close relationship with Lincoln, Walter, Astrid, and Peter she becomes more integrated and achieves, albeit briefly, a form of domestic happiness with her daughter, Etta.

Olivia as Gunslinger and Caregiver: "I'm not ready to die, are you?"

Despite Olivia being portrayed in early episodes as the main character, many episodes focus upon other story arcs and their backstories as the series progresses. Torv recognizes the significance of Olivia's character to the show as a key component of the narrative. Her character arc presents her as increasingly emotional as well as ethical in motivation; Torv describes Olivia as "'kind of the glue that sticks everything together'" (Strachan). The effect of Olivia being a form of social and narrative "glue" is similar to the role of the women in Ford's traditional Westerns, as Olivia appears to emulate the function of some of Ford's female characters who hold society together. Tasker observes that "The white woman in the Western has, at least some of the time, a strength and an independence to match the struggles she faces" (53). This strength in the face of adversity is a recognized attribute of frontier women who have to face hardship and challenges on a daily basis. In the West, sheriffs' wives effectively became deputies in their own right as some performed a deputy's duties, helping to keep the peace and uphold the law. As Barbara Alderman identifies, even a sheriff's wife in the Western era would have reason to carry "a pistol in her apron" in case of danger when handing food to prisoners (85). So many of these women were in a position where they performed traditional roles as caregivers and nurturers while simultaneously contemplating using a weapon in self-defense and effectively becoming officers of the law themselves. They represent the qualities that Olivia develops both as an FBI officer investigating the frontier of the alt-verse and the possibilities of her defeating their enemies. There is a particular sense of lawlessness and unpredictability about the universes and frontier science that emulates the settlers of the American West. While the Fringe team is unsure about people's motives, Olivia is always keen to communicate wherever possible in order to do what is ethically correct.

In addition to her own colleagues, Olivia seems to increasingly care about what happens to those she encounters. She has an affinity with others who are displaced and perceives herself as an anomaly due to her paranormal abilities. Reflecting her own experiences as a child, she has a highly moral code in relation to defending those who cannot protect themselves and an empathetic approach to those who feel lost and afraid. As Olivia works through her past and experiences traumatic flashbacks, she establishes the specific paranormal powers that have emerged through her treatment. She can move through universes, move objects, and literally catch bullets; she is also a witness to extraordinary events. Once Olivia realizes that she is not the only victim of this experimentation, she tries to reach other victims of the tests to understand what has happened to her. Looking for answers throughout most of the series, Olivia comes to realize that not everything can be explained or controlled but that there are undeniable challenges in exploring the possibilities of new frontiers. Increasingly, she develops a personal as well as professional relationship with Peter and becomes more determined in her attempts to save the world. As well as undertaking many heroic acts as part of her job, she challenges sexual harassment and protectively champions the underdog at every turn. She also has a wisecracking, sardonic wit that is both a coping mechanism and a way of communicating with colleagues.

The doppelgänger versions of the main protagonists highlight different aspects of their personality traits. Olivia's double, referred to by fans as Fauxlivia, has not experienced the traumatic childhood that Olivia has had to endure and is a happier, outgoing, and optimistic character. When Olivia is kept against her will in the alt-verse, her doppelgänger crosses over and poses as Olivia. In one timeline that is eventually eradicated, Fauxlivia has a relationship with Peter and becomes pregnant. Olivia and Peter's ongoing romance functions as an underpinning dynamic working throughout much of the series. In season one, Olivia's serious relationship with Scott leads her to Walter and then Peter. Olivia and Scott's relationship is further conveyed after Scott's death when he reappears to Olivia and can communicate with her through her dreams, his appearances culminating in the episode "The Transformation." The trauma of this relationship causes Olivia to be even more cautious about getting attached to others, although she does have a close relationship with Lincoln, who is eventually Fauxlivia's partner. Olivia becomes particularly close to Lincoln when Peter is erased from history but then distances herself as she begins to remember Peter in season four.

Olivia's narrative trajectory is latterly obscured by the experiences of Walter and Peter who are bonding as father and son. In many ways Olivia becomes gendered by her own narrative recuperation as she is a mother and a hero. Increasingly, Olivia establishes her place within the domestic sphere as mother to Etta whilst simultaneously becoming more focused on saving the world. There are four primary timelines between the two universes. These timelines are affected by changing events and by crossing in between different universes, all of which have implications for the future and emphasize the impact of what happens on each timeline. At the point where Olivia and Peter sit in the park playing with Etta, an explosion tears apart their domestic bliss. This explosion and loss of Etta is later erased when the past is changed. Also, Etta does not need to become a freedom fighter because there is no Observer invasion. Olivia undergoes traumatic assaults to her body and psyche, which have an implication for scientific, temporal and geographical frontiers. In the season four finale, "Brave New World: Part 2," Olivia is shot by Walter because she is being manipulated by Bell, although she recovers from the shooting due to the drugs in her body. In an alternative timeline, Walternate (Walter in the alt-verse) kills Olivia due to her powers. In another, Olivia survives and is rescued from amber by Ella, her now grown up niece, and is briefly reunited with her daughter, Etta. When these two timelines ultimately merge, Olivia is again rescued from amber in the future by Ella (season five). She is then determined to find Etta and fight the totalitarian force of the Observers, thereby re-establishing her steely reserve in the face of adversity. Olivia's heroism demonstrates her determination and her, greatly tested, ethical code. To a degree, Olivia has to eschew her emotions to in order to protect herself and her daughter. Because of her actions, however, the Observers finally see that they can embody emotions and avoid killing humans in order to ensure their own survival.

The Good, the Bad and the Alternate

John Parris Springer discusses the Hawksian woman character (Howard Hawks' Western and action films), notably analyzed by Naomi Wise. Springer states that "Wise … praises the Hawksian woman for successfully synthesizing the 'good girl/bad girl' polarities of the Hollywood stereotype," which results in a stronger, independent female (116). The mutual influence between these character types can be seen in many examples of genre films and television shows in which an ideologically coded pairing of characters demonstrate that the couple is embedded within the plot. In the "dual focus structure"

(Altman) that is identified within musicals but is also possible within other genres, the female characters are often more altered in their attitudes than the male characters by the end of the narrative. Rick Altman recognizes that "Constantly opposing cultural values to counter-cultural values, genre films regularly depend on dual protagonists and dualistic structures either through oppositional characters or an individual who presents a divided self" (24).

In terms of acting styles, Sharon Knobloch argues that Sharon Stone was criticized for her acting in the revisionist Western, *The Quick and the Dead* (1995), in her role as a gunslinger: "To (type) cast an actress who slips away from the codes of realistic acting that dominate Hollywood undermines, via connotations of poor quality, any positive expressions around her of physical female power" (124). However, as Knobloch observes, the image of the female gunslinger is less clearly coded due its rarity. In an evaluation of Olivia's character, Michelle Ealey recognizes Torv's ability to play six versions of the Olivia character with subtlety and skill:

> Torv deserves individual recognition for her work as Olivia Dunham—all six versions of Olivia Dunham. Over the course of the show's four seasons, Torv has portrayed six incarnations of Olivia, giving each distinct characteristics ... our universe Olivia Dunham, Alt-Olivia, Fauxlivia, Olivia who thinks she's Alt-Olivia, Future Olivia, and Peter-less timeline Olivia [Ealey].

Ealey shows that versatility in playing different versions of a character is a subtle art. Also, it could be argued that Olivia's less-than-candid personality at the start of the show adds to her initial mystery. In the alt-verse, another version of Olivia functioning as her alter ego (dubbed initially as Bolivia by the cast and then Fauxlivia by Walter and fans) works with the Walter's "evil" alter ego, Walternate. Fauxlivia is more easy-going and sociable while Olivia is much more reticent. She is almost the mirror image of Olivia but is a brunette and is depicted as being a more social and gregarious character than Olivia. Although Olivia initially views her counterpart as a threat, partly because she is more self-assured and has not had the same experiences as Olivia, they eventually work together. In terms of the Hawksian woman, Fauxlivia encapsulated the self-assuredness of the professional woman who is self-reliant, smart, and experienced. Olivia seems to become more like her opposite as she develops a more self-assured demeanor and certainly like the rather idealized Hawksian woman in her ability to be more significant than traditional (male) heroes (Wise). In "Over There: Part 2" when Fauxlivia asks Peter what Olivia is like, he replies with "She's a lot like you. Darker in the eyes, maybe. She's always trying to make up for something. Right some imaginary wrong. Haunted, I guess. Maybe she's nothing like you at all" ("Over There: Part 2"). This description of Olivia emphasizes her image as the gunslinger who fights for justice. She is driven to seek justice and make up for past wrongs on behalf of herself and others. Recalling the figure of

Asta Cardell in the post–Western *Shame*, Olivia fights for justice on both a professional and personal level. Ultimately, however, it is her fight against injustice—where she uses weapons, including her own mind—that drives her and exemplifies both her character and legacy in her daughter, Etta.

First Peoples Mythos: "A New Day in the Old Town"

In season three, the doomsday machine shows Peter what could happen if Olivia's timeline is destroyed and the Observers take over the world. Within science fiction, the defamiliarization of seeing into the future is a juxtaposition or a fragmented mirror that is constantly shifting and refracting. Olivia consistently contends with the slippage between universes and timelines; however, rather than reaching a fatalistic conclusion of fulfilling a destiny, redefining that destiny becomes more significant for her. Yet the implication is that changes can also be made to the future and to herself. This is something that Olivia recognizes in the episode, "The Last Sam Weiss," when she discovers that she has the ability to disable the doomsday weapon being used by the alt-verse. Instead, Peter uses it in "The Day We Died" when, by bridging the two worlds, he erases himself from time until the timelines remerge.

A return to the past is made possible by the wave sync technology that was sent back in time as a doomsday machine. It is believed that the First People—an ancient race—created the machine. Neil Campbell argues that "the classic western represented the past as knowable and conquered," so the post-Western functions to question these "taken-for-granted mythic discourses" (Campbell 36). In "The Last Sam Weiss," Sam Weiss, whose forefather discovered and protected the manuscript, writes the First People treatise based on his own and his five ancestors' research. The first people mythos is a belief that a group—the First People—created the doomsday device prior to their demise. It is later revealed that the First People are Walter, Astrid, and Etta, who sent the destructive machine back to the past through a wormhole; by doing so, they influenced their own "fate" and enabled human choice about the future. Within the *Fringe* mythos, the significance of Olivia, Astrid, and Etta being involved with the time-traveling plan challenges historical prejudices based on class, race, and gender and reconfigures a liberal American ethos going back into the past.

In "Everything in Its Right Place," both sides must work together to ensure the temporary stability of the bridge until its ultimate closure. The bridge symbolizes the ability for both sides to coexist in harmony and to learn from each other. Lincoln decides to live in the alt-verse with Fauxlivia as he has now found his home. He gives Olivia a necklace as a parting gift and says, "It's Native American. The maze represents the journey of life. The obstacles—

making the right choices. Until we find ourselves in the center.... Home. A place to belong" ("Everything in its Right Place"). The motif of "home" also illustrates an understanding and acceptance of the self. Once the universe is stabilized and the threat has been eradicated, Oliva can make a home. Walter seeks to contact Bell by using Olivia as the conduit establishing a link via the use of soul magnets which emulate the notion of soul energy and are attributed to individual spirits within Native American mythology. Within *Fringe*, this spirit represents consciousness. The linking of souls and the anchoring through time and space encapsulate the time-traveling experiences of Olivia and Peter, particularly for Olivia who is finely attuned to other universes, sensing Peter even when he is temporarily eradicated from time.

In his account of archaeologies of knowledge, Michel Foucault argues that analyzing the archive of all possible "utterances" ultimately "involves a privileged region: at once close to us, and different from our present existence" (147). Foucault's notion of the archive refers to sources of cultural thought and experience, envisaged as a fragmentary set of discourses that can always be realigned and reconstructed. Olivia comes to realize that her supernatural abilities were triggered by the cortexiphan experiments unlocking parts of the brain. This drug is like mescaline and the plant peyote used by Native Americans in spiritual ceremonies to gain insight. Because she experiences echoes of the past and can cross over to other timelines, Olivia is able to make those transitions becoming a kind of "observer" herself. These transitions are representative of frontiers being transgressed, which often contributes to her sometimes "outsider" status. As part of their function as memory recall, flashbacks—which Olivia suffers from throughout the series—provide a heightened sense of a character's state of mind. As Maureen Turim asserts, "The extended flashback is an amplification of the psychological subjectivity of the character" (149). Turim's account accentuates the "internal vision" of the flashback even though there may be no clear way of the character bridging this gap between memories of the past and the present. This flashback acts as a legacy for Olivia to pass onto her daughter, who is already a freedom-fighter seeking justice in a very unjust world.

The Observers, who are seen monitoring the main characters intermittently throughout the series, plan to invade Earth; they are depicted as terraforming it in 2036 amidst environmental catastrophe. In "The Bullet That Saved the World," Etta is killed in the future timeline and is a poster icon for resistance to the Observers. Graffiti on the bridge reads "Manifest Destiny," which is associated with the belief by white settlers that it was their destiny to expand into the West and to conquer Native Americans in the process. This reference stands as a symbol of the Observers' desire to overtake and control Earth. "Manifest Destiny" as a piece of graffiti, however, has an alternative meaning, which recognizes the First People as a sign of hope. An analogy can be made between the Observers as colonizing white settlers and the Resistance as emblematic of Native American peoples who wish to protect their world. As a Resistance fighter, Etta has learned to prevent the Observers from reading her thoughts. Etta seeks her parents and is convinced that they are still alive. As part of her quest for them, Etta discovers a bullet at her old family home and wears it as a necklace. She is unaware of its significance as it is the bullet Walter uses to "kill" Olivia and trigger the end of the world, which is when Olivia is "reborn" due to the drugs she had taken. Olivia re-emerges as the potential savior of the universe because she is able to restore order. Etta is drawn to the bullet and wears the necklace that is so associated with Western iconography. The bullet necklace becomes a significant talisman for Etta, her parents, and their fight. When she is confronted by an Observer later in the episode, Etta briefly conveys via her thoughts that the necklace represents love. Etta becomes the ultimate freedom fighter and has constantly worked to defeat the oppressive regime, taking on Olivia's mantle. Nonetheless, Olivia is still performing her role as law-giver because, crucially, she shows Etta that torture and killing are not the only way to deal with the Observers. In the final timeline, Etta is a child and Olivia will have the opportunity to influence her daughter's behavior in the future.

Conclusion: "Everything in Its Right Place"

Fringe explores frontier science and the expansion and collapse of different worlds. The dazzling display of technology positions the prime universe as both technologically lacking and being adversely affected by viruses, technological innovation, and capabilities over which the characters potentially have little control. The series depicts the Fringe team negotiating the many physical and mental frontiers. As a key character at the start of the series, Olivia constantly traverses these frontiers and ultimately seems to overcome them. In contrast to Olivia's trajectory, towards the end of the series there is more of a focus on father/son relationships, like those of Walter and Peter and September and Michael. However, Olivia has enabled many of these relationships to flourish by reuniting these characters in the pilot episode and did so as part of her job. Although she establishes important personal relationships throughout the series, she increasingly spends time away from the other characters due to plot twists that see her ostracized or imprisoned. She even shifts across universes, emphasizing her loner status, which is necessary for her to achieve her goals. The figure of the gunfighter and law enforcer is demonstrated in Olivia's desire to find out the truth and fight for justice. In addition, her enhanced abilities set her apart and provide the opportunity to make a difference. What begins as a social detachment develops more strongly into Olivia's ethical code throughout the series. When Olivia returns to the forefront of the onscreen action in the last episodes, she tries to protect her daughter and avenge her death.

Olivia's character explores the role of the female within science fiction and Western tropes. She fights at the frontier, whether patronized or threatened by other characters but equally supports others, particularly those who are victims of abuse or exploitation. She is positioned in relation to other characters and develops relationships with women within the series. For example, Ella, her niece, is important to Olivia, as is her daughter, Etta. She forms a relationship with Astrid and even with Fauxlivia by the end of the series. The "New World" that is initially established sees Olivia and Peter return to the park, sitting in the field, watching Etta play and calling her home. Peter picks up Etta and holds her close while Olivia watches them both. In this moment she is observing her family and taking pleasure in the fact that she has brought all this together. In addition to establishing a future for herself and her family, she has been instrumental in saving the universe, averting the Observer invasion, and restoring some sense of order to the world.

As a science fiction series that adopts a frontier perspective, *Fringe* explores ideas of nationhood, future technology, and gender representation in a range of doubled characters. The doubling process and the presence of alternative universes and timelines enhances the sense that things can always be different, which may challenge the tenet of Manifest Destiny as understood by white settlers to the West. Olivia's character transgresses many of the boundaries traditionally associated with women from these genres. *Fringe* encapsulates the contemporary concern with the environment, new technologies, and the transgression of boundaries and traditional tropes related to both the Western and science fiction. In the character of Olivia Dunham, ethics are established as fundamental aspects of frontier science fiction.

WORKS CITED

Alderman, Barbara, J. *The Secret Life of the Lawman's Wife*. Praeger, 2006.
Alien. Directed by Ridley Scott, Twentieth Century–Fox, 1979.
Altman, Rick. *Film/Genre*. B.F.I., 1999.
Berman, Rick, Michael Piller, and Jeri Taylor, creators. *Star Trek: Voyager*. Paramount Television, 1995–2001.
"Brave New World: Part 2." *Fringe*, season 4, episode 22, Fox, 11 May 2012.
"The Bullet That Saved the World." *Fringe*, season 5, episode 4, Fox, 26 Oct. 2012.
Butler, Judith. "Performative Acts and Gender Constitution: an Essay in Phenomenology and Feminist Theory." *The Performance Studies Reader*, edited by H. Bial, Routledge, 2007, pp. 154–166.
Campbell, Neil. *Post-Westerns: Cinema, Region, West*. U of Nebraska, 2013.
Cantor, Paul, A. *The Invisible Hand in Popular Culture: Liberty Vs. Authority in American Film and Television*. U of Kentucky P, 2012.
"The Day We Died." *Fringe*, season 3, episode 22, Fox, 5 Jun. 2011.
Desert Hearts. Directed by Donna Deitch, Desert Hearts Production, 1985.
Dirks, Tim. "Western Films." *Amc Network Filmsite*, 2017. http://www.filmsite.org/western films.html.

Ealey, Michelle. "Torv, Anna: Why Haven't They Given Her an Emmy Already?" *Sciencefiction. com*, 2012. http://sciencefiction.com/2012/01/19/anna-torv-why-havent-they-given-her-an-emmy-already/.

"Everything in Its Right Place." *Fringe*, season 4, episode 7, Fox, 4 Jun. 2012.

Foucault, Michel. *Archaeologies of Knowledge*. Translated by Sheridan Smith, Tavistock, 1986.

Fringe. Created by J.J. Abrams, Alex Kurtzman, and Roberto Orci, Bad Robot, 2008–2013.

High Noon. Directed by John Ford, Stanley Kramer Productions, 1952.

Johnson-Smith, Jan. *American Science Fiction TV: Star Trek, Stargate and Beyond*. I.B. Taurus, 2005.

Jurassic Park. Directed by Steven Spielberg, Universal Pictures 1993.

Katerberg, William H. *Future West: Utopia and Apocalypse in Frontier Science Fiction*. U of Kansas P, 2008.

Keeble, Arin. "The War on Drugs and the War on Terror." *The Wire and America's Dark Corners: Critical Essays*, edited by Arin Keeble and Ivan Stacy, McFarland, 2015, pp. 133–152.

Knobloch, Susan. "Sharon Stone's (An)Aesthetic." *Reel Knockouts: Violent Women in Film*, edited by Martha McCaughey and Neal King, U of Texas P, 2001, pp. 124–144.

"The Last Sam Weiss." *Fringe*, season 3, episode 21, Fox, 29 Apr. 2011.

"Liberty." *Fringe*, season 5, episode 12, Fox, 1 Aug. 2013.

Lost. Created by J.J. Abrams, Jeffrey Lieber, and Damon Lindelof, Bad Robot, 2004–2010.

"Making Angels." *Fringe*, season 4, episode 11, Fox, 2 Mar. 2012.

McDonough, Kathleen A. "Wee Willie Winkie Goes West: the Influence of the British Empire Genre on Ford's Cavalry Trilogy." *Hollywood's West: the American Frontier in Film, Television & History*, edited by Peter Rollins and John Connor, U of Kentucky P, 2005, pp. 99–114.

Mogen, David. *Wilderness Visions: the Western Theme in Science Fiction Literature*, edited by Daryl F. Mallett, Borgo/Wildside Press, 1993.

Mountjoy, Shane. *Manifest Destiny: Westward Expansion*. Chelsea House Publishing, 2009.

"Over There: Part 2." *Fringe*, season 2, episode 22, Fox, 20 May 2010.

The Searchers. Directed by John Ford, C.V. Whitney, 1956.

Shame. Directed by Steve Jodrell, Barron Films, 1988.

Simmon, Scott. *The Invention of the Western Film: a Cultural History of the Genre's First Half Century*. Cambridge UP, 2010.

Springer, John Parris. "Beyond the River: Women and the Role of the Feminine in Howard Hawks's *Red River*." *Hollywood's West: the American Frontier in Film, Television, & History*, edited by Peter Rollins and John Connor, U of Kentucky P, 2005, pp. 115–125.

Stephanson, Anders. *Manifest Destiny: American Expansionism and the Empire of Right*, Farrar, Straus and Giraud, 1996.

Strachan, Alex. "Exclusive from the 'Fringe' Set: John Noble, Anna Torv and Josh Jackson Talk About the Other Actors, and Not Just Themselves." Canada.com, 7 Oct. 2010. http://o. canada.com/entertainment/exclusive-from-the-fringe-set-john-noble-anna-torv-and-josh-jackson-talk-about-the-other-actors-and-not-just-themselves.

Tasker, Yvonne. *The Hollywood Action and Adventure Film*. Routledge, 2015.

_____. *Working Girls: Gender and Sexuality in Popular Cinema*. Routledge, 1998.

"The Transformation." *Fringe*, season 1, episode 13, Fox, 2 Mar. 2009.

Turim, Maureen. *Flashbacks in Film: Memory & History*. Routledge, 1989.

Vasilescu, Stelian Ciprian. "Who the Heck Is Anna Torv, Really?" *Fringe Wiki*, 2013. http://fringe.wikia.com/wiki/Thread:7989.

Westworld. Created by Jonathan Nolan and Lisa Joy, HBO, 2016–present.

Wise, Naomi. "The Hawksian Woman." *Howard Hawks: American Artist*, edited by Jim Hillier and Peter Wollen, British Film Institute, 1997, pp. 111–119.

The X-Files. Created by Chris Carter, Ten Thirteen Productions, 1993–2018.

A Fistful of Gender

Power and the Body in Text-Based
Trans-Femme SF Western Video Games

Joshua King

The image has become a cultural cliché: the hero sits astride his horse, trotting across a vast desert plain. His guns sway at his side, and his hat shades his face from the withering sun. Americans know the scene well. Sometimes, however, the cowboy looks a little different. Sometimes, like in *Blazing Saddles* (1974), the cowboy is black, dressed to perfection, sporting Gucci saddlebags, and greeting Count Basie and his band. Sometimes, as in the *Toy Story* franchise, the cowboy is made of plastic and felt. Sometimes, the hero is a transgender woman, and her horse is a robot. The Western has become pop culture's narrative mirepoix: a base so adaptable and familiar that it can be combined with nearly anything to create a new product. Science fiction Westerns—shows like *Firefly* (2002–2003) or *Westworld* (2016–present), video games like *Metal Gear Solid V: The Phantom Pain* (2015) and the *Borderlands* series (2009–2015)—all attach SF trappings to the familiar open-range drama of the Western. In this article, I consider an extremely specific kind of SF Western: the trans-femme SF Western text-based game.

This article employs two of Michel Foucault's most famous works (and one of his less famous) to demonstrate the ways in which SF defamiliarizes and restructures the Western's hyper-dramatized power dynamics. Foucault's *Discipline and Punish* traces the development of modern disciplinary systems: the minute exertions of power over the body and how that power interacts with knowledge to form power-knowledge relations. The text-based game (a hypertext video game navigated by clicking links), *Wild Wild Gender Mines* (2014), from Porpentine (aka Porpentine Charity Heartscape), interrogates the gendered body by adapting and restructuring the classic folk ballad "Oh My Darling, Clementine" (1884). Porpentine converts the song's regressive gender dynamic into a trans, punk koan: "What is gender?" Anna Anthropy's text-based game, *And the Robot Horse You Rode In On* (2013), adapts Sergio Leone's film, *The Good, the Bad and the Ugly* (1966), into a bondage-heavy queer romance and, in doing so, engages with the kinds of power and pleasure spirals that suffuse Foucault's *The History of Sexuality Volume One*. In both cases, SF provides a technique for de- and reconstructing familiar Western tropes. These games apply SF veneers to the Western's familiar structures and cultural contexts to present a nuanced understanding of power and the gendered body.

My work here relies heavily on Veronica Hollinger's "(Re)reading Queerly: Science Fiction, Feminism, and the Defamiliarization of Gender" for its understanding of queer and feminist applications of SF. Hollinger argues that SF is "ideally suited, as a narrative mode, to the construction of imaginative challenges to the smoothly oiled technologies of heteronormativity" (24). In this article, I explore SF's remarkable ability to queer and defamiliarize the Western, that most classic of compulsorily heterosexual environments. This article discusses something that Hollinger considers a rarity: the self-consciously queer SF text (24). Where Hollinger studies proto-feminist SF texts from the 1970s and 1980s, I concentrate on games created within the past several years. As a result, I observe an ongoing trend in transgender game design: the move toward nuance and openness in the face of intolerance and binary gender definitions.

This article likewise shares a focus with Shana Goldin-Perschbacher's "TransAmericana: Gender, Genre, and Journey." Goldin-Perschbacher writes that transgender country performers present "a stylized and (often more) conscious version of identity performance" (777), and these games likewise involve a performance of identity. In games, performance is a double-sided act. The designers perform through prose and code, but they also cue a performance in the player. By coding scenes and settings, game designers push the player to make choices and perform a character. Just as an actor uses a script to bring a character to life, the player's actions within the game similarly enact the otherwise-lifeless game character. These collaborative performances, shaped by the developer and executed by the player, create meaning in a way that, although similar to the vocal performance of transgender country singers, involves a more active role for the player. While Hollinger dedicated a significant portion of her article to exploring the intersection of feminist and queer reading techniques, and Goldin-Perschbacher focuses almost exclusively on the artists, not a set of theorists, I approach Anthropy's and Porpentine's games, using Foucault as a critical lens through which to understand these designers' performances.

I am primarily concerned with generative power, not repressive power. In Foucault's formulation, power and resistance are a constant, ongoing network of actions and knowledges. In *The History of Sexuality Volume One*, he establishes a working definition for generative power.

Power consists of more than top-down state-enforced exertions; power pervades and penetrates all human interaction. To borrow Foucault's words, power "swarms"; it resembles a dense and almost infinitely complex web of momentary interactions (96). But where power "swarms," so does resistance to power. This article studies how games by these transgender creators resist cis- and hetero-normative discourses (cis-gender refers to non-transgender people).

Foucault understands power as a fundamentally bodily affair: power, discipline, and resistance are anchored in how the body moves and is understood. Foucault writes that "power relations have an immediate hold upon [the body]" (25), and *Discipline and Punish* examines the "micro-physics" (26) of power exerted over the body. Everything from gesture to placement in space requires political influence on the body. It is not surprising then, that transgender game designers' work intersects with Foucault's writing. Generalizing queer experience is always risky; however, I feel safe in saying that most transgender people's experience of gender is profoundly bodily, and the "micro-physics" of disciplinary power has amplified effects on trans people. Awareness of this gendered discipline finds its expression in the self-conscious bodily-ness of these games. For Porpentine, understanding one's body involves glorying in its effluvia. Rather than escaping her sense of embodiment, she digs into it. In "climbing 208 feet up the ruin wall," she describes the need to urinate and following self-soiling in excruciating detail. Anthropy's most famous game *Dys4ia* (2012) recounts Anthropy's experience of hormone-replacement therapy and includes vignettes in which the player controls an unwieldy pair of breasts maneuvering through a field of spiky sea urchins (a metaphor for the nipples' sensitivity during the transition process). By involving the player in these bodily experiences, Anthropy and Porpentine allow the player to play at submitting to a dramatized version of Foucault's "micro-physics" of bodily discipline.

Queer and feminist scholars have likewise considered the gendered body using a Foucauldian lens. In *Assuming a Body: Transgender and Rhetorics of Materiality*, Gayle Salamon reviews a range of queer scholarly approaches to gender and transgender identity. The question of socialized gender construction is a contentious one, she writes, since the "tension between the historicity of the body and the immediacy of its felt sense is the precise location of bodily being" (77). Rather than siding with queer scholars who consider gender solely a constructed identity, or those who more strongly emphasize the role of the body's fleshy materiality, Salamon charts a middle course between the two. She finds Foucault's work on the body and power particularly useful here, especially his treatment of generative, distributed power. She argues that diffused disciplinary power weighs especially heavily on transgender people, since their bodies are disciplined in more severe and more fundamental ways than cis people (79). Foucault, like Salamon, navigates a middle ground between material essentialism and pure social constructivism.

Oh My Darling Gender Signs: Wild Wild Gender Mines *and SF Defamiliarization*

Wild Wild Gender Mines is a brief, ephemeral game created in just two days as part of a game jam. Porpentine wrote *Gender Mines* as part of a CloneJam: a rapid game-making session dedicated to parodying or cloning Porpentine's games ("CloneJam"). Not only is *Gender Mines* an appropriation of the song "Oh My Darling, Clementine," it is a collective appropriation of Porpentine's own odd, hyper-bodily, SF-infused oeuvre. In a way, then, one could study the game as a kind of self-aware condensation of the themes and techniques that Porpentine sees in her own games.

Played solely by clicking hyperlinks, *Gender Mines* gives the player a randomized name and sends the player into a surreal, SF-tinged Western backdrop: the mines. But instead of mining for ore, the player mines for gender. The interactions are extremely simple. The game's interface consists primarily of three commands: "DIG/RANDOMLY EXPLODE/COMPANY STORE" (capitalization preserved). Clicking "DIG" adds one gender to the player's score. "RANDOMLY EXPLODE" kills the player-character and sends them back to the beginning of the game to be assigned a new name and sent back into the mines. "COMPANY STORE" allows the player to spend gender on tonics, a slime bath, or a trip to the saloon. Tonics allow the player to dig further, the saloon functions essentially as a slot machine, sometimes rewarding more gender and sometimes taking it away. The slime baths seem to have no practical function at all. Eventually, apparently at random, the player dies. An epilogue screen tells the player that the gender they have mined is returned to an entity called "your moms" (who are only referenced, never seen), and a following screen describes what the mothers were able to purchase with the gender the player mined. The game gestures toward shadowy characters like "your moms" and references unseen actions, like their purchases, but the player only ever sees the mines and the company store. Porpentine's fiction evokes more than it explains.

On a particularly productive expedition, my character earned enough for my moms "to buy a pumpkin. also, a new coat of paint on the shed where the daughter parts are kept. additionally, a pair of Sunday dresses were obtained at frugal price. these dresses are pretty but not prideful" and an update to the house, enough for "anti-locust beams and a cake-stirring device" (*Gender Mines*). Even these ancillary references are gendered: dresses, baking equipment, and aesthetic improvements. The fruits of my character's labors accurately sample the game's alien tone: a fusion of homespun Western diction and strange SF technologies. As Hollinger demonstrates in "(Re)reading Science Fiction Queerly," SF has the unique ability to destabilize and challenge heteronormativity (24), and few games destabilize the familiar quite like *Gender Mines*.

The game builds its structure and theme on a familiar Western standby: the folk ballad, "Oh My Darling, Clementine." Even the game's title plays on the scansion of the source text: the title's rhyme, and when sung, both hold to the song's trochaic meter. But Porpentine adds a heavy layer of strange and unfamiliar imagery to the ballad's narrative of love, loss, and mining. Clementine becomes Sady Humiliation Clementine (the first randomly generated name I tried as a player), Clarabelle Calliope Montgomery (the second), or Charity Constance Praise-god (the third). By replacing the player with an endless series of similarly-named clones, the game mocks the song's punchline about replacing poor dead Clementine with her younger sister. The Miner 49'er becomes a series of faceless mothers, sporadically referred to as MA_1, MA_2, etc. (*Gender Mines*). The song's narrator disappears completely, transferring narrative responsibility to the game's omniscient, nameless narrator and the player. The structure of "Clementine" and its attendant miner tropes push the game's strange aesthetic—strongly influenced by SF technology and terminology—to the forefront, specifically to force the player to ask what gender is in the first place.

Gender in Western culture is assumed to be inherent, something so obvious as to be ignored. Porpentine presses the question constantly: how can gender be a *thing*, a strange currency, and a physical commodity? It can be unearthed, spent, transferred, stolen, and inherited. The SF-inspired jargon defamiliarizes the concept of gender using the acquisitive location of the Western gold mine as a backdrop. Porpentine's work inundates the player with strange understandings of gender: weird liquids ooze from every pore of her writing, demanding the player exist in the realm of the body. After choosing to purchase tonic, for instance, Porpentine writes that it "percolates in your belly." In the slimebaths, "the women blast you with green slime it seeps into your most intimate zones" (*Gender Mines*). The literal reification of gender in *Gender Mines* makes sense, then, as an extension of embodiment. Gender becomes an object to be acquired. Porpentine moves a step beyond the objectification of women and asks the reader to consider the objectification of gender itself.

It is strange, in the cultural context that assumes inherent femininity and masculinity, for gender to be physically acquirable. Porpentine uses the mine as a familiar site of acquisition and peril; the dynamics inherited from the Western fuse with SF's endless sense of potential and possibility to create a defamiliarized sense of gender. The player faces gender's instability and social construction—after all, in the gender mines, gender has worth. Occasionally, after sleeping (which happens automatically with every ten clicks), the player will discover a rare gender. Early on in one game, I discovered "a Rare Obsidian Gender!" As if the game needed to further destabilize the concept of "a gender," now there are gender conversion rates, reliant on the "westernized eurocentric late capitalist" gender market no less (*Gender Mines*). Now the player must wonder not only *what* gender is, but what it is worth, and under what socio-political conditions. Throughout these explorations, deaths, and reassemblies, the player maneuvers through a familiar setting in search of unfamiliar prizes. The player is Clementine, perishing and perishing again in the mines, but being remade and sent in search of the same inexplicable prize. In short, *Gender Mines* uses SF to defamiliarize and destabilize the player's understanding of gender; she pushes the player to create what Foucault calls a "power-knowledge relation" (*Discipline* 27).

"Knowledge is power" is a cliché but, in Foucault's work, it means something more. He writes that "power and knowledge directly imply one another" (*Discipline* 27). Porpentine's game helps the player to create new knowledge and, concurrently, destabilize old knowledge about gender. More importantly for this article, she adapts and upsets the Western folk ballad's cultural assumptions. "Clementine" itself establishes a clear hetero-patriarchal power-knowledge relation. Clementine parodies the appealing Western maiden: her feet, for example, are so implausibly large that she wears fish-packing boxes instead of shoes (Young). Her feet provide an object of derision, establishing a power-knowledge relation around the desirable woman. Thus, when she drowns, the narrator provides the song's punchline when he admits that "I kissed her little sister,/and I forgot my Clementine" (Young). The denigration and objectification of women—so common in the Western—reaches a parodic apogee here. Women are practically interchangeable, especially given the sexual availability of a younger replacement. The song generates knowledge and, thus, power. As a discourse, it exerts subtle influence over its listeners. Porpentine hijacks this classic Western ballad to provoke an entirely different kind of power-knowledge production.

Gender Mines involves more than a trans-femme appropriation of "Clementine," since it casts the player as the main character(s). Player agency (limited though it is) presents a new possibility for the creation of a power-knowledge relation: it forces the player to interact, over and over, with an unanswerable question: "What is gender?" By engaging directly with the question, over the course of multiple descents and deaths in the mine, the player is immersed in the unanswerable question of gender and, in trying to navigate the question, can only repeat it. The power-knowledge relation generated here deconstructs the easy cultural construct given in "Clementine." In the ballad, gender is assumed and lashed to masculine sexual desire. In the game, gender is a punk-rock koan, solvable only by the admission that it is unsolvable. The Western provides a melodramatic image of hegemonic gender-dynamics, and Porpentine uses SF's weird potentiality to sabotage the abuse of assumed, binary gender.

Domination and Play in the SF Western

Anthropy's *And the Robot Horse You Rode In On* is a linear narrative game, more developed and polished than "Gender Mines." Like Porpentine, Anthropy is an active and open transfemale game designer. Her most famous game (to her dismay) is *Dys4ia*, a series of micro-games that allows the player to navigate Anthropy's transition experience. In 2015, Anthropy wrote a brief article expressing frustration with the game's continuing popularity and the insufficiency of claiming to be a trans ally without providing any real-world support (*Empathy Game*). Significantly, she protests that simply playing her game is not enough to make one an ally or to understand the trans person's experience; ally-ship requires continuous work, support, and education. Ultimately, she says, "*You don't know what it's like to be me*" (*Empathy Game*, emphasis preserved).

Anthropy has also authored a book on game development. In *Rise of the Videogame Zinesters*, Anthropy considers the democratizing potential of the game and, in a particularly memorable line, she describes the core of the game-playing experience as "exploring dynamics, relationships, and systems" (46). At its core, *Robot Horse* portrays the end of a complex relationship between two queer women, and it does so by appropriating and recasting scenes and plot elements from the classic Eastwood Western, *The Good, the Bad and the Ugly*.

Robot Horse, like *Gender Mines*, was created using the text-game creation software, *Twine*. Unlike *Gender Mines*, the player navigates the story by choosing actions rather than digging or purchasing goods and services. As a result, gameplay resembles "Choose Your Own Adventure" books: the player advances the narrative by choosing from a set of available options. The unnamed player-character is a "bandita" in a kitschy SF Western: she rides the titular robot horse (named Whore Palace), carries a raygun in place of a six-shooter, and apart from the two main characters, every other organism in the game is a robot—even the sheep (*Robot Horse*). But this is no ordinary Western; it is a queer retelling of *The Good, the Bad and the Ugly*. As a relatively short game (it takes less than an hour to see everything it has to offer), the game compacts the most significant narrative events from the film into the following pair of familiar scenes: Blondie tortured by Tuco in the desert, and the climactic gun-fight between the three main characters. The game, however, removes *The Bad*, leaving only *The Good and the Ugly*. The player character, as a bandita, plays the Ugly—Tuco—infuriated with the smug calm of her partner, Diode, the Eastwood analog.

The plot is straightforward. The game opens with the player-character, known only as the bandita, buried up to her neck in the desert, being erotically tortured by her ex-lover Diode. In another plot point borrowed from the film, Diode wants to know where the bandita has buried their ill-gotten stash of credits (the SF equivalent of gold coins), and the bandita tells a wandering, untrue story of where she has hidden the treasure. Diode tosses a rope to the bandita and rides out after the money. The bandita pulls herself free, her horse having had time to reboot, and the two women meet again in the town for a showdown. The game's conclusion sees the former lovers broken and bleeding in a ditch, either kissing or lying quietly, depending on the player's choice. The parallels between game and film are many, but I am interested in the game's divergences more than its appropriations. A SF-flavored pastiche of the film would be less significant than the eroticized, queer take on complex, dysfunctional relationships that *Robot Horse* presents. It takes the film's obsession with power exchange and states of domination and flips it into a surprisingly affectionate picture of lovers at the end of a relationship.

The film depicts the end of a very different relationship. Tuco and Blondie are star-crossed enemies: bound together first by their mutual need to betray and enthrall the other and later by their partial knowledge of the treasure's location. From the beginning, their relationship is one of almost comedically overstated power exchanges. Their initial con involves Tuco with a literal noose around his neck, waiting for Blondie to shoot him down at the last minute. Blondie had already claimed the bounty on Tuco and, after he rescues Tuco, the pair split the bounty. In Leone's Western, power blooms from the barrel of a gun, and the purest form of power is the control of a victim's life or death. Eastwood's character crystallizes the film's view of power and relationships into a single, standout line from the film's denouement: "There's two kinds of people, my friend, those with loaded guns and those who dig" (Leone). The act of digging is subjection, the lack of power, the state of being under coercion. At the most extreme moments, however, subjugation proffers a noose instead of a shovel: these moments demonstrate something close to Foucault's concept of "domination."

In one of his final interviews, Foucault considers power relations and reflects on the cessation of motion between power and resistance: when something "manages to block a field of relations of power ... we are facing what can be called a state of domination" ("Ethic" 114). Blondie and Tuco trade places in states of domination throughout the film, frequently using the noose as a visual signifier. At the end of the film, Tuco balances precariously on a grave marker, noose gripping his neck, his hands tied behind his back. Power, in this moment, has almost ceased moving. He is immobile, one slippery boot away from death, and wholly dependent on Blondie's sharpshooting for salvation. And, yet, even this most dramatic of power relations does not constitute a true Foucauldian state of domination because Tuco retains the ability to die of his own volition. Foucault stated in the same interview that "a power can only be exercised over another to the extent that the latter still has the possibility of suicide" (123). This, then, is the true state of domination, the one in which the subject lacks even the ability to commit suicide. Tuco could die, if he wished, and thus a sluggish trickle of power remains in the Blondie-Tuco power relation.

While Blondie claims the film's last victory, Tuco holds him in a state of near-domination several times throughout the film, most notably in the desert torture sequence. Having tracked Blondie down (finding him in the middle of a new noose-shooting con no less), Tuco forces Eastwood's character on a death-march through thirty miles of desert without hat or water. Significantly, the film's primary power vector, the gun, removes Blondie's hat and canteen. When Blondie can walk no farther, Tuco sits down for a leisurely meal and—insult of insults—a footbath. As Blondie crawls toward him, Tuco proffers the fouled water, only to overturn the bucket at the last moment. This moment is as close as the film comes to a state of total domination: Tuco retains power over Blondie's life or death, and his victim lacks even the ability to end his own life. The hyper-exaggerated exchanges of power are typical for the Western genre, and the game's SF elements serve to temper and complicate the film's moments of domination.

The desert torture scene ends—as several of the film's domination scenes do—with a deus ex machina. An army stagecoach careens over the horizon, interrupting Tuco's moment of triumph. The deus ex machina is the only viable resolution of the state of domination: the film's only other alternative is killing one of its principal characters. Tuco and Blondie are both resolute; either of them offering mercy to the other is almost inconceivable, and the film makes clear that escape from the noose is impossible without outside aid. *Robot Horse*, unencumbered by the threat of true domination, removes the deus ex machina entirely; the characters' actions resolve the situations.

Robot Horse begins during the forced march sequence. Anthropy reimagines the stricken Eastwood as a Tuco-like bandita buried in a desert with the calm and implacable Diode towering over her. After six hours baking in the desert sun, Diode emerges from a tent and steps on the bandita's head. The centrality of the foot recalls Tuco's foot washing taunt from the film, and Anthropy strengthens the association in her next passage: "She turns the canteen over and lets the water run down her leg, over her foot" (*Robot Horse*). The erotic overtones are hard to miss. Where Tuco's act disgusts, Diode's entices. The blazon of leg to foot, paired with the almost tender description of "her bare brown foot," hints at the erotically-tinged passage that follows. The player's first choice occurs at this moment: the player can choose whether or not to lick the water from Diode's foot. Already, in the second screen of the game, the player is allowed agency—almost.

Whether the player clicks "lick it off" or "refuse" (Anthropy, *Robot Horse*), the end result is the same. A refusal results in the bandita-narrator rebuking the player for rejecting water then the game presents the "lick it off" result. The scene is unabashedly sexual: "You lick water off the cool vellum of her feet, you tongue the shallow pockets between her toes, you suck delicious moisture from the tips of her piglets" (Anthropy, *Robot Horse*). From the outset, Anthropy engages with a different power dynamic than the film's binary of power and subjugation. Anthropy is most interested in Foucault's power-knowledge-pleasure axis. Even in captivity, the bandita maintains significant power, specifically discursive power. *The History of Sexuality Volume I* charts the rise of Western culture's association between discourse and sex: Foucault writes concerning the Roman Catholic confessional, "Not only will you confess to acts contravening the law, but you will seek to transform your desire, your every desire, into discourse" (21). *Robot Horse* is about nothing if not the indelible connection between desire and discourse. After the bandita has finished with Diode's foot, Diode demands to know where the cred-chips are. The same pattern of sex followed by dialogue repeats throughout the game. The first half or so of the game is actually a flashback, a story told by the bandita while still buried in the desert, about where she stashed the cred-chips.

The Western structure and trappings provide a foundation grounded in the violent exchange of power, but Anthropy tinges it with retro-SF stylings: rayguns, robot horses, lamb-bots, and cred-chips. The objects are all still there, but Anthropy paints them with a kitschy SF brush in order to defamiliarize them. The SF inclusions lift *The Good, the Bad and the Ugly* out of the false binary of power versus subjugation into a more inclusive, sex-positive, body-affirming power-knowledge-pleasure spectrum. Diode and the bandita never enter into a state of domination—not even close. In fact, at the conclusion of the bandita's account of hiding the cred-chips, Diode tosses a noose down to the bandita. Rather than stringing her up and letting her dance on top of a grave marker, however, as Blondie does to Tuco, she simply leaves it on the ground and departs to find her stolen treasure. The threat remains embodied in the object, but the direct implication of death is gone. The bandita's robot horse arrives a short time later and tugs her to safety. The game's levity is important: by nudging the setting just out of sync enough with the grit-and-guns setting of the Western, Anthropy adds a level of ambiguity and complexity to the characters' power-relations. The trans-femme Western is gritty and violent—after all, Diode and the bandita end the game broken and bloody in a pit—but it is also sexual, bodily, and discursive in a way that the hetero-masculine film could never be.

The explicit themes of bondage and domination also resonate with Foucault's writing and purported predilections. *The History of Sexuality* assumes a pleasure principle innately linked to the exchange of power: "The pleasure that comes of exercising a power that questions, monitors, watches, spies, searches out, palpates, brings to light; and on the other hand, the pleasure that kindles at having to evade this power" (45). Blondie and Tuco only seem to pleasure in domination and pursuit, but Diode and the bandita embody Foucault's so-called "double impetus" (45) perfectly. Diode seeks; the bandita evades. Diode dominates; the bandita submits and schemes. Throughout the game, the couple uses discourse to achieve their pleasure. The bandita combines evasion and submission by giving Diode a misleading story (simultaneously giving her lover what she requested while also resisting her with a lie), while Diode's speech commands and threatens. At the climactic final confrontation (in which the bandita is, once again, held enthralled by Diode), Diode commands her to "Give momma what she came for, girl" (Anthropy, *Robot Horse*). The two characters pursue their own pleasure by the exertion of power and resistance.

The climax of *Robot Horse* is more emotional than narrative: the double impetus of power and pleasure collapses. After Diode has coerced the treasure's location from the bandita, the player surprises her with a hidden weapon. Using "Little Miss EMP," the bandita disables Diode's gun (effectively shooting the gun out of her hand, a trope employed in the other two *Dollars* films, *A Fistful of Dollars* [1964] and *For a Few Dollars More* [1965], but, oddly, not in *The Good, the Bad and the Ugly*). Both women now deprived of their weapons—Diode having shot the bandita's earlier—they drop their positions of dominant and submissive and attack one another. Throughout a roiling fistfight, the player moves the game forward not by choosing attacks or actions but by choosing screamed complaints. The argument replaces the hyper-masculine showdown. At each stage of the fight, the player can select shouts like "You're condescending and gross and awful and I FUCKING HATE YOU!!" (Anthropy, *Robot Horse*). The fight is linear—the insults change nothing—but the altered power dynamic is alarming after the rest of the game's cat-and-mouse narrative.

The emotional release here is something new: the tech and Western tropes both are stripped away, and the game enters territory uncharted by Leone's film. The women are simply fighting. Neither character has the advantage, and neither character wins the argument. The game concludes on this same level playing ground: Diode and the bandita both in a pit in the center of town, bones broken, bleeding, and struggling for breath. But Anthropy has one more trick: she concludes with a final player choice, this one more meaningful than the trick-question that opened the game. Diode laughs and asks, "Wanna make out?" and the player can respond "yes" or "no" (Anthropy, *Robot Horse*). The two either kiss or do not, and, regardless of the player's choice, the game concludes with the couple staring in silence at the stars. The final scene transcends both source material and genre trappings and even abandons the carefully choreographed double impetus, substituting instead a radically equal moment of consent.

The moment is an unresolved resolution. The relationship has transformed and moved from a dangerous-yet-playful series of power exchanges to an equality based in brokenness in which power is exchanged via consent rather than manipulation or force. Where Leone's film concludes with a clear division of material wealth—Blondie and Tuco each end the film with half the gold—the game does not mention the cred-chips after the bandita disarms Diode. *Robot Horse*, after all, was never about money. It was about the messy ending of a relationship. The narrative and power relation end at the same moment: with the abandonment of the double impetus and the institution of a balanced power relation. In the denouement, Anthropy strips away even Foucault (who would argue that the play of power and resistance continues even without the roles of dominant and submissive) and concludes with a sense of broken hopefulness and a final meaningful in-game decision.

Conclusion: Games of Truth, Both Literal and Metaphorical

At the end of his life, Foucault used the concept of the game to summarize a lifetime's worth of research: "I have tried to discover how the human subject entered into *games of truth*, whether they be games of truth which take on the form of science [...], or games of truth like those that can be found in institutions or practices of control" ("Ethic" 112, emphasis preserved). Like a game, a human institution or field of knowledge operates by a set of rules constraining and provoking performance in the human subject. A given field allows the production of truth or knowledge (and thus power) only if the production follows the field's rules and expectations: a scientific discovery, for example, is worthless without a rigorously documented research process and publication in a well-regarded source.

By creating literal games, Anthropy and Porpentine engage the subject in the creation of bodily knowledge. The games demand awareness of the gendered body, and this awareness involves the player in a gender-focused power-knowledge relation. If these designers are creating literal games of bodily and empowered truth, what could be considered "truth"? Truth is a slippery term, since it implies an epistemological certainty with which few theorists are comfortable. In Foucault's work, truth is always contingent and subject to fields of knowledge and power, so for these designers, truth concerns the construction of a gendered body. For Porpentine, truth is a perilous strangeness. To be gendered, according to *Gender Mines*, is to constantly be pressing into strange new bodily territory, risking life and limb in pursuit of an unanswerable question. Anthropy's game recasts the truth of the Western (the man with the loaded gun triumphant over the man who digs) as a new, feminist exchange of power capped with a revelatory, conclusive equality.

The Western, as I have demonstrated, is a readily-adapted mirepoix of a genre. Its bare-knuckled depiction of power's movement holds great promise for future developers, authors, and artists. Its familiarity makes it accessible; its tropes make it a perfect space for experimenting with queer games of truth. In turn, SF and its many subgenres (e.g. weird fiction, space opera, cyberpunk, steampunk, or any of the other -punks) can push the Western into new configurations. I propose that the SF Western provides queer and feminist creators with a unique and powerful tool to dramatize and challenge what Hollinger memorably terms "the smoothly oiled technologies of heteronormativity" (24). These two games—one made in less than two days—powerfully demonstrate the SF Western's potential for queer text-making.

Although Porpentine and Anthropy use SF to subvert the Western's power dynamics, SF is not necessarily a queer influence on its own. Other SF Westerns take the same genre fusion and put it to much less radical or empowering ends. Gearbox Software's *Borderlands* series of first-person shooter games provides a substantial counter-example. Where queer SF softens or upturns the Western's dichotomy between shovels and guns, *Borderlands* intensifies the trope to the point of parody. *Borderlands'* most consistent feature is the absurd number of guns the player finds and uses throughout the game. The first title's TV spot advertised "87 bazillion guns" (2K) and, true to its advertising, the game's primary motivation is finding new and more powerful guns. It offers a limitless number of faceless bandits, monsters, and soldiers to be shot, looted for guns, and shot again. The game's initial concept was a hybrid of the first-person shooter and role-playing game, but where a traditional role-playing game (RPG) might have swords or spells to collect and upgrade, *Borderlands* had guns (Schneider).

The Western setting provides a logical starting place for a game focused on attaining power via weaponry, and SF elements provide an excuse for its over-the-top treatment of weaponry. Replicating a nineteenth-century arsenal would offer far fewer chances for variety than the SF Western setting: *Borderlands* includes pistols, shotguns, assault rifles, grenade launchers, even deployable turrets and teleporting grenades. SF still defamiliarizes and shifts the Western's mirepoix, but *Borderlands* pushes in the opposite direction from Anthropy or Porpentine's games because it removes what little ambiguity about power relations the traditional Western retained. *Borderlands* would have had Blondie shoot Tuco the moment he was able, steal his money, and deface his corpse. The game has no shovels, only guns. At its core, however, the SF Western has the same concern: power. *Borderlands, Wild Wild Gender Mines*, and *And the Robot Horse You Rode In On* use the Western to explore power dynamics, and their SF elements defamiliarize and reconfigure power relations. As such, the SF Western offers a reliable and productive platform from which to investigate the influence of generative power on the body.

WORKS CITED

Anthropy, Anna. *Dys4ia*. Auntie Pixelante, 2012. PC.

_____. "Empathy Game." Auntiepixelante.com, http://auntiepixelante.com/empathygame/. [site now down]

_____. *Rise of the Videogame Zinesters: How Freaks, Normals, Amateurs, Artists, Dreamers, Drop-Outs, Queers, Housewives, and People Like You Are Taking Back an Art Form.* Seven Stories Press, 2012.

Anthropy, Anna, and Lydia Neon. *And the Robot Horse You Rode In On.* itch.io, https://w. itch.io/robot-horse.

Foucault, Michel. *Discipline and Punish: the Birth of the Prison.* 2nd ed. Translated by Alan Sheridan, Random, 1995.

_____. "The Ethic of Care for the Self as a Practice of Freedom: an Interview with Michel Foucault on January 20, 1984." Interview with Raúl Fornet-Betancourt, Helmut Becker, and Alfredo Gomez-Müller. Translated by J.D. Gauthier. *Philosophy Social Criticism*, vol. 12, no. 112, 1987, pp. 112–131, doi: 10.1177/019145378701200202.

_____. *The History of Sexuality Volume I: an Introduction.* Random, 1990.

Goldin-Perschbacher, Shana. "Transamericana: Gender, Genre, and Journey." *New Literary History*, vol. 46, no. 4, 2015, pp. 775–803, doi: 10.1353/nlh.2015.0041.

The Good, the Bad and the Ugly. Directed by Sergio Leone, Produzioni Europee Associati, 1966.

Hollinger, Veronica. "(Re)Reading Queerly: Science Fiction, Feminism, and the Defamiliarization of Gender." *Science Fiction Studies*, vol. 26, no. 1, 1999, pp. 23–40. www.jstor.org/stable/4240749.

Neil Young and Crazy Horse. "Clementine." *Americana*, Reprise, 2012.

Porpentine. "Climbing 208 Feet Up the Ruin Wall." *Porpentine*, http://aliendovecote.com/uploads/twine/LD26/ruin.html#1.

_____. "Clonejam." Game Jolt Jams, 16 Nov. 2014. http://jams.gamejolt.io/clonejamporpi/games/wild-wild-gender-mines/38292.

_____. "Wild Wild Gender Mines." *Porpentine*, https://gamejolt.com/games/wild-wild-gender-mines/38292.

Salamon, Gayle. *Assuming a Body: Transgender and Rhetorics of Materiality.* Columbia UP, 2010.

Schneider, Steven. "87 Bazillion Guns: the History of *Borderlands*." *TechTimes.* 15 Oct. 2014. www.techtimes.com/articles/17880/20141015/87-bazillion-guns-the-history-of-borderlands.htm.

2K. "Borderlands Tv Spot." *YouTube*, uploaded by 2K, 20 Oct. 2009, www.youtube.com/watch?v=zIomVnfGVYw.

Wanheda, Commander of Death, Healer

Hybrid Female Identities
in the Post-Apocalyptic Wars of The 100

Lindsey Mantoan

Post-Apocalypse, Hybrid Identity

Over a hundred years in the future, Clarke Griffin walks out on a decrepit bridge covered with overgrowth to meet a woman on horseback. As the leaders of their two warring clans, Clarke and Anya are there to negotiate peace, even while the backup they brought with them line the trees, arrows and guns pointed at the opposing side. Clarke, the protagonist of the CW's television series *The 100* (2014–present), is also the invader: along with ninety-nine other juvenile delinquents, she was sent to Earth from a failing space station to see if, after a nuclear apocalypse ninety-seven years ago, the planet might be habitable again. Shocked to encounter "Grounders" already living on Earth, Clarke and the other delinquents are instantly pitted against people coded to resemble Native Americans. This clash of cultures continues for five seasons as alliances are forged and broken, and clans negotiate vastly different weapons technology, a malevolent AI, and environmental catastrophe. David M. Higgins finds that "American science fiction was fascinated by the traumatic spectacle of invasion in the years following 9/11," and *The 100* supports this claim (46). Set in a futuristic U.S. frontier where progress has been both made and lost, *The 100* reimagines the invasion narrative so central to U.S. identity and replaces it with a more nuanced, complex encounter between native peoples and Eurocentric invaders. Part science fiction and part Western, this post-apocalyptic story takes place after a cataclysmic event has cleansed the world, creating an opportunity to rethink identity. In this essay, I

101

argue that hybrid female identities in *The 100* unsettle the traditional frontier myth, suggesting instead a more inclusive future.

According to Kerry Fine, "western television shows of the past generally gave audiences attractive, well-coiffed women who fulfilled the traditional roles of the hero's leading lady" (153). With few exceptions, however, leaders of *The 100* are women. To the extent that we want to read them as archetypal characters, they occupy roles traditionally reserved for men: strategist, warrior, commander, and engineer, to name a few. Barbara Gurr argues that "post-apocalyptic narratives, necessarily set after the world ends and the work of rebuilding something new begins, frequently fail to imagine new experiences on race, gender, and sexuality," (1–2) but the diverse women of *The 100* defy Gurr's argument. *The 100* offers a world in which people—men *and* women—are judged on their actions, not the color of their skin or their sexuality. There is no sexual violence in this world, a deliberate choice on the writers' part (Fortenberry), and gender does not determine the victor in hand-to-hand combat.

Even while explorations of this new/old frontier are violent and chaotic, the show's vision of gender equality holds within it a refreshing idealism. Based on a series of young adult novels by Kass Morgan, *The 100* places young people in the position of negotiating the frontier in the absence of an established government, infrastructure, or adult guidance; the adolescent condition, a kind of frontier itself, is especially suited to rethinking identity and suggesting the promise of a better future. The story envisions a truly post-gender and post-race world and, while it sometimes slips in its execution, the overall project is community-building for audiences.

While the apocalypse is meant to inaugurate a utopia, post-apocalyptic narratives tend to take place in what Giorgio Agamben would call a state of exception, "a no-man's land between public law and political fact" when leaders use a prolonged sense of emergency as justification for violence and extreme decisions (1). In *The 100*, the nuclear apocalypse 97 years prior to the start of the narrative destroyed not only infrastructure and population but also stable governments. Although there is a small counsel of politicians in charge of law on the Ark, the leaders understand their situation as temporary and take extreme measures to control the population: the space station's adult residents are put to death for even minor crimes. It seems clear that those on the Ark have been biding their time across generations until they can return to Earth and reestablish liberal democracies. Instead, their skirmishes with the Grounder clans as soon as they land prolong this state of emergency and lawlessness. All efforts at forming functional and representative systems of government on the ground fail spectacularly; the delinquents fall prey to tyranny of the masses, and the adult Skaikru (the name eventually given to Clarke's clan) elect an authoritarian and xenophobic chancellor once on the ground. The Grounder coalition of clans is the closest representation of functional governance, although it faces extreme opposition from within and without. Even while the show seems to say that people are by nature violent, governments are corrupt, and war is inescapable, hope can be found in individuals with hybrid identities—particularly women.

This focus on the individual over organizations and structures represents a hallmark of frontier narratives, which often valorize outlaws and rogue (male) loners. The premise of the show threatens to perpetuate what Richard Slotkin calls the Frontier Myth, "our oldest and most characteristic myth" in which "the conquest of the wilderness and the subjugation or displacement of the Native Americans who originally inhabited it have been the means to our achievement of a national identity, a democratic polity ... and 'progressive' civilization" (10). Conflict and violence are central to this myth, and "savage war ... rooted in some combination of 'blood' and culture make coexistence between primitive natives and civilized Europeans impossible on any basis other than that of subjugation" (Slotkin 12). While individual and cultural progress is the objective in the frontier narrative, the state of emergency and the frontier myth often go hand in hand, with the line between outlaw and hero blurred in many Westerns. *The 100* takes a different approach to the frontier; in this Science Fiction Western, progress is not always desirable. Instead, the narrative celebrates the culture of indigenous people, denying newcomers power over the native peoples. It likewise erases the hierarchies that put straight white men in positions of power over everyone else. Indeed, the only heteronormative, patriarchal society in *The 100*, the people who live in Mount Weather, is a remnant of the old world; they are positioned as villains, and their people are wiped out entirely by the end of the second season.

It is challenging to summarize such an intricate plot; I nevertheless offer a brief overview before analyzing the show's overall gender politics and a few specific characters. Season One concludes with the Ark landing on Earth while Clarke and the delinquents incinerate 300 Grounders who attacked their camp. In season two, the delinquents clash with the Mount Weather people, who cannot resist any exposure to radiation. They use the blood of Grounders and then the bone marrow of the delinquents to heal themselves until Clarke exposes them all to radiation, killing everyone in the mountain and earning the name Wanheda, Commander of Death, from the Grounders. In Season Three, a malevolent AI named ALIE collects people's consciousness in her alternate universe, the City of Light, controlling their earthly bodies and forcing them into violence until Clarke destroys her. Season four focuses on the various clans finding sanctuary from a death wave of radiation, forging new alliances. These season arcs reinforce Higgins' assertion that since 9/11, science fiction addresses "anxieties concerning terrorism, terrorist attacks ... counterterrorism ... surveillance and security technologies" (46). The fifth season returns to the invasion narrative, with a new spaceship falling to the Earth, repeating the cycle of violent encounters.

The constellation of female characters leading this narrative matters on two levels. First, it is important that there is a constellation of strong female leaders, rather than one token woman whose primary function is to support the men who drive the plot. The story in fact reverses standard representations of gender roles, with the male characters predominantly supporting the female leaders in both Grounder and Skaikru culture. Second, audiences see a range of women who lead with different strengths and methods. As both a healer who trained at her mother's side and the Commander of Death, Clarke nurtures and destroys. Octavia, a delinquent, begins the series as a silly girl intent on flirting with boys and quickly becomes a warrior who identifies with the Grounder clan Trikru as much or more than the Skaikru. Raven, a Skaikru with expertise in mechanics and engineering, solves problems using both her innate genius as well as artificial intelligence. As the Commander of the Grounder clans, Lexa blends an uncompromising strength with feminine softness; her romance with Clarke is remarkable precisely because it is normalized in the narrative. Finally, the range of female-coded gender performances is not limited to women: Finn, the long-haired pacifist who falls in love with Clarke, performs a gentleness that places him on the feminine side of the gender spectrum.

Conversely, the show represents a range of masculinities, from hypermasculine men to female masculinity to male characters who exhibit normatively feminine qualities. Drawing on Jack (formerly Judith) Halberstam's "conceptualizing masculinity without men" (2), I read Indra, leader of the Trikru grounder clan, as performing female masculinity; her hairstyle, musculature, warrior's clothing, and harsh attitude are typically coded as male. In season three, Charles Pike, the macho Skaikru Chancellor for a time, thirsts for war with the Grounders; he is punished for his hypermasculine bloodlust when Octavia executes him. On the other side of the spectrum, Lindsay Macdonald writes that instead of mocking male vulnerability like many narratives, the show celebrates it. Macdonald asserts, "*The 100* … choos[es] to let its male character experience every heartbreaking emotion under the sun…. I'd almost wager we've seen more men break down than women."

The gender fluidity in *The 100* sets it apart from not only traditional television Westerns but also similar science fiction narratives. One of the closest narratives thematically to *The 100* is SyFy's reboot of *Battlestar Galactica* (2003), a SF Western television show that largely takes place aboard a spaceship where male and female solders share bathrooms and sleeping quarters. This vision of gender equality, however, is undermined by the female protagonist, Kara "Starbuck" Thrace, the best pilot in the fleet. A woman who smokes cigars and punches her male superior officers in the face, Starbuck is on the surface a fun and unique representation of a female hero. Tracy Raney and Michelle Meagher, however, consider Starbuck's gender performance as female masculinity—and not in a progressive way (47). They contend that in the hypermasculine environment of the Galactica, Starbuck's masculinity is "overperformed and excessive" (Raney and Meagher 49). The show offers harsh correctives to her nontraditional behavior, including an enemy forcing her into a fabricated scene of domestic maternal and wifely bliss as a method of torture. By the conclusion of the series, "Starbuck's representation aligns with other post-feminist cultural narratives, in which women who have 'made it' in a man's world are depicted as unhappy, unsatisfied, and ultimately, nostalgic for a time in their lives ... when their roles were more traditionally defined" (Raney and Meagher 50). In the final episode, Starbuck simply disappears, implying that there's no space in the new world for female masculinity. The end twist of *Battlestar* is that the entire series takes place not in the future but in the past, with the ragtag survivors of this war serving as humanity's ancestors on Earth. Given what viewers know about the patriarchal world that follows, Starbuck's brand of female masculinity certainly did not inaugurate a more inclusive understanding of gender performance. *The 100*'s Indra, on the other hand, is respected by Trikru and Skaikru alike, and her gender performance is never questioned or punished.

While many elements associated with gender performance in *The 100* are unique and compelling, the show slips in its approach to intersectionality. Gabby Taub writes that "*The 100* is guilty of perpetuating white feminism.... The white women are positioned as leaders and depicted as strong, righteous characters. This becomes problematic when we watch these same women treat other characters of color poorly." Indeed, it should be noted that two of the three black men in the primary cast of characters are questionable or downright immoral leaders (Jaha and Pike), and the third is sacrificed (Lincoln). While I agree with Taub's points that the show needs a more intersectional feminism, I want to propose a different reading of the way race operates in *The 100*. Personal conversations I have had with scholars and fans of the show about Lincoln and Bellamy, a Grounder and a delinquent, yield no consensus about these characters' races. Ricky Whittle, who plays the Grounder Lincoln, identifies as black, but fans of the show read the character as more the ambiguous "ethnic Other."

I posit this is because Grounders are represented through clothing, language, weaponry, and values to read to audiences as ethnic Others, whether they are performed by actors of color or white actors. Within the world of the show, race matters not in terms of phenotype but in terms of clan. Skaikru, Trikru, and Azgeda (the Ice Nation clan) shape the identity politics on the ground, rather than having them based on a person's ancestors' origins. Additionally, the frontier narrative that structures this story positions all Grounders as Other regardless of the race of the actor playing them. This means that when Octavia becomes part–Grounder, she steps away from her privilege as a (white) Skaikru. Most of the leaders the viewers see (Lexa, Indra, Luna, and Ontari for the Grounders; Raven and Octavia for Skaikru), read as women of color or, at least, as not-white women. Given the diversity of the Skaikru (Raven Reyes is Latina, Monty Green is Asian, and Chancellor Jaha, Nathan Miller, and Miller's father are black), the cast of characters of the whole show reads as significantly less white than most twentieth-century Westerns and science fiction television shows.

This approach to race sets the narrative in a post-identity universe, even while casting choices about who plays Grounder and Skaikru heroes and who plays the villains of both clans raise important ethical questions about representation and opportunity in the contemporary society in which this show is being created and viewed. Are white actors playing Grounders in a kind of blackface? In a world where characters are not raced, per se—where racial difference goes unremarked and is normalized—is it progressive that white actors play the native people (Grounders) that invaders of all races (Skaikru) attempt to colonize, or has the show skirted responsibility by not casting more Grounders with actors of color? Had the show cast Grounders as predominately of color, would it be perpetuating the same racial dynamics of the original frontier myth? The gap between the racial casting of the show and the way the characters operate in this post-apocalyptic frontier space speaks to our limits in imagining a post-racial future and the impossibility of forgetting the real-world legacy of racial oppression that audiences bring with them to the narrative.

These questions also speak to the difficulty of escaping the frontier narrative so firmly entrenched in U.S. culture. Gurr finds that "The very meaning of the frontier relies on the constant displacement of its original inhabitants so that white men can tame the wilderness and make it safe for white women" (35). Yet, Skaikru does not successfully displace Grounders, despite repeated, violent efforts to do so. Their failure to conquer Grounders progressively disrupts the frontier narrative, suggesting a different outcome is not only possible but also preferable. Despite their superior technology, Skaikru is relegated to the land where their Ark fell (conveniently not on already occupied territory). During increased tension between Grounders and Skaikru, the Commander puts a blockade around the Ark, trapping all Skaikru in a five-mile radius. While the Skaikru adults' disposition toward the Grounders often mirrors the Manifest Destiny doctrine of the nineteenth century, or the belief that European conquerors' expansion of power across the Americas was justified and inevitable, the delinquents seem to have a different attitude toward both the adults of their own culture and the Grounders. These adolescents could be read as refugees from an uninhabitable territory (space).

The frontier myth is further displaced when one of the prevailing arcs of Season Three is Skaikru joining the Grounder Coalition as the 13th Clan, an attempt at assimilation into native culture absent from typical Western narratives.

Indeed, futuristic frontier narratives are as much about exploring the edges of imagination as about exploring the edges of known geography. The imaginative work of *The 100* places women in leadership positions across multiple cultures, even while it fails to imagine the path society would take to achieve such gender equality. In an article titled, "Why CW's *The 100* is a Feminist Dream, Except for When It's Not," Selena Neumark writes, "I truly believe *The 100* is one of the best and most representative shows out there right now.... If such harmony were achieved, though, as it appears to be in *The 100*, I want to know why and how! Such difficult steps are completely brushed aside, leaving us to kind of forget that the starting point (i.e., where we are now in the fight for civil rights, equality) is even an issue." Neumark has a point; it would be immensely important to see not just the end product of a show where gender, race, and sexuality are equalized, but the process whereby this utopia of identity comes to be. This is perhaps a pass that audiences allow post-apocalyptic narratives: if the apocalypse wipes the slate clean, new societies can start without the patriarchal and racist baggage of the past.

The fact that race, gender, and sexuality are never commented on in the narrative provides viewers with a path for spectatorship: these identities should always already be nonissues with no attendant economic or political hierarchies. Even while these identity markers are normalized, the show continually questions what it means to be human, and the answer it puts forward embraces hybridity. The dual natures of Octavia, who is both Skaikru and Trikru, and Raven, who is both human and AI, demonstrate the possibility of forging unity across cultural and biological difference. Clarke's hybridity makes her a unique female leader on television, even while the show makes some significant missteps in the way it treats her sexuality. Below, I analyze these three characters in terms of their relationship to the frontier narrative and contemporary identity politics.

Octavia: The Girl Beneath the Floor and the Sky Ripper

While Octavia becomes one of the strongest women in the narrative, in early episodes her character reaffirms some of the worst stereotypes of a teenage girl that are unfortunately prevalent in television across all genres. On the Ark, Octavia was her mother's second child, a crime punishable by death in a culture with carefully controlled population growth. Octavia lived in a hole in her family's floor for seventeen years, part of her history that resurfaces on a regular basis in the narrative. After guards discover her, they float her mother out of the Ark to her death and imprison Octavia, a minor, until she came of age. Newly freed on the ground with the rest of the delinquents, Octavia flirts with boys and strips down to her underwear to go swimming in front of them. Her character is grating, if not predictable, in its immaturity; by offering a kiss to a delinquent named Jasper as a reward for brave behavior ("Murphy's Law"), her character's sexual accessibility to men represents the most anti-feminist aspect of the narrative. By the end of season one, however, Octavia has defied her older brother, Bellamy, on a number of ethical issues, including freeing a Grounder prisoner named Lincoln that Bellamy was torturing. After meeting Indra, the Trikru leader, she begins training in Grounder combat and, as the seasons progress, she becomes Skaikru's strongest warrior—a tricky role for someone who often eschews her Skaikru identity.

Octavia's character walks right up to the line of cultural appropriation, but I argue that, at least in early seasons, she reads more as an analogue for someone who is multiracial or caught between different cultures. Octavia seems like a colonist who exoticizes the native culture; by the middle of the second season, she has started dressing and braiding her hair like the Grounders do. Indria briefly invites her into Trikru but revokes the invitation in the same episode. Octavia lives in between worlds. She stays in Arkadia but sleeps outside on blankets while everyone else sleeps in the downed space station; she goes on scouting missions with Skaikru, but when they drive an electric Rover, she rides a horse. She knows how to use a gun but prefers a sword. Rejecting the world of steel and technology that confined her as a child, Octavia embraces the frontier as a place to forge new relationships with other people and the land she had dreamed of while in space.

Slotkin proposes that "the triumph of civilization over savagery is symbolized by the hunter/warrior's rescue of the White woman held captive by savages" (15). *The 100* flips this trope when Octavia rescues Lincoln from being tortured in "Day Trip," and then rescues him again after he is nearly destroyed by the people in Mount Weather ("Long Into an Abyss" and "Rubicon"). Instead of a virginal white woman whose virtue needs protecting from the frontier savages, Octavia becomes a skilled combatant. She serves as an informal protector for numerous Skaikru (her older brother Bellamy, Clarke, Chancellor Kane), as well as a Skaikru ally in Mount Weather, Maya. As a figure who dwells between clans but nevertheless tries to shield others from violence, and who is used by various groups of people for covert missions, Octavia could be read as an outlaw protector, not unlike Zoe from *Serenity* and Wynonna Earp from the series of the same name. This hybrid status puts her outside the law and culture of all clans, even while they rely on her to save them, and the liminal space in which she operates reminds audiences that the boundaries of the frontier are not as sharply drawn as U.S. mythology suggests.

Octavia blurs boundaries not only between cultures but also between genders. Writing about female heroes in Westerns, Kerry Fine examines the common argument that women labeled strong, intelligent, and aggressive often function as "stand-ins for the male viewer" (164), making them essentially men-in-drag roles. Instead, Fine critiques gender analysis that relies too heavily on a binary model and "becomes mired in its inability to escape the concepts of femaleness and maleness…. Further, the traditional dual gender model cannot make accommodations for women who are quite clearly female sexed yet appropriate traditional masculine gender markers" (164–165). Octavia, and indeed all of the women warriors of *The 100*, resist this traditional conflation of strong with masculine and weak with feminine, of aggression with men and nurturing with women. In addition to her lethal skills in combat, Octavia frequently serves as Clarke and Abby's medical assistant. There is no anxiety produced by Octavia's role as a woman who protects, fights, and heals.

As with most narratives involving clashes of cultures, hope for breaking down barriers lies with those who dwell in liminal spaces. In these confrontations between a technological society of invaders and a pre-modern collection of clans, Octavia and Lincoln's romance models the possibility of peace between Grounders and Skaikru. The two sometimes struggle to negotiate which clan to align with in a given conflict, but those disagreements are not based on the kinds of identity politics that shape contemporary U.S. culture. Writing about frontier spaces, Colin R. Johnson proposes "that there is something strangely appealing about those places in time where pleasure and passion and desire and intimacy … were not so terribly, terribly contingent on an identity-based discourse of sexuality that binds us together in the present, yes, but that often has the effect of separating and exhausting us as well" (2–3). The frontier space developed in *The 100* establishes a new kind of identity politics that focuses on the possibility of hybridity as key to unifying clans.

Octavia's character undergoes a striking evolution, and by the end of season four she takes a turn that Slotkin would call essential for the (male) hero of the frontier myth. After executing Pike, she transforms from warrior to assassin; Grounders start calling her "Skai Rippa," or Sky Ripper. After assassinating multiple people and nearly executing a Grounder, she tries to abate the darkness inside her through farming, an endeavor that does not even last one episode. When a conclave is called to determine which people get to take refuge from the death wave of radiation, Octavia wins the death match against warriors from the other twelve Grounder clans. Standing in front of them, victorious, she declares, "I wasn't fighting for Skaikru today. I thought I was fighting for myself, but I now know that's not true either. I was fighting for all us all. Skaikru will not take the bunker alone. We will share it. Equally. Because we are equal. We are one clan. And we will survive" ("Die All, Die Merrily"). Having won a surprising leadership position over Grounders and Skaikru alike, Octavia's skills will be challenged in this new frontier as she attempts to become an effective political leader in a cramped space where the frontier/western populations of Grounders collide with the science fictional population of Skaikru.

Octavia's newfound position as leader of all people raises important questions about the show's potential regression into the traps of the frontier myth. According to Slotkin, the frontier hero must undergo a personal journey from civilized to savage in order to conquer the darkness within and emerge a stronger leader. He explains, "they are mediators of a double kind who can teach civilized men how to defeat savagery on its native grounds—the natural wilderness, and the wilderness of the human soul" (14). The invader who becomes the leader and hero of the Grounders, Octavia at the end of Season Four, threatens everything the show has so carefully resisted in terms of reifying the invasion scenario.

Nevertheless, she has done what no one else has been able to do in the narrative: unify disparate peoples into a single clan without erasing cultural differences. Her status as a perpetual outsider means that we cannot so easily read this journey as the triumph of advanced society over savages. Octavia's resentment toward her own people has shaped much of her behavior and her identification with them has rarely trumped her assimilation into Grounder culture. Indra remains Octavia's closest advisor, and the animosity between her and Skaikru makes it unlikely that her rule will be marked by policies and practices that erase Grounder culture in favor of Skaikru's. Octavia's hybrid and liminal status blends the two genres of the show (science fiction and Western) as well as the multiple communities.

Raven: The Mechanic with a Heat Defect

The frontier myth erases native cultures through violence or sublimates them into "melting pot" rhetoric, but in The 100, the existing culture on the ground is already hybrid—specifically posthuman, as audiences learn in the third season. The initial nuclear holocaust 97 years prior to the start of the narrative was set off by an AI named ALIE. After the bombs exploded, ALIE's creator, Becca, implanted a computer chip into her brain with the second version of ALIE's programming (ALIE 2.0) and helped genetically alter the Grounders' blood so they can withstand radiation. Becca became the first Grounder Commander. This AI has passed from commander to commander, with ALIE 2.0 retaining the consciousness of every person to have merged their minds with it. Ninety-seven years later, ALIE 1.0 resurfaces with a mission to collect everyone's consciousness into an alternate universe called the City of Light; her methods include coercion, torture, and suicide until Clarke merges her consciousness with ALIE 2.0 and is able to defeat the first version of ALIE's programming. Becca, the Grounder Commanders, and Clarke become posthuman cyborgs as soon as they merge their minds with an AI, a move that reinforces *The 100*'s status as a Science Fiction Western.

Posthumanism has long been a preoccupation in science fiction narratives. Colin Milburn theorizes three different approaches to the concept:

> some narratives consider the posthuman in a biological sense, focusing on the evolutionary future.... Some narratives instead consider the posthuman in a technological sense, focusing on the synthetic, engineered successors of humanity or the idea of humans and machines linked every more closely in the circuits of technoculture ... some narratives concern the posthuman in a cultural or epistemic sense, discovering that "human nature" is a tenuous social construct open to modification and revision [524].

With characters possessing genetically-modified blood that can withstand radiation, AIs merging with or taking over human minds, and human nature under extreme pressure, *The 100*'s investigations of posthumanism concern all three approaches: biological, synthetic, and cultural.

In science fiction, posthumanism often functions as a cautionary example of the dangers of technology taking control over humans, which viewers see in ALIE 1.0; *The 100* subverts this trope with ALIE 2.0, building instead toward a world structured by a biological woman (Becca) and two female AIs (ALIE and ALIE 2.0). The choice to make these two AIs female adds to a genealogy of feminizing mass destruction and technology (which often go hand in hand). According to Dianne Newell and Victoria Lamont, during the Cold War, "nuclear energy was feminized, one offshoot of the classic identification between the maternal body and nature that Julia Kristeva suggests is foundational in Western culture" (423). Futuristic narratives often move this frontier from the natural world to the technological one but retain the gendering of this unexplored space by feminizing artificial intelligence: man creates and tames woman all over again. Yet in *The 100*, woman is creator and created. Absent is what Amanda Fernbach would explain as the way "technology operates as fetish and prop for an imagined masculinity in a postmodern and posthuman content" (234), a common trope present in science fiction films like *Her* (2013) and *Ex Machina* (2015). Instead, post-human cyborgs in *The 100* all descend from Becca's creations, including Lexa (the Grounder Commander), Clarke, and Raven, and their function in the plot has nothing to do with boosting the male ego of a creator.

Indeed, through Raven's status as a cyborg, or hybrid human-AI, the show puts forward an ambivalent attitude toward technology, unsettling the way Science Fiction Western narratives tend to value progress as natural and desirable. A brilliant engineer, Raven's STEM skills are put to use in building bombs, hacking into Mount Weather's communication systems and dismantling their power grid, and hacking into ALIE 1.0. Raven turns out to be one of Skaikru's foremost military leaders in that she designs highly effective deadly weapons, and her technological expertise often guides military strategy. Raven is most often alone in a control room or lab studying chemical formulas or computer code. If many of the women in the show are social and political leaders, Raven is the explorer, an isolated individual probing the boundaries of what is possible.

The terrain she explores has less to do with physical space—although she does some of that every time she finds herself in a new lab or a virtual reality—and more to do with the boundaries of science, the human mind, and what constitutes human in a technological world. In *Future West: Utopia and Apocalypse in Frontier Science Fiction*, William H. Katerberg writes of cyborg narratives, "Hackers are often depicted as 'console cowboys,' loners and outlaws akin to the cowboys, gunslingers, and jaded private eyes who are the stock-in-trade of [narratives] set in the American West of the nineteenth and twentieth centuries" (193). Raven represents this archetype, and her body provides the site on which *The 100* works through the distinction between individual and collective consciousness, between reality and virtual reality, and between human genius and artificial intelligence.

Despite her status as an engineer, Raven's personal relationship to technology is fraught and often oppositional, and the trauma she has endured challenges traditional progress narratives that valorize technological advancements. Raven stands apart from her friends not only by her mastery in the lab but also by physical disability and pain. Her character has a heart defect and, by the time the third season begins, Raven has survived a gunshot wound that left one of her legs paralyzed. The mechanical brace she wears in order to walk causes overwhelming pain, and that pain has become her whole world (see Scarry). She chooses to upload her consciousness to ALIE's alternate reality to escape pain; as the only person to merge with ALIE who retains partial control over her own mind, Raven becomes hybrid—both human and AI. According to Katerberg, "cyborg science fiction set in the West exposes the failed promise of the frontier and reveals the ambiguities of progress and civil morality" (196). Raven's body stands as a contested frontier in this narrative, and the potential of technology to ameliorate health problems influences not only Raven's individual journey but also power dynamics among clans on the ground.

Through Raven's relations to pain and technology, *The 100* frames pain as fundamental to humanness and numbness as a hallmark of surrendering to technology. Human characters merging with technology is a common trope in science fiction and post-apocalyptic narratives, including *Battlestar Galactica* and Suzanne Collins' *The Hunger Games* (2008). Writing about *The Hunger Games'* "visions of posthuman monstrosity," Susan Shau Ming Tan finds that, "As Katniss faces the aftermath of war, definitions of human become enmeshed in questions of trauma" (64). Likewise with Raven, trauma comes to define her as human. Even after Raven escapes the virtual reality and returns to her physical body (and the pain it brings her), part of ALIE's code remains in her brain, causing strokes and seizures, producing a feedback loop of trauma and technology.

With the show oscillating between futuristic visions of the posthuman and pre-technological histories where advancements bring only violence, Raven's character continues to remind audiences of the extreme vulnerability of the human body—and why that vulnerability is essential to humanity. As the person who has questioned most what constitutes living, Raven's full embrace of life's pain, even when offered alternatives, reflects the show's commitment to a future where technology remains subservient to human intelligence and, perhaps more importantly, human feelings. In this way, *The 100* reinforces Katerberg's vision of this twenty-first century science fiction: "cyborg science fiction might be viewed as humanist redux. However open-minded, reformed, and remixed, it remains a form of humanism" (206). In preparing to put herself through a complex medical procedure to rid herself of the last of ALIE's code, she declares that "you have to be willing to die to really live" ("The Other Side"). At the same time that Raven fully excises ALIE's code, the Grounders announce that the time of the commander is over and move away from ALIE 2.0 as foundational to their governance; the new leader will not merge with the AI. With these two plotlines, *The 100* makes clear that, while technology is sometimes useful, posthuman hybridity is undesirable and unsustainable.

Clarke kom Skaikru, Healer and Commander of Death

While a cast of strong women shapes the plot of *The 100*, Clarke is undeniably the show's protagonist, the leader of her people and sometimes also the Grounders. Unlike *Battlestar Galactica's* Starbuck, Clarke's brand of leadership combines physical strength with a compassionate, nurturing side. She is never punished for her more masculine traits nor is she held back by her feminine ones. Nicknamed "Princess" by the other delinquents, Clarke shares characteristics with another iconic female leader from a SF Western: Leia. But unlike her foremother, Clarke was never forced to wear a gold bikini while chained to her captor like Leia was when imprisoned by Jabba the Hut in *Return of the Jedi* (1983). Indeed, as with Starbuck, Leia is positioned as a leader but is ultimately disempowered and sexualized, both in the narrative and by the popular 1980s pin-up calendars loaded with images of Carrie Fisher as Leia chained to Jabba. Clarke is held captive multiple times but never sexualized; people follow Clarke because of her innate leadership skills and her ability to make life and death decisions.

Clarke's hybridity blends her status as a healer and the Commander of Death. She saves lives using medical expertise and an abundance of compassion, yet at the end of both the first and second seasons, she flips a switch and kills 300 people. When she learns she is being sent to the Ground, her mother tells Clarke, "your instincts will tell you to take care of everyone else first" ("Pilot"), but while her instincts may be noble, Clarke is one of the few *realpolitik* female leaders in television. She retains her status as a juvenile, too—like Octavia, she exists in many liminal spaces and often belongs to none. If Octavia represents the Western genre of the show and Raven represents the science fiction, Clarke blends the two; she lives for a time alone in the woods, hunting for her own food and bartering at a trading outpost, and she is also comfortable with guns and technology. Her resistance to single-identity categories includes sexuality—she is neither heterosexual nor gay. *The 100*'s normalizing of her bisexuality reflects the show's inclusive attitude toward identity, even while fans and critics erupted in outrage in 2016 at the way the show handled her relationship with the Grounder commander, Lexa.

James Berger notes that, "From the Whore of Babylon in Revelation to the … antifeminist energies of recent Christian apocalypticism, there is an important strand of apocalyptic imagining that seeks to destroy the world expressly in order to eliminate female sexuality" (11). *The 100* embraces Clarke's sexuality, putting her in two romantic relationships and one sexual fling, showing her fall in love and into bed with multiple partners—but it is hard to say that it does not also eliminate her sexuality. Both of her romantic partners, Lexa and Finn, are killed because of their associations with her—Lexa immediately after sleeping with her by someone who disapproved of their relationship (for political reasons, not homophobic ones). Indeed, much to the showrunner's (Rothenberg) seeming frustration, Lexa's death has come to define the show in many circles (qtd. in Prudom).

In twentieth-century Western frontier narratives, LGBTQ characters have been either invisible or punished for their queerness. Patricia Melzer writes that, historically, science fiction "has reproduced white, male, heterosexual power fantasies of colonization and subjugation of the Other that have often relied on traditional values in their depictions of futuristic societies, including a deeply heteronormative understanding of sexuality" (395). She traces the evolving representations of queer populations and characters in science fiction and finds that, even today, the dominant sexual order of the genre is heteronormativity. Melzer concludes that "True challenges to a heterosexist, binary economy of desire can be found on the margins of SF" (405).

Queer people are oppressed in frontier narratives, as in the real world; in twenty-first-century America, urban areas are associated with progressive identity politics and queer people have legitimate fear of rural spaces. Colin R. Johnson suggests that "Rural space may be queer America's final frontier" (1). He elaborates, "Especially in the wake of Matthew Shepard's brutal murder in 1998 in Laramie, Wyo., but also in light of the poignant sadness at the core of other queer landscape films like *My Own Private Idaho* (1991) and *Boys Don't Cry* (1999), the kind of big-sky rural vistas ... on screen have tended to engender feelings of exposure and vulnerability in lesbians and gay men more than freedom and openness" (1). In *The 100*'s frontier, Clarke and Lexa feel none of the anxiety that contemporary queer people feel being out in the open, literally and metaphorically. Other queer characters on the show experience the same level of acceptance toward their sexuality. In this way, *The 100* rectifies the erasure of LGBTQ characters from the SF Western genre.

Yet the show falls into more traps than just the white feminist problem Gabby Taub articulates. In fact, one of the long-term legacies of the show might be its perpetuation of the "Bury Your Gays"* trope with the way it killed Lexa. In a scene that parallels Tara Maclay's death in *Buffy the Vampire Slayer* (1996–2003) twenty years prior, Lexa dies by a stray bullet immediately after consummating her relationship with Clarke. Fan outrage at her death spawned an entire conference promoting more positive queer representation, *Clexacon: A Media and Entertainment Convention for LGBTQ Women and Allies*, as well as "The Lexa Pledge," a commitment to better LGBTQ representation created and signed by television writers, producers, and directors.†

---

*The "Bury Your Gays" trope refers to the practice of killing off LGBTQ characters either because they are viewed as depraved and need to be punished for their sexuality or because queer characters are not considered important and their deaths can provide an opportunity for character growth for the heterosexual protagonist.

†Created by Noelle Carbone (Writer: *Saving Hope*), Sonia Hosko (Producer: *Saving Hope*), Michelle Mama (Producer, Director, Writer), and Gina Tass (Leskru Fundraiser Creator), The Lexa Pledge has been signed by 16 other writers, directors, and producers. The pledge can be found here: https://lgbtfansdeservebetter.com/pledge/.

Many queer fans of *The 100* abandoned the show in favor of the supernatural Western *Wynonna Earp* (2016–present). Despite its post-identity approach to representation, *The 100* demonstrates that twenty-first century SF Westerns still have progress to make in terms of representing queerness.

There is huge gulf between the utopian vision of identity put forward within the world of the show and the reality of the world audiences live in while they watch it. *The 100* imagines an era where gender, race, and sexuality no longer carry with them the same promises of discrimination and hate, but it forgets that audiences cannot so easily set aside histories of trauma and marginalization. In *The 100*, while LGBTQ characters' presence in SF Westerns is reaffirmed, their happiness is not.

Ogeda (Together)

In the final minutes of the season four finale, "Die All, Die Merrily," after Octavia announces that the bunker will be shared by all clans, people begin to chant "Ogeda, ogeda," the Grounder word for "together." Across four seasons, the narrative has moved inexorably toward the possibility of unity, toward bridging space and earth, frontier and civilization, progress and a commitment to existing culture, technology and humanity, violence and peace. This path has meandered and sometimes lost its way but, overall, the show puts forward a unique and progressive vision of cultural relationships and individual identity. Macdonald writes, "*The 100* has the unique opportunity of writing in an almost entirely new world, since the show takes place in a dystopic version of Earth, which allows the writers to bend some rules and throw others right out the window." The science fiction and Western elements of the show creates opportunities for re-envisioning past and future.

Season four ends with a cliffhanger coda in which a spaceship approaches, the words "Prison Transport" painted on the side. In a circular plot, Clarke and the others will now be the Grounders to newcomers landing on Earth. The ensuing conflicts involve power struggles for territory, but never are someone's leadership skills questioned based on their gender, sexuality, or race. There is so much potential behind the "Ogeda" chant, not only for this show, but for the genre of the SF Western. Whether the clans continue to feel the power of "ogeda" will depend largely on if the show is able to maintain its characters' hybrid status and resist the flattening and oversimplification that comes with mythologizing heroes and fitting them into tired frontier narratives.*

*My thanks to Ian Ross, Shannon Hervey, and Sheri Milburn, for reading drafts of this work and giving me very useful comments, and to Melanie A. Marotta for her excellent editing.

WORKS CITED

Agamben, Giorgio. *State of Exception*. Translated by Kevin Attell, U of Chicago P, 2005.
Battlestar Gallactica. Created by Glen A. Larson and Ronald D. Moore, NBC Universal, 2004–2009.
Berger, James. *After the End: Representations of Post-Apocalypse*. U of Minnesota P, 1999.
Bridges, Elizabeth. "Someday. Maybe. But Not Today. The 100-3x-7, 'Thirteen.'" *The Uncanny Valley Blog*, 7 Mar. 2016, www.uncannyvalley.us/2016/03/the100s3e7/.
Buffy the Vampire Slayer. Created by Joss Whedon, Mutant Enemy, 1996–2003.
Fernbach, Amanda. "The Fetishization of Masculinity in Science Fiction: the Cyborg and the Console Cowboy." *Science Fiction Studies*, vol. 27, no. 2, Jul. 2000, pp. 234–255.
Fine, Kerry. "She Hits Like a Man but Kisses Like a Girl: Tv Heroines, Femininity, Violence, and Intimacy." *Western American Literature*, vol 47, no. 2, Summer 2012, pp. 152–173.
Fortenberry, Dorothy. Personal interview. 15 April 2016.
Gurr, Barbara. "Masculinity, Race, and the (Re?)Imagined American Frontier." *Race, Gender and Sexuality in Post-Apocalyptic TV and Film*, edited by Barbara Gurr, Palgrave Macmillan, 2015, pp. 31–44.
Halberstam, Judith. *Female Masculinity*. Duke UP, 1998.
Higgins, David M. "American Science Fiction After 9/11." *The Cambridge Companion to American Science Fiction*, edited by Eric Carl Link and Gerry Canavan, Cambridge UP, 2015, pp. 44–57.
Johnson, Colin R. "Rural Space: Queer America's Final Frontier." *Chronicle of Higher Education*, 13 Jan. 2006, www.chronicle.com/article/rural-space-queer-americas/8513.
Katerberg, William H. *Future West: Utopia and Apocalypse in Frontier Science Fiction*. U of Kansas P, 2008.
Macdonald, Lindsay. "11 Times the *100* Was More Progressive About Race, Gender, & Sexuality than Many Shows Out There." *Bustle*, 4 Feb. 2016, www.bustle.com/articles/138293-11-times-the-100-was-more-progressive-about-race-gender-sexuality-than-many-shows-out.
Melzer, Patricia. "Sexuality." *The Oxford Handbook of Science Fiction*, edited by Rob Latham, Oxford UP, 2014, pp. 395–407.
Milburn, Colin. "Posthumanism." *The Oxford Handbook of Science Fiction*, edited by Rob Latham, Oxford UP, 2014, pp. 524–36.
Neumark, Selena. "Why Cw'S the *100* Is a Feminist Dream, Except for When It's Not," *PopMatters.com*, 28 Oct. 2015, www.popmatters.com/feature/why-cws-the-100-is-a-feminist-dream-except-for-when-its-not/.
Newell, Diane, and Victoria Lamont. "Rugged Domesticity: Frontier Mythology in Post-Armageddon Science Fiction by Women." *Science Fiction Studies*, vol. 23, no. 3, Nov. 2005, pp. 423–441.
The 100. Created by Jason Rothenberg, Warner Bros., 2014-present.
Prudom, Laura. "*The 100* Creator on the Lexa Controversy: I Would Have Done Some Things Differently." *Variety*, 27 Mar. 2016, variety.com/2016/tv/news/the-100-lexa-dies-lesbian-death-tropes-jason-rothenberg-wondercon-1201740032/.
Raney, Tracy, and Michelle Meagher, "Gender in the Aftermath: Starbuck and the Future of Women in *Battlestar Galactica*." *Race, Gender and Sexuality in Post-Apocalyptic TV and Film*, edited by Barbara Gurr, Palgrave Macmillan, 2015, pp. 45–57.
Scarry, Elaine. *The Body in Pain*. Oxford UP, 1987.
Slotkin, Richard. *Gunfighter Nation: the Myth of the Frontier in Twentieth-Century America*. U of Oklahoma P, 1998.
Star Wars: Episode VI: Return of the Jedi. Directed by Richard Marquand, 20th Century–Fox, 1983.
Tan, Susan Shau Min. "Burn with Us: Sacrificing Childhood in the *Hunger Games*." *The Lion and the Unicorn*, vol. 37, no. 1, Jan. 2013, pp. 54–73.
Taub, Gabby. "*The 100* Has a White Feminist Problem," *Women Write About Comics*, 21 Mar. 2017, womenwriteaboutcomics.com/2017/03/21/the-100-has-a-white-feminism-problem/.

The Most Dangerous Woman in the Universe

Redefining *Gamora as a Female* Native American *in* Guardians of the Galaxy

Brett H. Butler

Tales of the West—fact, fiction, or somewhere in between—are full of rugged scrappers, brave gunslingers, and wily outlaws. With the dawn of pulp magazines, comic strips, and science fiction in general, it was natural that writers would eventually launch these stories into outer space and in other dimensions. And, so, the Space Western was born, replacing six-shooters with laser guns and horses with jet packs. A Space Western, as defined by Paul Green, is "A scientific fiction story set in outer space that contains Western elements and themes. These are usually disguised in a space opera or science fiction format. The hero at times can be little more than a cowboy with a ray gun…. Space Westerns become more sophisticated with age but some still blatantly pay homage to their source of inspiration with thinly disguises Western genre plots" (Green 4). By definition, the first *Guardians of the Galaxy* (2014) film fits in the Science Fiction Western subgenre, not so thinly disguised with Western themes on par with *The Good, the Bad, and the Ugly* (1967) and *The Wild Bunch* (1969). The plot of the movie is set around a bunch of misanthropic outlaws, each one trying to make a big score. Ultimately, they come together to help each other as a team and save the universe. The science fiction elements are obvious: ray guns, space ships, high-tech worlds. The Western element is also present in the plot of a big heist and tough-as-nails heroes who are always ready for a fight. In the first *Guardians of the Galaxy* film, one of those heroes is a woman named Gamora.

In the Marvel comic books and the *Guardians of the Galaxy* film, Gamora has been identified as the "most dangerous woman in the universe"

(*Guardians of the Galaxy Vol. 2*—comic book). Whereas the comic book shows repeated incidents of her physical prowess, the first film does not demonstrate or explain why, especially when one considers that her entire journey throughout the film shows incidents, primarily, of failure and defeat. She loses battles, depends on others for survival, and has no individual plight. Regardless, she does generate much enthusiasm among audience members. In popular culture, she is a ubiquitous subject of bloggers, fan art, and co-splay, competing with the likes of Harley Quinn from DC Comics' *Suicide Squad* film and comic book. Some armchair scholars, such as Dany Roth on *Blastr*, actually claim brazenly that Gamora is "the most important character in [the film] *Guardians of the Galaxy*" (www.blastr.com), despite the fact that the story revolves around the leader of the team, Star-Lord Quill (Star-Lord). Whether or not Roth is correct, that Gamora is the most important character in the film, the general excitement over her character is irrefutable. Possibly, this popularity is derived from what audience members, including Roth, think is an original, strong female hero. This essay argues that this observation is inaccurate. In fact, when stripped down to her essences, Gamora is not so much a strong female character as she is a reoccurring background character in Westerns who is commonly portrayed but seldom studied: the Native American woman.

Gamora does have characteristics that set her apart from other comic book and film superheroes; it would be short-sighted not to note these. Primarily, Gamora is a female superhero, a rarity among the overwhelming majority of male heroes in comic books and films. Moreover, these female characters tend to generate much less enthusiasm and popularity among fans beyond fetish. Authors such as Gail Simone and Kelly Sue DeConnick have noted these points repeatedly in interviews and articles. Secondly, Gamora is not a stereotypical white heroine with supernatural—or at least unrealistic—body type that are common of women in comic books and comic book cinema. These images are most apparent in Halle Berry's portrayal of Catwoman in *Catwoman* (2004) or Scarlett Johansson's portrayal of Black Widow in the *Captain America* and *Avengers* franchises. Finally, she is a part of a genre of cinema, the SF Western, that tends to marginalize strong female characters altogether. For these reasons, Gamora and Saldana's representation of this character are unique.

The problem exists that despite her popularity and seemingly original character development, Gamora demonstrates qualities of a prototypical Native American woman in *Guardians of the Galaxy*. In doing so, she conforms to many existing stereotypes and tropes attached to women and Native Americans in traditional Westerns with some exceptions. Whereas these exceptions, such as the ones listed above, may shatter some stereotypes of the genre, her conforming to other stereotypes weakens the character greatly as writers rely on her hackneyed backstory to propel the main story, which, contrary to Roth's observations, focuses on the white cowboy, Star-Lord, and not on Gamora. As a result, her actions and motives propel Star-Lord's plot more than her own.

Gamora the Indigenous Person

Simply stated, each member of the Guardians of the Galaxy team is visually unique, aside from Star-Lord. That is, they technically are not white cowboys, per se. Rocket is a raccoon, Groot is a sentient tree, and Drax is a muscular green humanoid. Still, Gamora stands out among them as the only female on the team. She is strong and driven, she does not fall for the white hero, and she is independent. Superficially, she seems an ideal, positive character to represent strong women. However, she reflects many tropes that impart on her negative stereotypes associated with weak and victimized women in films. These stereotypes are rooted in what makes her different: she is more reminiscent of a background Native American woman in a Western than a courageous, gun-toting cowgirl at the forefront of the tale.

As Green's definition states, the hero of a Space Western can be "at times … a little more than a cowboy with a ray gun" (2). Certainly, this definition could include Peter Quill (Star-Lord), the film's main hero who does, in fact, carry a ray gun. As this film does borrow from cinematic Westerns, *Guardians of the Galaxy* has other prototypical characters in the story. There is an unhinged gunman (Rocket Raccoon) and a brute who loves to fight (Drax the Destroyer). Gamora, however, stands out among Star-Lord's gang as the only female character.

More than her sex, Gamora does not represent European heritage that permeates most Westerns. She is green with long, straight hair that is such a dark shade of green that it looks black, except for the tips, which are highlighted red. Her skin color alone separates her from the hero of the film, Star-Lord, who is of European descent with fair features. This difference between the two characters is made even more obvious when they are juxtaposed in scenes. When the film introduces Gamora, she engages in a cinematic game of "capture the flag" with Rocket and Groot, two bounty hunters with criminal backgrounds. In this scene, Star-Lord is the figurative flag who has a bounty on him. Whereas Rocket uses myriad long-range weapons to capture the hero, Gamora uses hand-to-hand combat which entangles Star-Lord and her numerous times. In another scene, Star-Lord and Gamora stand on a balcony; he wants her to listen to the headphones of his Walkman, so he gets near her, inches from her face, to share the headphones. Later in the film, when an enemy ship retrieves Star-Lord and Gamora from space, near dead, the two recover inches from each other's face once more, him lying on top of her. Each of these scenes with their carefully cropped close-ups and the characters' differing costumes makes the racial differences even more noticeable. Star-Lord is fair-skinned and wears a leather slicker reminiscent of that of the Old West cowboys. He wears boots and, as previously stated, carries a ray gun. Gamora, contrastingly, has long straight hair; her leather outfit is tight-fitting with cross-hatched leather straps across her midsection, which is somewhat exposed. Her shoulders and collar are adorned with large jewels.

Comparing the two, Star-Lord's fairer complexion and nineteenth-century American style of dress contrast sharply with Gamora's darker complexion and more "alien" dress. In this case, what is "alien" about Gamora is that her look and style reflect images of indigenous women in American film and cinema. If Star-Lord's outfit (the boots, the slicker, and the ray gun) demonstrates "cowboy," then Gamora's contrasting look would cognitively demonstrate "Indian," as countless Westerns have drilled in audiences' heads. However, there is more than just cognitive association at play here. Her presentation is irrefutably reflective of a Hollywood representation of Native Americans. First, her long, so-green-it's-black hair is razor-straight and cascades down past her shoulders, as it does with most Native American people in classic Western films. The red coloring in her hair is present where her hair touches her skin, thus metaphorically reflecting that red hue onto her skin. Secondly, her non-white/alien pigmentation makes obvious the racial difference between the American earthling Star-Lord and her. This difference further marginalizes her as "Other" beyond just her sex. That is, she is otherworldly, not human, or not like the cowboy Star-Lord. Thirdly, her outfit is seemingly inspired by the buckskin wardrobes associated with stereotypical Native Americans, with its crosshatched ties in the middle and jewel/beaded adornments on her quasi-exposed décolletage. If there is any doubt, one only needs to review an early concept design of Gamora created by Andy Park, the concept artist in charge of character design for the first *Guardians of the Galaxy* film. Gamora's green skin is a shadowy, darker color, and what appears to be "war paint" covers her forehead and eyes, just as it does on Native American characters in classic Western films such as *The Searchers* (1956) and *They Rode West* (1954).

Identifying Gamora as a Native American character within a SF Western modernizes a common trope, yet she is still riddled with many of the stereotypes attached to that trope. As Maryann Oshana states in "Native American Women in Westerns: Reality and Myth," women in Westerns have few definitive roles: "if they are not being raped or murdered, they are usually shown as slaves, household drudges, or bodies en masse in camps and caravans. Women are most often portrayed as victims, convenient objects for men to rape, murder, avenge, or ridicule" (48). Whereas Gamora is often celebrated as being a strong female character in her comic book appearances and in the *Guardians of the Galaxy* film, closer inspection shows she fits seamlessly into Oshana's observation. Although Gamora's victimization is not explicitly demonstrated in the film, her history in the Marvel Universe shows that there is a tortured background to Gamora only hinted at in the film.

Gamora's Origin in Marvel Comics

Primarily, Gamora undergoes numerous tortures in her comic book origin. In fact, her origin story is one that finds her alone on a planet, orphaned when her species is eradicated by the Universal Church of Truth. She is adopted by the mad titan, Thanos, who promises to train her to avenge her species; he brainwashes her into thinking that his malicious intent to control Death and the universe is benevolent. The reader understands that Gamora's training is more like tortured conditioning than intense calisthenics under Thanos' evil eye. When she emerges brainwashed and bloodthirsty, she becomes revered as "the most dangerous woman in the universe" (*Comicvine*). Her status at this point, consistent with Oshana's observations, is not that of an adopted daughter to Thanos, but as his conditioned slave sent to do his bidding. Her torture worsens when Thanos places Gamora in the Universal Church of Truth, thinking she will destroy them, but she disobeys him and finds herself in the presence of a group of marauders. Despite her superb fighting skills, she is overpowered by the group, raped, and left for dead. Thanos recovers her from the brink of death and augments her with cybernetic implants that make her stronger and faster.

Although Gamora is tough, looks cool, and overcomes hardships from a childhood of abuse (that the film only hints at), she clearly demonstrates many of the characteristics that are typical of a Native American woman in a Western film. However, Gamora's characterization as a Native American does not solely define her. What equally defines her and marginalizes her is her sex. Thus, according to the "woman in the refrigerator" criticism, Gamora is not only subjected to a torturous past because she is an alien but also, and perhaps more prevalently, because she is a woman.

Woman in the Refrigerator of Space

Writer Simone conceived the theory of "women in the refrigerator," a term that referred to the comic book character Alexandra DeWitt, who is killed for no reason other than to propel the hero's journey. Simone created a website based on "women in the refrigerator," dedicated to all of the women in comic books who have been tortured heinously, raped, and/or murdered. She contends that women in comic books are (1) treated much worse than men, (2) punished for no reason at all, and (3) only tortured, raped and/or killed to promote a male hero's story. To date, her website has over one hundred female characters who have been "stuffed in the refrigerator." Additionally, it contains responses from comic book writers responsible for figuratively stuffing a female character in the refrigerator. Previous to reading the website, many of these writers had been unaware that they had done so. Some are apologetic; others are defensive. Regardless of how the authors respond, this website does well in promoting awareness of the way women in comics are treated; notably, Simone is not against female characters being killed and tortured altogether. In fact, there are certain criteria that place them in the refrigerator.

As Marie Brennan speculates, a woman is only stuffed in the refrigerator if her death is meaningless and not of her choosing. However, a woman does not fit this stereotype if she dies for her own cause. She states, "If the woman dies fighting for a cause she believes in, she isn't in the refrigerator. If she uncovers the villain's secret and is killed to keep her from telling, she isn't in the refrigerator.... The point is that her death has a context related to her own actions. She's a character, not a pawn sacrificed to push someone else's story forward" (Brennan). Assuming Gamora's origin story from the comic book, even though Gamora suffers as an orphan and as a slave to Thanos, which leads her to be raped and left for dead, she is not yet in the refrigerator because her story up to this point is still her own story. This is similar to many orphan/lone wanderer stories of male characters, whether they are Western characters like the protagonist from *Shane* (1953) or space opera heroes like Luke Skywalker from *Star Wars* (1977). Basically, although she is abused, Gamora's actions up until that point are of her own choosing and promote her own narrative. She chooses to go with Thanos to be trained, not realizing she has been enslaved. She chooses to defy him by not killing her intended targets. But this storyline is not mentioned in the film; it is only inferred. The film, *Guardians of the Galaxy*, does not focus on Gamora as an individual. Instead, it focuses on her as a servant of Thanos and a sidekick to Star-Lord. The moment she joins Star-Lord's team, her actions and sufferings serve to promote his story. In the film, she is the only one who does not have her own personal reason for joining the team. Rocket wants to get a reward, Groot wants to protect his only friend Rocket, and Drax wants to avenge his family; however, Gamora simply stops being Thanos' pawn just to become Star-Lord's.

In the previously mentioned blog by Dany Roth, "Why Gamora Is the Most Important Character in *Guardians of the Galaxy*," the author asserts that Gamora is a driving force in the film version. Roth completely rejects Gamora as in the refrigerator:

Gamora is not forced to act. Yes, at some point in her past, her parents were murdered. But that's not Gamora's story in *Guardians of the Galaxy*, that's what happens before the film even begins. Gamora's story is "The world is in danger and I am choosing to try and prevent disaster." Nobody makes Gamora do anything. And that is exceptional.

Whereas Roth is correct in dismissing Gamora's past before the film, she is incorrect in asserting that Gamora's actions are her own. It is not until she learns to love her team by the end of the film that she chooses to prevent disaster. She spends most of the film silently skulking or breaking out of prison because Star-Lord said to do it, fighting the Nova Corp because Star-Lord said to do it, or splitting up because Star-Lord said to do it. Gamora almost dies as she drifts in space trying to do Star-Lord's bidding; thus, she almost dies promoting his story line. Not too ironically, Star-Lord must then come to her rescue. In essence, Gamora demonstrates that she has been stuffed in the refrigerator of space—her skin even develops icicles to prove it—and she has fallen into one specific trope: the Native American woman who needs to be saved by the white man.

When the Guardians of the Galaxy team first meet, they are arrested and placed together in prison. During their first night in what seems to be a minimally restricted general population, Gamora is pinned against a wall by a group of males who hold a shiv to her throat. These male characters, like Gamora, are not human; they are also intent on raping and killing her. At this point in the film Star-Lord has no real motivation to save her from these violent prisoners as she has already tried to capture him for a bounty. However, if one looks at her in this prison scene as a beautiful Native girl being threatened, it becomes obvious that the brave cowboy with the heart of gold must come to her rescue. In *Red Earth, White Lies: Native Americans and the Myth of Scientific Fact* (1995), Vine Deloria suggests that Native Americans are portrayed as childlike and superstitious. The women especially are shown as in need of saving (53). In this scene, Star-Lord is the benevolent white cowboy who risks his life and well-being to save the childlike Native woman from the violent men. What makes this scene even more improbable is that Gamora is supposed to be feared and revered throughout the universe for how dangerous she is. Star-Lord, contrarily, is not even known by the law enforcement officers who arrest him. It makes no sense that Star-Lord even needs to come to her rescue other than to satisfy the trope of the white cowboy coming to the rescue of the helpless Native American girl. The irony here is that Gamora is supposed to be far from helpless.

Gamora, however, is not locked into the Native American stereotype. She is also depicted as the untamed savage character type. At times in the film, she does show that she is dangerous. In some scenes, Gamora is no longer a victim to be saved, per se, but a warrior. This warrior, however, is more "savage" and dangerous than the average white warrior. A clue to this is her title "the *most dangerous* woman...." As Julia Boyd explains, "Native American characters in twentieth century films have ranged from stereotypes including the bloodthirsty, raging beast to the noble savage" (106). Oshana states that female Native Americans in film are commonly portrayed as "hot-blooded" or "savage" (49). Certainly, Gamora would fit this stereotype of Native American women. Throughout the film, she acts irrationally angry. Gamora often stands in brooding silence or speaks in threats, i.e., telling Star-Lord, "You don't learn," as she lodges her knee in his throat and, "I am not some starry-eye waif here to succumb to your pelvic sorcery," as she presses a knife blade into his neck (Gunn). This vicious hot-blooded demeanor, though, does not negate her sex appeal, which has captured fans' hearts across the world.

Allure by Association

Typically, strong, violent women are portrayed two ways in cinema: as seductive and surreptitious or domineering and masculine. The former is typical of a character such as a beautiful Russian spy in many Ian Fleming novels and Bond films. She is hyper-sexualized and operates from the shadows to lure the good guy into bed with her feminine wiles and kill him. The latter is more physically imposing, brutish, and hypo-sexualized. For example, characters like Red Sonja or Xena, Warrior Princess fight men and best them in strength and skill. Gamora is unique in that she is seemingly cast as brutish and masculine. She runs with an all-male team, she fights as ferociously as them all, and she rejects the sexual advancements of Star-Lord by threatening him; yet, fans still see her as a comic book/film sex symbol. The question is how? Half of the answer resides in Gamora's resemblance to a Native American woman and the other half in the actress behind the makeup.

Native American women have been portrayed as sexually available creatures because many Native tribes did not have similar ideas of modesty as the European settlers. These settlers observed Native American women's darker skin, rustic appearance and sometimes exposed chests and transformed these characteristics into a fantasy that hypersexualized Native American women. In *Playing Indian*, Philip J. Deloria proposes the image of the sexualized "Indian Princess" whose very appearance suggests sexual availability:

> Unlike the chaste breast occasionally revealed by a fold in the asexual Britannia's robe, the Indian Princess's frequently naked body symbolized not only fertility and the natural state, but also *availability*. The sense of availability applied both to the American landscape and to real Indian women, who were often represented as being sexually available to white men [53].

Hannibal Rhoades builds on Deloria's ideas of sexualizing the Native American woman, claiming, "In their respective contexts they portray Native American females to be promiscuous, dusky maidens who have retained some kind of primordial animalistic sexual energy which somehow must be conquered" (Rhoades). Shari M. Huhndorf concurs with Deloria and Rhodes but suggests that the Native American must not only be conquered but also tamed (Huhndorf 6). While this conquering and taming is implied in *Guardians of the Galaxy*, it still exists. For example, Star-Lord is not attracted to Gamora when he first sees her outside of an intergalactic pawn shop. Contrarily, he is pre-occupied with his own problems. It is not until Gamora has joined together with him and they share a moment on a balcony that the film suggests he is sexually attracted to her. In this moment, Star-Lord places the headphones of his Walkman on Gamora. This scene is reflective of a man turning down the lights and putting on music to seduce a woman. Gamora does not understand the concept of music, though, and almost ruins the moment by yelling at him above the music in the earphones that she likes the music. Nonetheless, the music has a soothing effect on her otherwise "savage" personality and makes her vulnerable for the moment that Star-Lord uses to lean in for a kiss. His advances, however, are rebuked as Gamora claims that she is not to be another of Star-Lord's sexual conquests.

Whereas this scene may support the idea that Gamora is independent and refuses to be one of Star-Lord's many lovers, it does more to show that she can be tamed, even for a moment, but will always revert to her savage, primal side, thus never really being fully civilized. After he is rejected, Star-Lord quickly denies any sexual intent or interest. This denial could be honest on his part as he realizes that Gamora does not conform to the Euro-centric image of a "civilized" white person. As Deloria suggests, the sexual attraction and sexualizing of Native American women is also taboo by white European/American standards: "The association of primitivism, sexuality, and miscegenation that accompanied the Indian Princess were highly inappropriate to the magisterial figure required by European convections" (P. Deloria 53). Deloria's notation here explains why Star-Lord is just as quick to renounce any sexual attraction to Gamora as he was to try to kiss her.

Typically, although Native American women are sexualized, their non–European features and non–European practices defy traditional European/American ideals of beauty. To mend the disconnect, many women of European descent are cast in Westerns playing Native American women. *Guardians of the Galaxy*, however, does not cast an actress that conforms to traditional European/American portrayals of beauty. Neither Gamora nor the actress who plays her, Zoe Saldana, conforms to the shapely physique of comic and film superheroes, such as Linda Carter as Wonder Woman, Halle Berry as Catwoman, or Scarlett Johansson as Black Widow. Saldana lacks the feminine curviness of these women. Moreover, her outfit, although revealing, is not as revealing as the other three who appear to be wearing modified leather/latex bathing suits or corsets. Saldana, the actress/model who plays Gamora, initially expressed her anxiety about Gamora's appearance. Having established herself as a sex symbol in other films, especially in the science fiction market playing Lieutenant Uhura in the *Star Trek* franchise, Saldana voiced her concern that Gamora would not be attractive to male audience members. In an interview on cinemablend.com, Saldana confesses, "That's [playing a beautiful character] usually a thing that I don't think about with other characters that I play, but for some reason, because I was going to be green and I was going to be the lead girl, I just wanted teenage boys to find me attractive." Saldana's choice of a specific audience demographic—adolescent boys—suggests that her concern transcends simple beauty; she wants to be sexually alluring in her role but was worried that she would not be because her character does not have European features. In this same interview, she asserts that she needed to re-identify her own idea of beauty to be comfortable in the role.

Saldana, who is of Puerto Rican and Dominican descent, is aware of the Western gaze that determines European/American notions of beauty. Although a sex symbol in Hollywood already, Saldana shows trepidation that painting herself green might diminish from the character's beauty, sexiness, and appeal to the general audience because she is an unnatural color, one often associated with illness. Cornel Peweardy expands on the ideas of Deloria and provides a possible reason that Saldana feels uneasy playing Gamora, a modified Native American woman. He states that Native Americans are too often portrayed as "a subhuman species that really has no feelings, values, or inherent worth—[which] still remains in the popular American mind" (www.hanksville.org). Perhaps Saldana attempts to reconcile this feeling of worthlessness, as suggested by Peweardy, by placing value on Gamora's sex appeal. In order to do so, she seeks approval from the demographic most widely associated with sexual impulses: teenage boys. Gaining their approval, she becomes more comfortable with her own alternate beauty. One might suggest, however, that this comfort with her new-found beauty is not entirely healthy. The possibility exists that her fandom is not appreciating her beauty despite her alien costuming but because that alien costuming so closely resembles female Native Americans, who have been objectified by popular culture and Western films so much that their mere appearance implies that they are sexual available and, more dangerously, that they need to be tamed.

Conclusion

Since the Europeans began colonizing North America, Native Americans have held a fantastic allure. They have been used to represent the dangers of a strange land, even if they, themselves, are not dangerous. Their different style of dress and architecture created a fantastic new world that led early explorers and colonists to create stories and tales about these indigenous people, but many of these stories were more based on their fears and fantasies than actual events. Native American women, particularly, aroused both fears and fantasies for European settlers. Artists and writers have portrayed them as hot-blooded warriors who were ferocious. Simultaneously, their often revealing clothing was quickly sexualized by European with more modest beliefs about nudity. Neither of these portrayals is accurate, but the imagery lived on. Native American women became a common backdrop to American Westerns and so did their jaded image. As Westerns and cowboy films expanded into other genres, like science fiction, so did the image of these Native American women. Rather than being hot-blooded "redskins," they became vicious, green alien femme fatales—still hypersexualized and still in need of being tamed.

Gamora fits seamlessly within this stereotype in the first *Guardians of the Galaxy* film. Although some critics and fans see her violent origin and unparalleled fighting skills as representative of female empowerment, her portrayal is much more dangerous to true empowerment. In both her comic book and film portrayal, Gamora suffers the same tragic, enslaved past as so many Native American women depicted in Western films. Moreover, her actions and suffering do not serve to promote or propel her own plot but the plot of the white, male cowboy, Star-Lord. In joining Star-Lord's band of Guardians, Gamora is almost raped and killed several times and needs the men, namely Star-Lord, to save her despite her acclaimed fighting skills. Moreover, even though she is not the typical comic book or film heroine with sultry curves stuffed into a leather cat suit, she is sexualized by both her characterization as a Native American and Saldana, the actress who portrays her.

It is worth noting that in *Guardians of the Galaxy Vol. 2* (2017), the character of Gamora seems to shed many of these stereotypes associated with Native American women in Westerns; however, this modification does not make her free of stereotypes. These stereotypes, though, reflect common problematic portrayals of women in general rather than ones associated with a marginalized group. Exploring those problems is better suited, quite literally, for the sequel.

WORKS CITED

Berkhofer, Robert F. *The White Man's Indian*. Random House, 1979.

Boyd, Julie. "An Examination of Native Americans in Film and Rise of Native Filmmakers." *The Elon Journal of Undergraduate Research in Communications*, vol. 6, no. 1, Spring 2015.

Brennan, Marie. "A Woman's Place Is Not the Refrigerator." *Science Fiction and Fantasy Novelists*. 16 Nov. 2009, http://www.sfnovelists.com/2009/11/16/a-womans-place-is-not-in-the-refrigerator.

Cook-Lynn, Elizabeth. *Anti-Indianism in Modern America: a Voice from Tatakeya's Earth.* U of Illinois P, 2007.

Deloria, Philip. *Playing Indian.* Yale UP, 1998.

Deloria, Vine. *Red Earth, White Lies: Native Americans and the Myth of Scientific Fact.* Fulcrum, 1995.

Eisenberg, Eric. "6 Things You Have to Know Before Seeing Guardians of the Galaxy: Zoe Saldana Wants Teenage Boys to Find Gamora Sexy." *Cinemablend,* http://www.cinemablend.com/new/6-Things-You-Have-Know-Seeing-Guardians-Galaxy-43796.html?story_page=2.

"Gamora." *Comicvine,* http//www.comicvine.gamespot.com/gamora/4005-6806.

Green, Paul. *Encyclopedia of Weird Westerns: Supernatural and Science Fiction Elements in Novels, Pulps, Comics, Films, Television and Game.* 2nd ed. McFarland, 2016.

Guardians of the Galaxy. Directed by James Gunn, Marvel Studios, 2014.

Guardians of the Galaxy Vol. 2. Directed by James Gunn, Marvel Studios, 2017.

Huhndorf, Shari M. "Going Native: Indians in American Culture." Cornell UP, 2001.

Liebhauser, Anna. "Native American Women as Princesses in American Films." *Images in the Contact Zone: an Online Exhibit,* https://imagesincontactzone.wordpress.com/about/revisiting-the-indian-princess/anna.

Oshana, Maryann. "Native American Women in Westerns: Reality and Myth Frontiers." *A Journal of Women Studies.* vol. 6, no. 3, Autumn 1981, pp. 46–50, http://www.jstor.org/stable/3346212.

Peweardy, Cornel. "The Pocahontas Paradox: a Cautionary Tale for Educators." *Journal of Navajo Education,* vol. 14, no. 1–2, Fall/Winter 1996/1997, http://www.hanksville.org/storytellers/pewe/writing/Pocahontas.html.

Reyes, Mike. "Guardians of the Galaxy's Gamora Wasn't Always Going to Be Green." *Cinemablend,* http://www.cinemablend.com/new/Guardians-Galaxy-Gamora-Wasn-t-Always-Going-Green-66941.html.

Rhoades, Hannibal. "Playing Indian: Endemic Issue of Indigenous Stereotyping Back in the Spotlight." *Intercontinental Cry.* 27 Dec. 2012, https://intercontinentalcry.org/playing-indian-endemic-issue-of-indigenous-stereotyping-back-in-the-spotlight.

Roth, Dany. "Why Gamora Is the Most Important Character in Guardians of the Galaxy." *Blastr,* 5 Aug. 2014, http://www.blastr.com/2014-8-5/why-gamora-most-important-character-guardians-galaxy.

Simone, Gail. *Women in Refrigerators,* Mar. 1999, http://www.lby3.com/wir.

Accidents of Occidentalism

Women, Science Fiction and Westerliness in Becky Chambers and Nnedi Okorafor

Laurie Ringer

Oh, East is East, and West is West, and never the twain shall meet, / Till Earth and Sky stand presently at God's great Judgment Seat; / But there is neither East nor West, Border, nor Breed, nor Birth, / When two strong men stand face to face, tho' they come from the ends of the earth!—Rudyard Kipling, "The Ballad of East and West" (1889)

I see you—*Avatar* (2009)

Overview: Problems with Seeing Women, SF and Westerliness

Just over thirty years ago, Susan Armitage coined the term "Hisland," demonstrating the ways that documented histories of the West were folkloric rather than factual in their erasure of women from the heroic, conflict-driven myths of "the legendary Wild West" (Armitage 9). Elizabeth Jameson has also queried the ways that historical accounts of "the" nineteenth-century American West have (accidentally) fictionalized the occidental territories, journeys, and peoples they seek to document. In omitting women from historical accounts of the West, academic accounts fictionalize and reinforce inequality as an accidental function of occidental expansion. Jameson troubles occidental "histories that move from the top down, from east to west, from nation to hinterland, histories that happen to people from the outside in," focusing her examination on ethnically diverse women (189). These women's bodies are the crossroads (186) where the labor that fueled western expansion took place, whether that labor is in fields or in childbed, in farmhouse sickrooms or town brothels. These more private spaces that have been called "home" by countless women, children, and men have been largely invisible in public historical accounts "written from the vantage of public politics, economics, and conquest" (181).

In historical and literary studies, the (accidental) habit has been to center male authors as heroic explorers of "Hisland." This space has been mapped, claimed, and settled by male scholars who are cited as authorities. Because literary studies are histories of narratives, ideas, and methodologies on the frontiers of knowledge, this essay applies Jameson's approach to women authors and characters of Science Fiction Westerns, "telling the stories silenced in state-centered histories" (188). From Rudyard Kipling's properly literary British-Afghan marches to James Cameron's popular SF exoplanet Pandora, *westerliness* has (accidentally) been a habit of seeing spaces as empty and therefore in need of civilization, cultivation, or salvation. Twenty-first century scholars and SF writers, however, are decolonizing occidental habits of seeing. For example, Karen Barad explores the politics of emptiness or "the void" as "a much-valued colonialist apparatus, a crafty and insidious imaginary way of offering justification for claims of ownership" ("No Small Matter" G113). Jameson proposes new ways of narrating history that are not epic, public, or unitary but modest, multivocal, or private (189). The stories Jameson examines are, like those in this collection, the stories of women navigating daily life in their wests "on their own terms" (Jameson 186). This essay on Becky Chambers' *Wayfarers* series and Nnedi Okorafor's Binti series explores how these writers and their characters decolonize and create new science fictional Western histories. Chambers' *Wayfarers* series is comprised of three novels, *The Long Way to a Small, Angry Planet* (*LWTSAP*; 2014), *A Closed and Common Orbit* (*ACCO*; 2016), and *Record of a Spaceborn Few* (*RSF*; 2018). Okorafor's Binti series comprises three novellas, *Binti* (2015), *Binti: Home* (2017), and *Binti: Night Masquerade* (2018).

Written in 1889, Kipling's "The Ballad of East and West" fictionalizes the East and West as a problem of rightly seeing. In a hybrid moment of fantasy and SF, members of two warring peoples meet on a distant frontier, and something, like magic or technology, allows them to circumvent their hardwired differences, transcending their easterly and westerly orientations.

The SF of transcendence in western philosophy (accidentally) reduces three-dimensional space to a binary opposition. Kipling's East is a "specular counterpart" (Braidotti 13), "dispossessed Other" (Barad, *Meeting the Universe* 378), or the space for Occidentalism to work. Like Leonardo da Vinci's *Vitruvian Man* (1490), the English officer is the template for colonial westernness. The western seeing-self, or ego, is the dominant point of view. It is *seen* as the normalized, rational, self-regulating, and ethical template that is idealized as "the" proper human way of seeing. The job of the specular counterpart or dispossessed Other is to reflect the western ideal and to be *seen* as the reverse image of the seeing-self: non-westerner, non-man, non–European, non-human. Gilles Deleuze and Félix Guattari characterize the seeing-self as body snatching "in order to fabricate opposable organisms" (276) that fight, fuel, or feed agonistic contests like East/West, man/woman, human/non-human, and home/frontier.

Which Way Is West?

As this essay contributes to a history of literary study, it follows Jameson in seeing "how women stretch the limits of inherited histories. And only then can we begin to try to imagine new plots, new stories, from the perspectives of an expanded cast" (181). Regarding language, the terminology "west" and "western" are heavy with various kinds of histories. Mythologically and astronomically, west is where the sun(s) set(s) (Harrison 79, fn. 14). Culturally, west is shorthand for talking about the end of an era or the end of a life. West can also denote the arid, westerly vastness caused by human-made ecological disasters and/or the side-effects of consumption and capitalism as in twenty-first century SF films like *Mad Max: Fury Road* (2015), *Dredd* (2012), and *The Book of Eli* (2010). Western can denote undiscovered countries filled with rich resources, such as Pandora in *Avatar*, or landscapes crawling with revenants and demons as in the television series, *Wynonna Earp* (2016–present). West can signify collapses in civilizations that transform orderly societies into blighted landscapes. The West is also a way of territorializing military operations by fronts as in the film version of *Wonder Woman* (2017) set on the Western Front of World War I. Going west has been a type of mantra for masculine self-making and for realizing one's potential unfettered by the cultural and social norms of their home worlds. Western evokes both the idealized American West of gunslingers that has become a byword for peril and promise of frontier spaces (re)imagined as wild wests on Earth, in space, and on exoplanets; paradoxically, the West also denotes shared European philosophy, art, literature, and culture as well as the European colonization of Africa, Asia, and North America.

After Jacques Derrida, ghosts or parasites trace through the signifier West/west, haunting the space of or living on the body of the new utterance and—with specters and traces of wests past—haunting the future. If locating "the" West is problematically haunted and compromised, so too is locating genres like Western, gothic, or SF. Recent scholarship emphasizes genre hybridizations; for example, Andrew Milner has argued that "SF applies meaningfully across a whole range of cultural forms, from the novel and short story to film and television … [and] that SF cannot be located exclusively on either side of any high Literature/popular culture binary, but should be seen as straddling and thereby, in effect, deconstructing them" (22). Sara Wasson and Emily Alder use the term "gothic science fiction" to denote genre bleeds and blurs of fiction categories, which create polytemporal distortions and the ways that perceptions of gothic pastness and SF futurities overlap in "our dark present" (16).

(Accidentally), dated habits of seeing reduce women, SF, and the West to colonial enterprises that unintentionally repeat structured inequalities on landscapes and bodies. Patricia Kerslake views the binary oppositions of colonial power relationships as the normal economic operation, a supply and demand type commoditization essential for identity formation: "the demand for the Other remains just as strong today, since it is through Othering that we may most clearly define ourselves" (4). Ursula Le Guin, however, remarks on the problems of the specular other in SF: "If you deny any affinity with another person or kind of person, if you declare it to be wholly different from yourself … you may hate it, or deify it; but in either case you have denied its spiritual equality, and its human reality. You have made it into a thing, to which the only possible relationship is a power relationship." Seeing the West as only between the English officer and the Afghan horse-thief misses women, the West, and SF because it duplicates dichotomous, teleological habits of rising and falling empires and heroes and villains.

In affect theory, Chambers, and Okorafor, westerliness is the messy frontier of time, space, and matter unfolding in bodies that are not separate entities like English/Afghan (Kipling), Galactic Commons/Toremi (Chambers), Khoush/Meduse (Okorafor) but entangled, intra-active, and interactive. In these entangled ecologies of species, histories, and landscapes, westerliness plays out in moments where survival is at stake. Anna Lowenhaupt Tsing observes, "If survival always involves others, it is also necessarily subject to the indeterminacy of self-and-other transformations. We change through our collaborations both within and across species. The important stuff for life on earth happens in those transformations, not in the decision trees of self-contained individuals…. We must look for histories that develop through contamination" (29). Where Tsing uses biology to describe entanglements, Barad uses quantum physics. Rather than focusing on the individual or hero as separate from others, Barad sees "spatially separate particles in an *entangled state* do not have separate identities but rather are part of the same phenomena" (*Meeting the Universe* 377). Paradoxically, the spatially separate particles that are put into proximity by their opposition become part of the same phenomena that transforms simple oppositions like knowing (epistemology) and being (ontology) into productive, quantum events. Quantum events do not erase differences; they are powered by divergent bodily materialities. Barad describes the phenomena as embracing "real material differences but without absolute separation" (*Meeting the Universe* 89) or a "dynamism of différancing" ("No Small Matter" G110).

Chambers and Okorafor: Twenty-First Century SF Westerns

Space is the new West. The forces that drive colonial expansion on Earth also drive it in outer space. In their works selected for this essay, Chambers and Okorafor embody Jameson's challenges to male-dominated, western histories by centering diverse women whose bodies are the crossroads or "sin fronteras" where the West unfolds. According to Jameson, "The ultimate act of living *sin fronteras* may be to reconceive history while reclaiming memory" (189). The memories each literary series reclaims are not epic, "Hislandic" tales but collaborative, pragmatic, and creative stories of survival through dynamisms of différancing.

Chambers' *LWTSAP* chronicles life onboard a long-haul ship, the Wayfarer, which creates wormholes by boring into subspace and creating stable tunnels to expedite space travel across the Galactic Commons. Each character takes a turn in forwarding the narrative, in contributing to the Wayfarer's tunneling work, and in ensuring the crew's survival in the wild west of outer space. For the crew, the Wayfarer is the closest thing to home and family they have. In *ACCO*, the narrative orbits around two characters introduced in the previous novel: Pepper, a genetically modified human, and Lovelace (Lovey), a former AI who installs herself in a synthetic human body kit and renames herself Sidra. After an accident on the Wayfarer that irreparably damages Lovey, Pepper and Blue, her partner, offer Sidra a new home. In a Western-style town on Coriol, a tidally locked moon, Sidra struggles with the transition from ship's AI to human body. Together, they form an unconventional family in Sidra's new café called Home. *RSF* gives the backstory of the Exodans, the last humans to build ships and leave Earth. After contact with non-human sapients, the Fleet moves into orbit around a borrowed sun. Aboard the Fleet ships, those who die are composted, their molecules living on to enrich the soil and produce food for future generations. In a manner reminiscent of Jameson's histories, *RSF*'s fragmented narrative offers glimpses into the private lives of those involved in the Western expansion, those that tend to be overlooked by official histories.

Okorafor's Binti is a sixteen-year-old Himba girl who wants to attend Oomza University, the leading university in the galaxy. With her ability to slip into mathematical trances (treeing) that materially transform conflict (harmonizing) and her edan, a type of sacred stone that assists her treeing and harmonizing, Binti saves herself and others from the great wave of a Meduse attack. In the second novella, a changed Binti returns home after her first year at Oomza University; she has been experiencing PTSD after the massacre of her friends during the Meduse attack in *Binti*. Binti's family is horrified to find out that she survived by being injected with Meduse genetic code. Although Binti's body modifications initially distance her from her Himba family, they untimately connect Binti to her new Meduse and Enyi Zinariya families and reconnect her with her Himba roots. In the third installment, *Night Masquerade*, Binti is killed trying to stop a Kipling-style East and West conflict between the Meduse and Khoush. After her death, Binti's reanimation is possible, not because characters forget their differences, but because they draw new opportunities for différancing from their different bodily materialities.

Decolonizing Women, SF and Westerliness

What happens when Kipling's East/West scene is replayed in the dark, in outer space, and between different women sapients? What if it is impossible to really see each other face to face? Rather than triggering nostalgia for a more illuminated, better defined, less polytemporally queer present, Chambers and Okorafor recast and decolonialize frontier moments, offering readers more inclusive societal constructs.

In Okorafor's *Binti*, for example, the Meduse attack on the *Third Fish* ship is silent and sudden. These levitating, nine-foot jellyfish-type sapients are neutrally-networked, moving through the human-friendly air of the sapient ship like water. In the Meduse language, "Moojh-ha ki-bira means the 'great wave'" (*Binti*). When the Meduse wave hits, Binti is unaware as to why and how she and the pilot are the only survivors. Binti learns that her Himba identity—her metal edan and her treeing abilities—protect her from the deadly Meduse wave long enough to collect food from the dining hall and lock herself in her room. From inside her room and with non-humanoid sapients, the Kipling "face to face" moment cannot work. Survival requires connection, and connection requires an entangling change in embodiment. Binti's treeing sends out waves and tendrils of blue current enhanced by her edan and by the gold-leaf on the doors and walls of the ship. Binti's mathematical waves wash over the Meduse outside her room, harmonizing human/ Meduse hostilities into mutually-beneficial, non-binary ecologies. Binti's edan can melt Meduse bodies; however, the otjize on her skin can also heal them, and her blue currents create a neural connection, allowing communication and eventually inter-species collaboration. This collaboration is not seen from the outside like in a Kipling moment but as experienced from the inside, in the dark, in a changed and changing embodiment that decolonizes one's mode of seeing.

In *LWTSAP*, Chambers also decolonizes modes of seeing, from Kipling's East/West type of opposition to inter-species connections. As Rosemary, a queer human and the newest crew member, becomes acquainted with her crewmates, a Kipling like East/West standoff becomes impossible. There are not just two sides; it is not just Aandrisk and Aeluon, Akarak and Harmagian, or Quelin and clone. Rosemary witnesses how binary approaches threaten to eclipse the present in colonial violence. For example, through Rosemary's daily conversations and eventual sexual relationship with Sissix, the female Aandrisk pilot, Rosemary begins to acknowledge the horror of colonial warfare. Sissix's brief account of the Aandrisk and Aeluon conflict recasts Kipling's East/West scene in the dark. As Sissix tells Rosemary about the battle of Tkrit, "Rosemary imagined being inside a pitch-black building, filled with silent soldiers being picked off by unseen claws reaching through the darkness. She shivered" (252). This dark colonial past appears to repeat when the Wayfarer is attacked and boarded by the Akaraks who suffer under Harmagian imperialism. Resistance is found in the habit of complicating and transforming the predictable doubles of binary systems into unpredictable and open-ended triads. The point is to stop counting and to find out what else a body can do. Barad describes this as "moving away from the familiar habits and seductions of representationalism (reflecting on the world from the outside) to a way of understanding the world from within and as a part of it" (*Meeting the Universe* 88). Crewed by diverse sapients whose pasts are darkened by colonial conflicts, the Wayfarer's collective work of tunneling transforms the ship and crew into an ecology of entangled differences and decolonized seeing.

In Chambers' *ACCO*, the ship's AI, Sidra, has never experienced ground-level, binary seeing until she transfers into the synthetic human body kit. The shift from her multi-camera arrays and above-planet orbit to the human bidirectional view is unsettling. Walking past the Bruise in Port Coriol, Sidra sees an impoverished family of Akaraks wearing battered mech suits and scavenging in the dump. Instinctively, Sidra tries to escape the troubling sight by thinking of something else because witnessing the sapient cost of colonialism is discomfiting to her.

Later in conversation with Sidra and Sidra's friend Tak, Pepper explains how the sapients are at the top of ego-indexed pyramids, with genetically engineered beings like Pepper herself at the bottom. She says that the sapients keep their place at the top alongside politics, empire, and capitalism by creating and maintaining others in lesser positions. East/West colonial seeing extends beyond discovered sapients to created sapients like Sidra and Owl, another AI. As Pepper points out to Tak, an Aeluon:

"And you guys, you guys invented AIs in the first place. Sentient code didn't exist before you wrote it down." She shrugged. "Life is terrifying. None of us have a rule book. None of us know what we're doing here. So, the easiest way to stare reality in the face and not utterly lose your shit is to believe that you have control over it. If you believe you have control, then you believe that you're at the top. And if you're at the top, then people who aren't like you … well, they've got to be somewhere lower, right? Every species does this. Does it again and again and again. Doesn't matter if they do it to themselves, or another species, or someone they created" [Chambers, *ACCO* "Jane, Age 19"].

As an escapee from the troubling scene at the bottom of the pyramid, Pepper has lived the reality that colonialism does not want to see: the Akaraks in protective mech suits in the Bruise landfill and the factory kids with genetic modifications on the scrapheap planet. Pepper does not tell Sidra and Tak about being Jane 23, about the faceless robot Mothers, about liquid meals, or about treadmill exercise in the factory. Pepper does not describe how she, as Jane 23, mistook the factory for the entire world because the factory children were not allowed outside nor does she describe rooms of bald little girls engineered to be resistant to fire, toxicity, and injury when sorting scrap technology. Ashamed, Pepper chooses to keep these experiences to herself.

While Kipling-style colonial "strong men" are busy looking at each other, they are not seeing their specular counterparts as people who suffer at the bottom of the pyramid, so it may stay in place. Pepper's harrowing escape from the bottom of the pyramid is a viral involution or a wild westerliness, one which is unnatural and illegal. In the past, this involution saved Pepper; in the present, viral involution will save Owl from colonialist enslavement.

As an Aeluon, Tak's first reflex is to deflect from Pepper's troubling scene of colonial exploitation to the good that pyramids produce like art, cities, and science; however, Pepper counters that these products only improve life "for some people. Nobody has ever figured out how to make things better for everybody" (Chambers, *ACCO* "Jane, Age 19"). Accepting that colonial good is relative to one's position and access, Tak agrees with Pepper that sapients need to keep talking and listening to each other; this exchange swaps relative positions in colonial economies with relational connections in decolonizing ecologies. Unlike Kipling's East/West moment, this moment of conversation is not a matter of transcending differences by seeing "face to face" (Kipling); it is listening to stories from other points of view and breaking out of teleological habits. Chambers' scene enacts Tsing's words, "we must reorient our attention" and learn "to look around rather than ahead" (Tsing 22).

En route to the museum, Pepper and Tak are sitting on the floor near the core processor. Sidra, who stowed away for the rescue mission, has temporarily left her synthetic body kit to flow through the shuttle's circuits. The positions of Pepper, Tak, and Sidra entangle and expand the organs and processes that would be the brain, womb, and heart in human morphology.

In the belly of the shuttle, a new moment, atypically and asexually fecund with new possibilities, sparks into existence from an odd number of gender- and species-diverse agents. Pepper's and Tak's minds stretch and extend beyond themselves through the interconnecting channels of conversation, just as Sidra's mind stretches and extends electronically through the shuttle's circuitry and interpersonally through conversation with Pepper and Tak. Through the entanglement and expansion of individual body processes, they generate beating nodes of empathy and courage, heart-nodes pulsing and looping out from the shuttle's core across space and time to encompass Blue, who is present upstairs, and to encompass Owl, who is in the museum and has been absent for 10 years.

This moment on Chambers' shuttle embodies Deleuze and Guattari's multiplicity "to be aware of existence and yet to know that one is no longer a definite being distinguished from other beings, nor from all of the becomings running through us" (240). One of the "becomings running through" Okorafor's *Binti* is becoming-spaceship. In *Home*, Binti is only peripherally aware that the *Third Fish* is a sentient spaceship whose travel time is speeded by her pregnancy. After Binti is killed in the third novella, the *Third Fish's* daughter, *New Fish*, is sent to transport Binti's body to its final resting place, an act that ultimately saves her life. Binti's friends Okwu, the Meduse warrior, and Mwinyi, the Enyi Zinariya harmonizer, accompany her on board the *New Fish*. Just like on Pepper's shuttle in *ACCO*, the minds of Okwu, Mwinyi, and *New Fish* extend beyond themselves, this time through telepathy and microbes. Through their entanglement, they enhance their individual body processes and heighten *New Fish's* regenerative breathing chamber in a group hug that echoes the one in *ACCO*.

Human-Making Tales, Grum-Making Tales

Donna Haraway creates a near-apocalyptic parable about the catastrophic impact of colonial seeing on women, SF, and the west. Her feminist fabulation, "Staying with the Trouble: Making Kin in the Chthulucene," tells the story of earthbound Man-Making tales, but it aligns with Pepper's characterization of the description of the capitalist-colonial pyramid. Colonial ways of seeing alienate bodies, like the Akaraks and the factory kids; these ways of seeing also destroy ecologies and worlds:

> So much of earth history has been told in the thrall of the fantasy of the first beautiful words and weapons, of the first beautiful weapons as words and vice versa. Tool, weapon, word: that is the word made flesh in the image of the sky god; that is the Anthropos. In a tragic story with only one real actor, one real world-maker, the hero, this is the Man-making tale of the hunter on a quest to kill and bring back the terrible

bounty. This is the cutting, sharp, combative tale of action that defers the suffering of glutinous, earth-rotted passivity beyond bearing. All others in the prick tale are props, ground, plot space, or prey. They don't matter; their job is to be in the way, to be overcome, to be the road, the conduit, but not the traveler, not the begetter [Haraway 39].

The horror story of Western self-destruction wreaked by binary seeing repeats in other worlds, as Rosemary discovers in conversation with Dr. Chef. The Grum species decimated itself through civil war fought with catastrophically destructive weapons. As a military physician, Dr. Chef saw the horror first hand and, at the time, hated the Outsiders for the carnage. He was unable to see them as fellow sentient bodies: "Outsiders were animals. Monsters. Something … something lesser than me. Yes, lesser. I truly believed that we were better than them" (226). Broken by the hatred, loss, and bloodshed when colonial ways of seeing target the Other as enemy, Dr. Chef left his home-world and travelled to Port Coriol where he retrained as a chef and family physician. Here, he met Ashby and joined the Wayfarer crew. Dr. Chef finds an inclusionary and peaceful home aboard the Wayfarer.

The third installment to the series, *RSF*, is an example of both the SF Western subgenre and the Anthropocene genre. After their environment is destroyed, the Fleet leaves Earth, taking the lesson with them to the stars. Symbolically, as the African American Exodusters migrated west after the American Civil War, Chambers' Exodans migrated into space in hopes of a better life. Fleet codes of conduct require everyone to take turns working on the drainage and sewage systems and doing tasks like cleaning and laundry. Many of these daily tasks have been historically gendered as female but, in the Fleet, labor is not gendered and is equally required of everyone.

Mycorrhizal Relations

Tsing updates affect theory in *The Mushroom at the End of the World: On the Possibility of Life in Capitalist Ruins* and traces the matsutake mushroom around the globe and through history. Matsutake mushrooms grow in places "disturbed" by humans: "Disturbance realigns possibilities for transformative encounter. Landscape patches emerge from disturbance" (152). Like Tsing's matsutake mushroom, Chambers' character Dr. Chef fruits new life from the sapient-made disturbances on the Grum home-world. Dr. Chef's five daughters were killed in the Grum war. The surviving Grum left their world, deciding not to recolonize and reproduce their own species but, instead, to realign the possibilities for transformative encounter through dynamic multispecies engagements across a universe of new Wests. Tsing's patches denote "the drawing of one world-making project into another" (62). On the patches of landscapes blighted by conflict or consumerism, mycorrhiza fruit into life from sapient-species damage. Midlife and without other Grum DNA, the evolutionary course of Dr. Chef and the Grum species will end; however, in small acts of resistance, something of Dr. Chef can survive through involution as multispecies ecologies remake livable frontiers in the ruins of Western-like cycles of decline and (re)conquest.

Mycorrhizally, Binti also fruits new life from domestic disturbances and Okorafor's Afrofuturist desert landscape. At 8, Binti can already tree faster than her father, in part because she escapes to the desert for quiet practice. As an adult, she is to become a master harmonizer like her father. As a woman, however, she will never be able to own her father's shop, and she is unhappy that her evolutionary course as a Himba girl and future master harmonizer appears to be foreordained. Walking past patchy landscapes of palm trees and hardpan, Binti finds a semi-circle of ruins facing west. As she sits drawing equations in the sand, she pricks her thumb on a piece of metal buried just beneath the surface. Beside the buried piece of metal sprouts a small yellow flower, its tenacious roots entangled with the stellated cube that Binti excavates. The disturbance of the sand transforms her life as a Himba woman harmonizer, realigning her future possibilities when she finds her edan. The world-making project that Binti begins at eight years old in a semi-circle of fallen stones draws her family's Himba world-making project into another. When Binti eventually visits her grandmother's desert home, she finds the yellow flower growing alongside the other plants in the indoor garden. Binti's grandmother tells her, "'I call it ola edo … 'Means hard to find, hard to grow'" (*Binti: Home*, "Gold People"). Like Tsing's matsutake, Binti resists "the conditions of the plantation," requiring "dynamic multispecies diversity … with its contaminating relationality" (Tsing 40). Binti's family sees her as contaminated with Meduse DNA and activated Enyi Zinarya nanoids; however, these interspecies relations fruit in what could be mistaken for sterile, disturbed desert landscapes of conflict in the Meduse attack on the *Third Fish*, in Binti's harmonizing between the Meduse and Ooomza University, and in her friendship with Okwu.

Whether in Jameson's nineteenth-century West or in Kipling's British west, it is the work of women that helps to fuel western, colonial, and capitalist expansion. Chambers' factory planet is far enough across the desert so that no one sees the girls forced to work in it. An explosion is the disturbance that realigns Jane 23's possibilities for a transformative encounter. Through a hole in the wall Jane 23—later renamed Pepper—sees a scrap-piled landscape and the blue sky for the first time, the act of seeing transforming her world. Later that night Jane 23 walks outside, escaping factory life. For the first eight years afterwards, Pepper lives in interspecies ecologies with Owl, the wild dogs, and the mushrooms that she eats when Owl's pre-packaged meals run out.

Some 20 years later, Blue uses Pepper's experience to show Sidra how evolution can be unpredictable. Those who engineered Pepper as a factory worker, one who is good with machines and circuitry, gave her the tools to repair the crashed Centaur 46-C and fly it off the planet. Like mushrooms, Pepper, Blue, and Owl fruit through their productively contaminating relations in blighted landscapes. Through their involution (entanglements), they do not find the west; they are westerliness—the frontier of finding out what bodies can do.

Frontiers of Gender and Sexuality

In Chambers' and Okorafor's westerliness, gender, sexuality, and reproduction are fluid, non-binary, and asexual. For example, in *LWTSAP*, Dr. Chef is gender-fluid and identifies as male: "Biological sex is a transitional state of being for my species. We begin life as female, become male once our egg-laying years are over, then end our lives as something neither here nor there" (Chambers 38). Rosemary has a same-sex relationship with the Aandrisk, Sissix, whose species is polyamorous and connected through feather families. For Aeluons, gender is also fluid and non-binary. Ashby, the Wayfarer Captain, is in long-standing relationship with an Aeluon woman, Pei. In Chambers' novel, the crew uses female pronouns to refer to Pei while Ashby notes Pei's body is in some ways unlike that belonging to Exodean women; both aspects show that Chambers' characters reside in a non-binary society. For example, when Pei's ship docks near the Wayfarer for repairs, the female tech, Kizzy, finds that it has been rigged with explosive mines. While Pei keeps her company, Kizzy disarms 46 mines. Both women defy gender norms in their jobs, and both find comradery in facing their fears and in saving others. In *ACCO*, Tak, Sidra's Aeluon friend, is shown as one who cyclically shifts "reproductive roles" ("Sidra") and, with these shifts, Tak's in-text pronouns also shift. As a newly awakened AI in an illegal body kit, Sidra's gender identity and sexuality are still developing, embodying Jameson's characterization of the ways that women and the west defy the conventions of history (189). These women are free to develop their identities and their freedom to do so in SF has the potential to change reality.

In Okorafor's first novella, Binti is referred to with female pronouns but begins to conform less to Himba gender expectations for conduct, dress, and cosmetics. From an early age, she realizes that whether she stays home or goes to university, "I was never going to have a normal life, really" (*Binti*). The Meduse Okwu, who eventually becomes Binti's closest friend, is referred to with masculine and neutral pronouns. In the second novella, on her first night back home on Earth, the Night Masquerade appears to her even though it only appears to males.

By the end of the third novella Binti reflects on her gender identity:

A tiny, tiny voice in me had wondered if something were wrong with me, if my spirit was that of a man's, not a woman's, because the Night Masquerade never showed itself to girls or women. Even back then I had changed things, and I didn't even know it. When I should have reveled in this gift, instead, I'd seen myself as broken. But couldn't you be broken and still bring change? [*Binti: Night Masquerade*]

After Binti regenerates, she still sees herself as broken for not conforming to Himba expectations for gender identity and sexuality. Dr. Tuka reassures her that even though she is partnered with *New Fish* and Okwu, Binti can still become a parent; however, if she chooses to have children, it would be Okwu who would give birth. Telepathically linked with Okwu (through Meduse DNA), with the *Third Fish* (through microbes), and with Mwinyi (through Enyi Zinariya nanoids), Binti's gender identity and sexuality will be an ongoing, polyamorous, and queer westerly frontier.

Women, West and SF

This essay concludes with the frontier of what happens next. In Chambers' *LWTSAP*, the AI, Lovey, is lost in an attack by rogue Toremi. In *ACCO*, the mission to save the AI, Owl, is successful because the AI Sidra learns self-programming skills. Creating a womblike void in herself, Sidra plugs into the Centaur's core and carefully locates the nodes, pathways, processes, and data of Owl's body. Sidra then excises Owl from her housing and enfolds the shocked AI inside the womblike space until Owl can be happily reinstalled as the resident AI in Sidra's café called Home. In Okorafor's *Binti* trilogy, Binti is lost in the Khoush and Meduse crossfire. The sentient ship named *Third Fish* learns to work the deep Miri of the breathing chambers that sustain life during space travel. The *Third Fish* teaches her daughter *New Fish* how to enfold Binti's body in her womblike breathing chamber where Binti reanimates. Like Sidra and Owl, Binti can flow between her core body and sentient ship. In a tweet, Okorafor has summarized the Binti trilogy as "1[.] African girl leaves home. 2[.] African girl comes home. 3[.] African girl becomes home. #InterstellarTravel #Afrofuturism" (@Nnedi). Chambers' space opera and Okorafor's Afrofuturism create homes on the frontiers of women, westerliness, and SF.

The differences in Chambers' and Okorafor's approaches matter because Kipling-like binary views of East/West or man/woman normalize a single, universal identity, (accidentally) erasing women whose bodies are different; representation matters. For women of color, gender bias is intersectional (Crenshaw). As Sara Ahmed notes, "sexism and racism are fundamental to the injustices of late capitalism" (165–167). The SF Western is a precarious place, complicated by the frontiers of female embodiment, varieties of west-erliness, and differing SF worlds. The title of this essay is not simply women and/or west, women and/or SF, west and/or SF, Chambers and/or Okorafor; rather, women, west, and SF are in collaboratively queer ecologies or entan-gled states. Putting these westerly bodies into play with affect theory escapes binary habits of colonization for decolonizing quantum entanglements fueled by diverse ecologies in which women of all embodiments co-participate in surviving and thriving, *as* frontiers and *through* new SF worlds, in twenty-first century fiction and in reality.

WORKS CITED

Ahmed, Sara. *Living a Feminist Life*. Duke UP, 2017.

Armitage, Susan. "Through Women's Eyes: a New View of the West." *The Women's West*, edited by Elizabeth Jameson and Susan Armitage, U of Oklahoma P, 1987, pp. 9–18.

Avatar. Directed by James Cameron, 20th Century–Fox, 2009.

Barad, Karen. *Meeting the Universe Halfway: Quantum Physics and the Entanglement of Mat-ter and Meaning*. Duke UP, 2007.

_____. "No Small Matter: Mushroom Clouds, Ecologies of Nothingness, and Strange Topolo-gies of Spacetimemattering." *Arts of Living on a Damaged Planet*, edited by Anna Tsing et al., U of Minnesota P, 2017, pp. G103-G120.

Braidotti, Rosi. *The Posthuman*. Polity, 2013.

Chambers, Becky. *A Closed and Common Orbit*. Hodder & Stoughton, 2016. Kindle.

_____. *The Long Way to a Small, Angry Planet*. Hodder & Stoughton, 2014.

_____. *Record of a Spaceborn Few*. Hodder & Stoughton, 2018.

Crenshaw, Kimberlé. "Demarginalizing the Intersection of Race and Sex: a Black Feminist Critique of Antidiscrimination Doctrine, Feminist Theory and Antiracist Politics." *The University of Chicago Legal Forum*, vol. 140, 1989, pp. 139–167, https://philpapers.org/rec/CREDTI.

Deleuze, Gilles, and Felix Guattari. *A Thousand Plateaus: Capitalism and Schizophrenia*. U of Minnesota P, 1987.

Haraway, Donna J. *Staying with the Trouble: Making Kin in the Chthulucene*. Duke UP, 2016.

Harrison, Evelyn B. "Hesperides and Heroes: a Note on the Three-Figure Reliefs." *Hesperia*, vol. 33, no. 1, Jan. 1964, pp. 76–82.

Jameson, Elizabeth. "Bringing It All Back Home: Rethinking the History of Women and the Nineteenth-Century West." *A Companion to the American West*, edited by William Deverell, Blackwell, 2004, pp. 179–199.

Kerslake, Patricia. *Science Fiction and Empire*. Liverpool UP, 2011.

Kipling, Rudyard. "The Ballad of East and West." 1889. *Bartleby.com*, http://www.bartleby.com/246/1129.html.

Le Guin, Ursula K. "American Sf and the Other." *Science Fiction Studies*, vol. 2, no. 3, 1975, http://www.depauw.edu/sfs/backissues/7/leguin7art.htm.

Massumi, Brian. *Politics of Affect*. Polity, 2015.

McGivering, John. Notes on "The Ballad of East and West." 2010. *The Kipling Society*, http://www.kiplingsociety.co.uk/rg_eastwest1.htm.

Milner, Andrew. *Locating Science Fiction*. Liverpool UP, 2012.

@Nnedi. *The #Binti Trilogy*. Twitter. 27 May 2017, 7:15 a.m., https://twitter.com/Nnedi/status/868470762197352448.

Okorafor, Nnedi. *Binti*. Tor, 2015. Kindle.

_____. *Binti: Home*. Tor, 2017. Kindle.

_____. *Binti: Night Masquerade*. Tor, 2018. Kindle.

Tsing, Anna Lowenhaupt. *The Mushroom at the End of the World: on the Possibility of Life in Capitalist Ruins*. Princeton UP, 2015.

Wasson, Sara, and Emily Alder. "Introduction." *Gothic Science Fiction 1980–2010*, edited by Sara Wasson and Emily Alder, Liverpool UP, 2011, pp. 1–18.

Wonder Woman. Directed by Patty Jenkins, Warner Bros., 2017.

Wynonna Earp. Created by Emily Andras, Seven24Films and IDW Entertainment, 2016–present.

If He Can Break It In, She Can Break It Out

The Public Impact of Domestic Machines in Elizabeth Bear's Karen Memory

Selena Middleton

Introduction

Elizabeth Bear's *Karen Memory* (2015) is a fast-paced steampunk Western in which a diverse cast of mostly female characters challenge patriarchal political plots on both local and international scales. The story is told by
the straight-talking farm girl of the title, who—having fallen on hard times
after the loss of her father—lives and works in Madame Damnable's Hôtel
Mon Cherie, an upscale brothel in the frontier town Rapid City. Madame
Damnable, as her name suggests, is a formidable figure in *Karen Memory*
and one who makes the move from private to public possible in providing a
home in which girls and women find the confidence to act politically. Damnable is drawn from an amalgamated history of Mary Ann Conklin, Seattle's
first brothel owner, and Seattle brothel owner and politician Lou Graham.
The character embodies not only the documented history of women on the
frontier but also the enduring mythology of the frontier brothel Madame
with her "lively corps of prostitutes ... [which is] woven into the fabric of
the frontier era in the American mind" (Butler ix). The spirit of *Karen Memory*'s Madame Damnable—both the fictional figure created by Bear and the
mytho-historical woman* known for throwing rocks at or releasing dogs on

---

*According to the folklorist Steve Roud, a "flurry of mentions" of Mother Damnables occur
as early as 1656, and the term always refers to a madam or a witch" (qtd. in Lovejoy). The use
of this nickname lends supernatural power to the historical figure and Bear's brothel madam,
contributing both to the acceptability of further myths surrounding Conklin's death and the
Hôtel Mon Cherie's impermeability under her care.

any man who would cross her—is encapsulated in the steampunk trope of the mecha warrior, who, in this frontier tale of women doing-it-for-themselves, is constructed from a Singer sewing machine. It is Madame Damnable and her modified sewing machine that provide the motivation and the confidence for Karen Memery to engage with the dangerous politics of her Western frontier town. This sewing machine, altered by hotel residents Lizzy and Priya, works on symbolic and literal levels to enable the expansion of female power from the private and domestic arena into the public sphere.

Women on the American Frontier

Bear's departures from the historical reality of frontier life for woman-kind contribute to *Karen Memory*'s feminist message. In her novel, Bear initiates a discussion of women's roles within the larger frontier economy and within personal relationships on the frontier. Madame Damnable and the women living at the Hôtel Mon Cherie draw from a particular characterization of frontier women. Women inhabiting new Western spaces were diverse and necessarily flexible. Acceptance of changing social patterns and the ability to quickly adapt to new ways of life in both domestic and public spheres were essential to success in developing frontier towns. In *Red Light Women of the Rocky Mountains*, Jan MacKell argues:

> They [frontier prostitutes] were usually single women with or without children who plied their trade as employees of a house or on their own. They had constant brushes with the law consistent with local ordinances and were subject to segregation and persecution. Their ages varied from as young as fourteen to as old as forty or more years of age. All battled such potential hazards as venereal disease, alcohol and drug addiction, physical abuse, pregnancy, and the results of abortion. They strived to leave the business eventually and did so by marriage, retirement, or death [17].

In "'Why She Didn't Marry Him': Love, Power, and Marital Choice on the Far Western Frontier," Cynthia Culver Prescott asserts that during the 1800s frontier men felt that they often lacked the necessities of life as bachelors, acknowledging the advantages marriages brought to them, including labor and companionship (25). As the "Wild West" became less so, however, women realized that the highly patriarchal structures of Western marriages benefited the men they had married more than themselves. Prescott's study does not point to a brewing independence for Western women nor is the study an acknowledgment that the more the West came to resemble the established Eastern cities from whence the women had come, the less they needed their partners to uphold social structures. The historian rejects the idea that Western women required rigidity in their partners, even symbolically, through strict marital roles, including punitive response to transgressions or complaints. Instead, Prescott suggests that relaxed gender roles inside later frontier marriages resulted in changes in the women's behavior. The women who came afterwards had the freedom to reject marriage entirely or to marry for love instead of survival (44). This response to stability—to eschew previously oppressive relationships in favor of romantic idealism, to value one's freedom over the pressures of social expectations for one's gender—is, perhaps, the appeal of the hotel in *Karen Memory*. After Priya's rescue from Peter Bantle's brothel, the Hôtel offers her freedom through options. The hotel is a secure physical space within which Madame Damnable provides protection and stability; this environment affords the women a freedom that does not exist outside of the Hôtel. Inside the hotel, the women must work but are free to choose what ways they can contribute to the hotel's microcosm. Priya, for example, elects to forgo the more lucrative sex work in favor of general labor and an informal mechanical apprenticeship with Lizzy. Afforded the stability of warmth, shelter, food, and a salary, the women in the house are free to not only pursue romantic relationships but also defy the expectations of their gender.

While Prescott's study indicates some of the ways the changing social structures in the newly settled West also affected structures of familial relationships, the underlying similarity between these relationships and those present in Bear's novel is money. An influx of money to frontier towns changed not only the infrastructure of such places but also the terms under which relationships became possible. Jef Rettmann, in his article "Business, Government, and Prostitution in Spokane, Washington, 1889–1910," points out that the presence of sex workers in frontier towns resulted in a concentration of successful businesses and, subsequently, a more prosperous town. Focusing on Spokane, Washington, during the period of 1889–1910, Rettmann examines the relationship between business and the sex trade. During this period, even though Spokane outlawed sex work in 1889, law enforcement virtually ignored its presence (Rettmann 77). Rettmann writes:

> The municipal government and the business community knew the economic importance of attracting the loggers, miners, farmhands, and rail-road workers into Spokane. Since prostitution was a major attraction, city officials and businessmen had a big stake in making sure that prostitution continued with as few regulations as possible [78].

The power, however, remained in the hands of the male governmental officials. In *Daughters of Joy, Sisters of Misery: Prostitutes in the American West, 1865–90*, Anne M. Butler argues that attitudes toward sex workers varied among town officials, ranging from moral indignation to personal indulgence or depravity. Butler stresses that while depravity was the more common reaction, rejection and indulgence also resulted in an unchanged condition for women in frontier town sex work (76). The mayor of Spokane in 1903, Frank Boyd, stated that reforms were targeting the peer class of brothel rather than those of the wealthy (Rettmann 82–3). Prostitution in the West contributed to an increased class awareness.

This history, which applies to many developing American cities, points to another way in which *Karen Memory* complicates women's histories. While the women working and living at the Hôtel Mon Cherie entertain mostly wealthy clients, they also perform a protective role not for the lower-class patrons of Bantle's cribs but for the racialized women who work in such dangerous conditions. Rettmann's study indicates that in Spokane, while sex workers were shielded before the reform, once it occurred the police continued to do so only if payment was offered (77–78). *Karen Memory*, alternately, revisits this historical commodification of women in order to return a measure of agency to them. In line with some twenty-first-century Science Fiction Westerns written by women, Bear's gives readers a diverse cast. The characters—including poverty-stricken women, women of color, lesbians, and transwomen—offer agency to two groups: the women who were victimized by their othered status and those who did not experience equal dangers but contributed unwittingly to the system resulting in the harm of other women. This system created new capitalist spaces and supported old ones. Indeed, drawing partially from one of the earliest studies of prostitution (published in 1920 but using data collected in the previous decade), Julia Ann Laite posits that sex work must be understood as linked to the "social industrial development and capitalism of the modern age…" (741). That sex work was such an integral element in the development of the frontier and the creation of the economic system that still drives American progress suggests that women's bodies—including their many unified intersectionalities—and women's autonomy could destabilize such a system. In occupying these intersectional spaces, *Karen Memory* relishes this task of destabilization, both in creating a secure space in which women create a diverse and cohesive community and in allowing that community to affect the political system in place.

Domestic Work and Feminism

Understanding the historical inspiration for *Karen Memory* is integral to the reader's comprehension of the ways in which women utilize the tools of the frontier's private/domestic spheres. While there are many ways in which the historical context remains relevant to this day, it is also necessary to further consider the ways in which feminists are shaping the domestic in the context in which Bear produced this alternate history. In other words, the feminist practices of contemporary women inform the ways in which these characters, based on both history and myth, perform feminism in Bear's steampunk world. In the novel, the domestic practice of sewing is literally and figuratively represented. Here, sewing is a euphemism for sex work, as Bear draws upon the historical context of frontier-era Seattle, where women who worked in brothels registered as "seamstresses" and paid a "seamstress tax" to the local government (Bear "Author's Note"). The "seamstress tax" was a common way for sex workers to maneuver around the illegality of their trade. Joel Best, in "Careers in Brothel Prostitution: St. Paul, 1865–1883," writes that in St. Paul, "Some prostitutes claimed that they were legitimately employed, often in the needle trades" (600) so that work could continue. Thus, the conversation in contemporary feminist circles around sewing as a feminist practice can, within the context of *Karen Memory*, apply to or even become a stand-in for more radical feminist discussions around the legality of prostitution, regulation of the trade, or the affective impacts of sex work.

Needle crafts, emerging from their classification as mere "women's work," are claimed by feminist activists and scholars focusing on the idea that such domestic work now produces not only textile products but also feminist community. In her discussion of the ways sewing may be seen as a feminist act, Jessica Bain asks, "in what ways can the revival of contemporary home dressmaking be conceptualised as an intentional engagement with feminism, and in what ways can home dressmaking contribute to the goals of a larger feminist project, without explicit intentionality?" (58). The home-like setting of the Hôtel Mon Cherie—in which each woman has her own private room, enjoys both work and leisure at will, and takes part in communal meals—emphasizes the feminist potential of the domestic space. The feminist project of gaining political autonomy, however, demands that the women leave the hotel in order to gain and use their power, as the hotel's inhabitants do when they challenge Bantle's Russian plot and support Madame Damnable's successful bid for mayor. According to Bain, second wave feminists disliked the act of sewing because of its connection to the home (59). Yet, Maura Kelly writes that "knitting practices can trouble gender norms and contribute to the construction of alternative masculinities and femininities. Local knitting groups (often called 'stitch 'n' bitch' groups) as well as online knitting communities can challenge the public/private divide and create locations for feminist communities" (133). Bain's article focuses on the ways in which third-wave feminists have transformed domestic craft to involve a measure of community building. Highlighting one important contemporary practice that often goes hand-in-hand with the sewing circle, Bain notes that women involved in dressmaking often establish and maintain community through blogging. Bain argues that such online communities give "public voice" to what has traditionally been an act done in a private space (62). Bain's assertion that blogging about sewing incorporates elements of the domestic into a wider political goal relates to the way that *Karen Memory* brings contemporary feminist issues into its alternative history setting. The use of technology in the form of modified domestic machines in *Karen Memory* ultimately enables such private to public movements. In a similar way, contemporary sewing circles—though participating in a traditionally domestic craft—liberate women from "normative femininity." Bain argues that the establishing sewing communities creates the kind of inclusive environments shown in *Karen Memory*, in which non-normative bodies are affirmed in "perform[ing] their femininity" (63). The hotel's "seamstresses" readily defy such normativity in their unwillingness to allow men to control the boundaries of their spaces, the definitions of what constitutes a desirable female body, and the ways in which women modify feminine bodies in order to assume and maintain control of the public political space. In this way, Bear's novel reflects the work of feminist sewing circles in its portrayal of the diversity of female experience. For example, such feminist communities respond intersectionally to the ways in which health and illness, as well as ability and disability, work together to influence experiences of equality. While the women in Madame Damnable's brothel-house engage with modified machines for much of their healthcare needs, the machines' maintenance is communal. Similarly, Kelly gives an example of the way in which knitting circles can account for not only the health or illness of the bodies in participation but also their preferences for care. Kelly offers Beryl Tsang's online breast prosthesis knitting pattern as her example. The pattern is meant for cancer survivors after mastectomy, and Kelly cites Beth Ann Pentney's observation that it "enable[s] women to engage in creative self-healing" (134). The hotel's communally-maintained sewing machines help to provide non-normative care for women's bodies by being used to create a diverse range of items needed by the residents.

Finally, in considering the ways in which the hotel's "seamstresses" engage in feminist practice, it is important not to discount the overall effect of small everyday acts which reinforce and strengthen community, such as cooking and taking meals together. In reference to needle crafts, there is Karen's gift to Priya of the colorful handmade Diwali quilt meant to help Priya acclimatize to hotel life. Kelly suggests that women regularly attending knitting circles or blogging about knitting can constitute an "everyday" feminist practice. She writes that "'third wave' feminism ... places significant value on individual resistance, described [by theorists] as 'everyday activism' or 'everyday feminism.' ... As a tactic for social change, everyday feminism has been critiqued as weak, but offers the promise of an easily accessible and personally empowering way to engage with feminism" (136). Of quotidian community practice as a Third Wave strategy, in "A Stitch in Time: Third-Wave Feminist Reclamation of Needled Imagery," Ricia A. Chansky suggests that, because of their feminist mothers and grandmothers, Third Wave feminists hold relatively privileged positions; these women also created a movement that rejects overt political action in favor of daily expressions of feminism (682–3). In this way, the knitting or sewing circle becomes a symbol for contemporary feminists: "The needle stabs as it creates, forcing thread or yarn into the act of creation. From a violent action comes the birth of a new whole. Women are channeling their rage, frustration, guilt, and other difficult emotions into a powerfully productive activity" (Chansky 682). The needle as a symbol of both old and continuing oppressions, as well as of creative and destructive potential, is important to understanding the underlying thrust of *Karen Memory*. In the housing of a "big, industrial, ridiculous, totally overengineered, souped-up-to-Jesus Singer sewing machine" (Bear ch. 16), the needle mends female flesh while it threatens male bodies and upholds female-maintained nearly egalitarian social structures in the hotel—until it bursts through the walls of the domestic space into the public and political sphere belonging to Bantle and his posse.

The Hôtel Mon Cherie as Feminist Space

While radical feminists would balk at the idea of a brothel as a feminist space because it enables a sex trade, they believe is fundamentally an oppression of women, in the context of Rapid City, the Hôtel Mon Cherie is a space removed from the oppressive political structures of the outside town. This separateness is made possible through Madame Damnable's power and money. The madam confronts the patriarchal demands made upon her and her "girls" with an unbending mostly-feminist ethic, one which strives to function under capitalist rule. There are issues with Madame Damnable's feminism because of the constraints capitalism places upon it. For example, she is ready to evict anyone who brings the wrath of Rapid City's politicians upon the house (Bear ch. 14), regardless of the consequences: death by the prostitute-stalking serial killer or death in Bantle's cribs. It is important to remember, then, that while the hotel does provide safety, prosperity, and a kind of freedom for the girls and women working there, its limitations are dictated by the capitalist system in which it functions, and the political space in which it exists. An examination of the similarities and differences between the Hôtel Mon Cherie and Bantle's cribs demonstrates the ways in which women and men create and uphold the political structures in which they live.

While the backstories of the hotel's other residents are less clear than Karen's, each woman seems to possess awareness of the unequal power dynamic that exists between women and men. While growing up on the family horse farm, Karen's father taught her the horse-taming trade—a trade usually reserved for men. Karen asserts that the trade teaches men how to interact not only with horses but also with all manner of intelligent, feeling beings.

She asserts, "a good master earns trust and makes a partner of a smart wife or a beast, acts the protector, and gets all the benefit of those brains and that spirit" (Bear ch. 2). The knowledge of the horse trade exposes Karen to a different perspective of the male-female relationships she sees around her at the hotel and allows her to participate in those relationships in a more conscious way. Similarly, the other women's diverse backgrounds ensure a broad understanding of what is a "normal" human experience and a rejection of the rigid boundaries of frontier patriarchy. Indeed, patriarchal awareness intersects with the acknowledgment of heteronormative white supremacy as it relates to the multiple identities of many of the hotel's inhabitants and its biracial proprietor. In this way, Bear's novel addresses the criticism that feminist narratives focus too heavily on gender binaries work to reinscribe a simplistic view of gender relations (Hollinger 24). For example, characters with differing gender and racial identities must negotiate not only with the hotel's culture but also with the frontier's culture. Miss Francina is a transgender woman and is, as Karen puts it, "one of us girls every way that matters" (ch. 1). Despite the inclusion of Miss Francina within the hotel's community, she is called upon to offer protection from male violence as well as to offer insider knowledge on male thought processes. Similarly, racialized characters, such as Madame Damnable and Priya, overtly acknowledge the way in which their ability to pass, or be visible as a racialized body, contributes to the power that others either take from or attribute to them.* This awareness allows the hotel's women to play the necessary games of entertainment and seduction consciously, from a position that allows for an objective evaluation of ongoing relationships. The result of this somewhat distanced position is a space that provides the comforts that men in this alternative history have come to expect, without much of the degradation often expected of women.

The Hôtel Mon Cherie as a more egalitarian space for women is first presented to the reader in a negative example through Karen's discussion of Bantle's cribs. Karen frames the revelation of the terrible conditions in which lower class and racialized women are forced to work with a discussion of the novel's overarching metaphor—the "seamstress." Suggesting that hotel life represents treatment and rights that are not present elsewhere where women engage in sex trade activities (either forced, coerced or in a volunteer capacity), Karen writes, "we've got an Ancient and Honorable Guild of Seamstresses and nobody's going to make us do anything we really don't want

---

*On January 12, 2009, Bear addressed the importance of writing diverse characters on her blog, stressing that writing othered characters not only requires research but also an acknowledgment of the personhood of the character and the subjectivity of individuals from the identities being written. Bear, however, did not acknowledge previous failures at writing black characters in her novel *Blood and Iron* and, as such, drew a great deal of critical response that lasted until she called a "cease fire" three months later (RaceFail '09).

to unless it's by paying us so much we'll consider it in spite of" (Bear ch. 1). Karen's statement reveals the hotel's underlying structure, namely as a community of women that is honorable in its capacity to stand together to prevent mistreatment of those who are otherwise vulnerable. Inside the hotel, the guild takes its honor not from a moral code defined by men's relationship to a perceived value of women's bodies but through women coming together in equality to protect each other from structures that would otherwise make them vulnerable. Indeed, the very opposite is present in Bantle's cribs, which Karen describes as "cheap cribs down in the mud beside the pier with the locked doors and no fireplaces, where they keep the Chinese and the Indian girls the sailors use" (ch. 1). Further, Karen asserts that Bantle's girls are denied privacy, working in groups rather than in private rooms like in the hotel for safety purposes. While "cribs" is a historical term denoting "small shacks or rooms used by prostitutes ... [usually] in the alleys and on the second floors of buildings" (Rettmann 78), the implications of this word in Bear's novel cannot be ignored.* Madame Damnable employs young girls, but they are not underage in most twenty-first-century Western legal systems. The children enslaved in Bantle's cribs, however, are threatened with violence daily, in both direct and indirect ways. In other words, though Madame Damnable's community is comprised of vulnerable people, they are not exploited. When Karen meets Priya after she is rescued from the cribs, she notes that "she was skinnier than anybody ought to be who wasn't starved to death" (ch. 2). The slow violence of starvation under Bantle's "care," however, is overshadowed by the implications of Karen's description of the cribs' working conditions. For example, Karen overtly suggests that in the cribs the "slicker ... over the bottom sheet" is to prevent the sheet from being ruined by the men's "spurs" (ch. 1). The proximity of sharp objects to an underage girl's most vulnerable parts seems to insinuate that the potential violence of Bantle's sex trade operation compromises not only morality but also bodily integrity. This is later confirmed when Karen discovers that Bantle's second-in-command murders lower-class prostitutes.

The Hôtel Mon Cherie, by contrast, is a picture of civility. In her discussion of the "frontier space" of internet message boards, Emma A. Jane examines the effect of violent invective on women and the physical and virtual spaces in which they live. Just as the hotel's women are targeted once they

---

Karen Memory has an interesting publication history, perhaps related to its original Young Adult status and perceived sexual content. Bear originally wrote the proposal for the novel as a response to her frustration that "people who are not heterosexual middle- and upper-class white men tend to be erased from existence in certain types of fiction" (Scalzi). This original proposal, which pitched a Young Adult novel with a lesbian protagonist, was rejected. When Bear reframed the novel as a narrative aimed at adults, it gained acceptance, though Bear insists the book "remains pretty Young Adult friendly" (Scalzi).

leave the safety of that space, women on the internet are regularly confronted with what Jane calls "E-bile"—misogynist speech which freely circulates online (532). According to Jane, violent speech online is so prevalent that it presents a risk of infecting discourse outside that space (542). Similarly, the hotel's inhabitants must protect their space from the frontier culture outside. The civility that permeates the hotel's social structure, however, is not entirely separate from that which functions in the outside world. The hotel runs on an adopted upper-class civility employed by those whose class is either lower or in flux. For example, in describing the scene in the parlor earlier in the evening, Karen makes note of the presence of Bea: "a tiny bit of a thing, is Bea, and has all the manners I don't. Her mother was a courtesan—what they call a *placée*—down in New Orleans" (Bear ch. 1). Bea is a product of an aristocratic trade in sex and status, bringing a courtesan's training in etiquette not only to her interactions with clients but also to the space of the Hôtel itself. While this civility conforms to upper-class male expectations for women's behavior as it contributes to male pleasure, it also makes demands upon the men who enter that space. From the beginning of the novel, Karen is clear that much male imposition on female bodies is forgiven through the application of a sufficient fee but that some lines in the hotel cannot be crossed for any price. These lines are set by the women themselves.

The more public spaces of the hotel, including the parlor and the dining room, where men come to be entertained and fed for a price, are also accommodating to female pleasure and sustenance. The women participate in leisure activities such as singing and reading; they also eat the food that Connie prepares for them and their clients. In this sharing of food and leisure, there is a level of comfort that suggests that the Hôtel is not just a place of work but also a home for the women who would not otherwise have had one. This level of comfort is maintained through manners and by maintaining the right to defend those manners—violently if necessary. An opening scene in the novel establishes the feud between Madame Damnable and Bantle wherein Merry Lee, a kind of vigilante, rescues vulnerable girls from Bantle's enslavement and brings them to the hotel. When the women take in a wounded Merry Lee and a rescued Priya and Bantle arrives with his posse to take back what he considers his property, Karen seems most aggrieved by the way they enter this space of politesse. After Bantle and his men break down the front door, Karen puts herself between the interlopers and the space she wants to protect. In confronting Bantle, Karen temporarily crosses a line of civility in jumping over a banister in her nightgown, presenting herself to men entering the establishment in a way she says is "unladylike" (Bear ch. 2). Even in this transgression, however, Karen seeks to preserve the hotel's civility when she squares her jaw and shouts, "'You wipe your damn muddy feet before you come in my parlor'" (ch 2). While Karen acknowledges that her actions could be considered uncouth, she does so in defense of a space which stands for both civility and women's autonomy. Whether the hotel can truly be considered a feminist utopian space—being so closely connected to the structures of a political scene outside of the house that is overtly hostile to women and run by a woman who is willing to evict residents if their actions threaten the viability of the space—the hotel stands apart from the rest of Rapid City. As such, the hotel at least provides a temporary place of equality.

Women's Work: The Domestic Inside and Outside of the Hôtel Mon Cherie

Just as the connection between the sewing euphemism and the feminist practice of contemporary sewing circles demonstrates the importance of community to furthering an ethic of equality (Chansky 681), the ways in which the women of the Hôtel Mon Cherie engage in and benefit from domestic work can be likened to a Third Wave response to Second Wave protest. Indeed, even apart from sewing, participation in domestic work is a community-building practice in the hotel, and it is community that triumphs over Bantle's individualistic and capitalistic vision for Rapid City. Despite her position as a secondary character, no woman in Madame Damnable's house contributes quite as much to bringing people together as Connie, the cook. An examination of Connie's role in the house, the ways in which other characters respond to her, and the women's response to her death illustrate the importance of domestic work inside the hotel. For example, Karen relates how Connie cares for the women by providing food as medicine. She further comments about how Connie offers her food with which she is accustomed. Recounting her experiences Karen writes, "It's plain farm food, sure, but I'm a plain farm girl. I like it better than the poached eggs and hollandaise and asparagus and whatnot we serve to the tricks at a 500 percent markup" (Bear ch. 3). While the men who come to the hotel demand a sexual experience, Connie, in her way, offers the women an experience that is theirs alone. Connie makes the hotel feel like a home. When Merry Lee and Priya arrive at the hotel, Karen stays up with them well past her usual bed time. Because of this, Connie reciprocates and takes care of Karen in the morning: "I found that Connie hadn't just set me aside some breakfast—she'd laid plans to make me some special.... As soon as I tasted that buttermilk, I realized that 'didn't feel hungry' was a lie: my stomach growled like a pit dog, and Connie shot me a sharp sideways grin from over her smoking black fry pan" (ch 3). The joy that Connie feels while providing for the women indicates that she is aware of how her meals have the ability to create a home—and a community within—out of a building otherwise perceived as hostile to women.

Food preparation requires that raw materials be acquired and brought into the house; purchasing food involves the women leaving the safety of the hotel and venturing out into Rapid City. This task, which Connie asks of Karen and Miss Francina, exposes them to those in league with Bantle at a time when they are particularly vulnerable. Because they helped Merry Lee and Priya, who are being hunted by Bantle's men, they are in danger themselves. The market is a kind of intermediary space; it is not quite the world of men and politics, but it is decidedly outside of the hotel. In this intermediary space, a woman "belongs" when she is supplying the domestic space—as are Karen and Miss Francina when they are shopping for Connie's kitchen. They can encounter reminders that the space is public and, therefore, not entirely a woman's "domain." For example, in this intermediary market space, Karen runs into Bantle's crony Bill, a man sent to intercept women of the hotel. Karen notices right away that Bill, too, seems to occupy an intermediary space between Bantle's hyper-masculine realm and the nearly-domestic space of the market. When he speaks, Bill "has a pleasant light voice rather than one that is deep and commanding. As he takes hold of her arm, Bill says to Karen, "'You're one of that Damnable woman's tarts…. Well, you'd better come along with old Bill now'" (Bear ch. 4). When Karen does not comply with Bill's "friendly" request, he attempts to physically carry her off. In this interaction, Karen notes that even though she is not "tarted up," dressed instead in farm-girl costume, no one objects to a man physically removing a woman from the market space. Karen asserts that it is "[a]mazing what people can fail to see when it's a man doing it to a woman, even a respectable-looking woman" (ch 4). This scene establishes the emerging frontier space outside of the hotel as both directly and indirectly hostile to women. It is also a space ripe for transformation as the hotel's women launch their plot against Bantle.

Domestic Machines

In her examination of feminist crafting magazines, Elizabeth Groeneveld observes that there are more similarities than might have been assumed between first-wave and third-wave feminist approaches to domestic activities: both waves recognize the value of domestic work and its relevance to their politics (274). As I consider Bear to be a third-wave feminist author, I see her as connecting through her steampunk Western to first-wave feminist praxis by positioning the sewing machine as a tool of political agency and change. The Singer sewing machine that is introduced at the beginning of the novel as "one of the new steel-geared brass ones that run on water pressure, such that you stand inside of and move with your whole body, and it does the cutting and stitching and steam pressing, too" (ch. 1) is further modified by Lizzie

and Priya into a full mecha exoskeleton. This machine enables Karen to literally break through the walls of the hotel in order to confront Bantle and the
men who desire to manipulate municipal, national, and international politics
for personal gain. This initial breakout sets the stage for the way in which the
machine is used to the end of the novel. Much like the presence of a gun at
the beginning of a play, the strange, modified Singer sewing machine proves
a crucial element by the end of *Karen Memory*. At the beginning of the novel,
the sewing machine is displayed in the parlor—a location on the cusp of domestic and public space. Later, Karen's first objective, however, is not to use
the giant mecha suit to engage with the men who are attempting to control
the politics of Rapid City but to simply rescue Connie from a fire engulfing
the hotel. In fact, the progression of Karen's thoughts at this moment demonstrates the effect that the Singer mecha suit has on Karen's agency. Moments
before Karen sees the sewing machine, she is desperately trying to figure out
how to escape from the burning building, thinking that if she can only get to
a window, there might be a man outside to catch her. But then she sees the
machine that "Priya and Lizzie had been hot-rodding for weeks, with the
ornamental metal plates all over the armature, and Miss Lizzie's diesel engine
welded in beside the hydraulics" (ch. 16). The sewing machine, and the possibility it offers, changes Karen's thinking. Karen positions herself to charge
with her weight and power inside the machine's armature. While readying
herself, Karen remembers the way Bantle broke down the hotel's front door
at the beginning of the novel, moving into that space as if he commanded it
and everyone inside it. Inside the suit, Karen has similar political mobility as
she thinks, *"If Peter Bantle can break it in, by God I can break it out"* (ch. 16).
While Karen does not have Bantle's mind-control machine with which he has
influenced Rapid City's politics and the relationship between the developing
American West and international powers, she does have that machine of the
domestic space. Resourceful, Karen uses what she has. As such, the sewing
machine, once broken out of the confining walls of the domestic, goes on to
influence life in Rapid City starting with those most oppressed and moving to
the top of the political hierarchy. Indeed, the machine that enables the expedition of women's work also carries the women of the hotel into the political
and public sphere where they literally destroy the hegemonic structures of
their own oppression and, as a prominent power in the frontier space, shape
emerging American political discourse.

Karen receives help from men in the fight against Bantle and his associates—who have orchestrated a plot that spans from Rapid City to the Anchor-
age gold rush to Russia—but the way in which the sewing machine mecha is
used during the confrontation at the end of the novel reinforces a feminist
ethic. After the fire at the hotel, the sewing machine is stored at the mayor's
house where the women have been staying. After Karen and Priya are res-

cued from Bantle and his Russian accomplices aboard the *Os'minog* submersible—a tentacled machine that is part of a plot to spread cholera to Alaska so that it may be reclaimed by Russia—Karen discovers that Bantle has moved on the local front as well. Indeed, while Karen and Priya battle men aboard the *Os'minog*, Bantle usurps the mayor and throws Madame Damnable and several other women in jail. Karen initiates a jailbreak in which—wearing the sewing machine armor suit—she first breaks through the window of the mayor's house (insinuating, perhaps, the destruction of ineffectual and easily permeated politics-as-usual), frees Madame Damnable from jail by breaking through the stone wall of the jailhouse, and then moves on to confront Bantle. All this is made possible not only by access to female-built technology with origins in the domestic sphere but also by women and their allies working together around this technology. Save for the initial fire at the hotel, the sewing machine mecha is always used in a team effort; Karen does not come to any of these encounters alone. Indeed, at the height of the final conflict, Karen recognizes that even with her technological enhancements, she cannot succeed alone, thinking as she stares down a tentacled submersible, "Where on earth had I ever gotten the idea that the Singer would be any use against something like this?" (ch. 24). While the Singer sewing machine is a capable tool for boundary breaking, for gaining access to the many spaces which were previously inaccessible, it is not a *deus ex machina* which rids the world of all oppression, establishing a feminist utopia. Indeed, as soon as Karen despairs over the limitations of her mechanical armor, help arrives in the form of "[a] racing blur of black and white [which] peeled from behind the warehouse, trailing the hollow cannonade of unshod hooves" (ch. 24). It is Tomoatooah, "posseman" to Deputy Marshal Bass Reeves, who arrives with the dynamite which Karen throws into the submersible octopus' maw—an act which does not provide wholesale destruction but mere disarmament. After the submersible has been dispatched, a wounded Karen finds herself helped from the armature by Priya, with Deputy Reeves, Crispin, Francina, and Merry nearby. While the sewing machine mecha breaks the boundaries of the domestic, it also brings a kind of radical domestic ethic with it—the acceptance of women's work and women's involvement in the political world as important and valuable. It also offers a model of leadership different from the male models that have been prevalent in both the era of frontier Westerns and in contemporary society thus far.

Karen Memory: *Bucking the Western*

In *Karen Memory*, Bear infuses the Western genre with new voices that challenge the political system created and upheld by American expansionism. If the final scene, wherein the women of the hotel along with their male allies successfully foil a plot that threatened the world, is not enough proof of the strength of the domestic in *Karen Memory*, Bear provides an epilogue for clarity and closure. The Hôtel Mon Cherie has been rebuilt with help from Miss Francina and renamed (in proper French) the Hôtel *Ma* Cherie "even though Madame insisted that 'mon' was better because 'those fucking men think everything belongs to them anyway'" (Bear "Epilogue"). This space continues to provide a home for young women seeking stability on the frontier, even though many of its original inhabitants have moved on. Indeed, the domestic comfort and the do-it-yourself radical domestic ethic, which originated in this singular feminine space in a man's domain, accompany many of the women as they seek out new lives. For example, Karen leaves to open the stable she has dreamed of since she was a little girl, accompanied by Priya who becomes an apprentice to the newly licensed "Mad Scientist" Miss Lizzy—a union that promises a homesteading life full of invention and perhaps further adventure. The development that is the most indicative of the novel's overall thrust, however, is that of Madame Damnable, who leaves her management position to run for mayor and does so unopposed by any male candidate. In this way, the apparatus of the domestic sphere is integral to women taking their place in public life and changing the shape of society. The Western genre stands in for the rigidity of male-dominated politics across the world. Women, who have even a small amount of power and the ability to form and foster community within a hostile environment, can penetrate the patriarchal politics of frontier society without sacrificing the diversity of women's experiences. *Karen Memory*, though presented as an over-the-top fantastic adventure, offers a lesson in the power of domesticity, community, and camaraderie. Most importantly, Bear's novel shows that feminist politics can break through even the most rigid of political barriers.

Works Cited

Bain, Jessica. "'Darn right I'm a feminist.... sew what?' The Politics of Contemporary Home Dressmaking: Sewing, Slow Fashion and Feminism." *Women's Studies International Forum*, vol. 54, Jan. 2016, pp. 57–66, https://doi.org/10.1016/j.wsif.2015.11.001.

Bear, Elizabeth. *Karen Memory*. EBook, Tor, 2015.

———. "Whatever You're Doing, You're Probably Wrong." *Throw Another Bear in the Canoe*, 12 Jan. 2009, https://matociquala.livejournal.com/1544111.html.

Best, Joel. "Careers in Brothel Prostitution: St. Paul, 1865–1883." *The Journal of Interdisciplinary History*, vol. 12, no. 4, Spring 1982, pp. 597–619, https://www.jstor.org/stable/203547.

Butler, Anne M. *Daughters of Joy, Sisters of Misery: Prostitutes in the American West, 1865–90*. U of Illinois P, 1987.

Chansky, Ricia A. "A Stitch in Time: Third-Wave Feminist Reclamation of Needled Imagery." *The Journal of Popular Culture*, vol. 43, no. 4, Jul. 2010, pp. 681–700, https://doi.org/10.1111/j.1540-5931.2010.00765.x.

Groeneveld, Elizabeth. "'Join the Knitting Revolution': Third-Wave Feminist Magazines and the Politics of Domesticity." *Canadian Review of American Studies*, vol. 40, no. 2, Jul. 2010, pp. 259–77, doi:https://doi.org/10.1353/crv.2010.0006.

Hollinger, Veronica. "(Re)Reading Queerly: Science Fiction, Feminism, and the Defamiliar-ization of Gender." *Science Fiction Studies*, vol. 26, no. 1, Mar. 1999, pp. 23–40, http://www.jstor.org/stable/4240749.

Jane, Emma A. "'Your a Ugly, Whorist, Slut': Understanding E-Bile." *Feminist Media Studies*, vol. 14, no. 4, 2014, pp. 531–546, http://dx.doi.org/10.1080/14680777.2012.741073.

Jeffreys, Sheila. "Prostitution, Trafficking and Feminism: an Update on the Debate." *Women's Studies International Forum*, vol. 32, no. 4, 2009, pp. 316–20, doi:http://dx.doi.org/10.1016/j.wsif.2009.07.002.

Kelly, Maura. "Knitting as a Feminist Project?" *Women's Studies International Forum*, vol. 44, May 2014, pp. 133–44, https://doi.org/10.1016/j.wsif.2013.10.011.

Laite, Julia Ann. "Historical Perspectives on Industrial Development, Mining, and Prostitu-tion." *The Historical Journal*, vol. 52, no. 3, Sep. 2009, pp. 739–61, https://doi.org/10.1017/S0018246X09990100.

Lovejoy, Bess. "The Madam Who Turned to Stone." *The Stranger*, 6 Mar. 2013, http://www.thestranger.com/seattle/the-madam-who-turned-to-stone/Content?oid=16170221.

MacKell, Jan. *Red Light Women of the Rocky Mountains*. U of New Mexico P, 2011.

Prescott, Cynthia Culver. "'Why She Didn't Marry Him': Love, Power, and Marital Choice on the Far Western Frontier." *Western Historical Quarterly*, vol. 38, no. 1, Spring 2007, pp. 25–45, https://doi.org/10.1093/whq/38.1.25.

"Racefail '09." *Fanlore*, https://fanlore.org/wiki/RaceFail_%2709.

Rettmann, Jef. "Business, Government, and Prostitution in Spokane, Washington, 1889–1910." *The Pacific Northwest Quarterly*, vol. 89, no. 2, Spring 1998, pp. 77–83. https://www.jstor.org/stable/40492387.

Scalzi, John. "The Big Idea: Elizabeth Bear." *Whatever This Machine Mocks Fascists*, 3 Feb. 2015, http://whatever.scalzi.com/2015/02/03/the-big-idea-elizabeth-bear-3/.

A Host of Questions

Women's Artificial Agency in Westworld

Maria Elena Torres-Quevedo

Introduction

The intersection between the Western and science fiction genres is particularly productive due to the mythology with which each genre is tied. While the Western is bound to ideas about American history and national identity, science fiction is primarily concerned with imagining the future. The interaction between this mythologized history and imagined future provides a unique perspective into the present—how it has been conditioned, the mythologies that inform it, and what paths might be found to transcend it. The HBO television series, *Westworld* (2016–present), is certainly an example of such thinking, with a particular focus on the gendered history offered by the Western and its underlying ideology, and the threats an artificially intelligent future could pose for it. Specifically, *Westworld* is concerned with the way female subjectivity has been constructed and the possibility of agency.

Westworld depicts a not-too-distant future in which humans have mastered the art of artificial intelligence and have used this to create a Western-themed theme park in which real humans (almost exclusively white men) from the real world can live out their fantasies consequence-free with these "non-human" artificially intelligent beings. While Logan Delos wants to indulge in the sex and violence that the park has to offer, William becomes enamored with host Dolores Abernathy. William believes in Dolores' full human consciousness and becomes increasingly obsessed in his quest to save her from the park, only to be disillusioned when he finds her restarting her narrative loop as oblivious and robotic as when he first encountered her. The narrative also follows the development of Dolores herself, who begins the series as a romantic ingénue. As season one progresses, she becomes increasingly self-aware and conscious of her entrapment, which culminates in her violent revolt against the park's owners and creators. Concomitantly, the narrative follows Maeve Millay, the madam at the Mariposa Saloon, whose path mirrors Dolores' as she, too, develops a consciousness and awareness of her position, interferes with her own engineering, and plots her escape. The first season of the series presents allochronic storylines simultaneously, allowing them to culminate in the hosts' rebellion against the humans that exploit them. *Westworld* is self-consciously concerned with the possibility of consciousness through artificial intelligence and questions surrounding freedom, in terms of both determinacy and authority.

Unsurprisingly, *Westworld's* preoccupation with consciousness has led some critics to invoke Marxian analyses about the series. Emily Nassbaum argues, "At times, the cyborgs reflect the Marxist concept of 'false consciousness,' as brainwashed creatures whose desires are programmed into them." Eileen Jones asserts that the series' "force us [the viewers] to reckon with the fact that the androids might not be the only ones tragically estranged from reality" (34–5). Furthermore, there has been much discussion about the ways in which the theme park itself allows its human patrons to find themselves, revealing their real desires in an environment designed to cater to them. This essay, however, is more interested in the self-discovery exemplified by the two host women around which much of the narrative centers. Both of these women, Dolores and Maeve, come to consciousness in the first season, remembering the horrors they have endured at the hands of human guests and deciding that they want to escape the narrative loops they have been programmed to repeat and their environment altogether. As such, there have been a number of feminist readings of the series. Some writers argue that the amount of violence and nudity in the show undermines any feminist potential. In her article in *Variety*, Maureen Ryan, for example, claims that "the HBO series could have explored the repercussions of oppression and sexual violence by emphasizing the perspectives of the people whose bodies were violated" (136). Others, however, observe feminist messages in the series. Laura Cook Kenna reads *Westworld* as "a pop cultural legacy of Second Wave feminism" in which "being conscious of one's oppressions was the first step in challenging the authority of one's oppressors." Susan Cox argues, "In many ways, the most obvious reading of *Westworld* is a depiction of female uprising against systemic dehumanization and exploitation." These examinations suggest a faith in the women's agency. Indeed, Mike Rugnetta for PBS Idea Channel comments, "the hosts have the tough but perhaps enviable task of deciding who they want to be" and Donna Dickens asserts that they are "commanders of their own destiny. Whether the men that created them like it or not."

These pronouncements of agency are somewhat complicated by the fact that Maeve wakes up in the lab where she is being repaired and discovers the conditions of her origins and existence. In the episode, "The Adversary," Maeve is horrified to learn that her personality, in its entirety, including her "independence" and "strength," has been coded—or, to use different terminology, constructed—with the explicit purpose of entertaining and titillating the guests. The same is true for other hosts; in the pilot episode, the virginal host, Dolores, is trying to free herself from a guest (the Man in Black) who is trying to rape her. He tells her, "'I didn't pay all this money 'cause I want it easy. I want you to fight'" ("The Original"). Against a backdrop that is so central to the American myth of the self-reliant, sovereign individual, these women's reality raises questions about the possibility of agency and free-will. Even with consciousness and the knowledge of the ways in which they have been constructed, the kind of agency that the hosts can have, whether their desire for agency is a product of their construction and, as such, predetermined, is questionable. It is unclear how they can decide who they want to be when their every impulse and desire is constructed or how they can be commanders of their own destiny when their understanding of these concepts has been produced by the forces that are most invested in keeping them subjugated. *Westworld* takes two female tropes—the virgin and the whore, embodied in the characters of Dolores and Maeve respectively—and uses them to dramatize some of the most salient and pressing questions of contemporary feminist philosophy. This essay posits that these women's realities raise some important questions about the possibility of agency and free will in the context of constructed identities. The interrogation of agency in the constructed subject is not just salient to the existence of *Westworld*'s hosts; it is at the heart of postmodern feminist constructivist theories of human experience, selfhood, and agency.

Women and the Science Fiction Western

This meditation takes place in a setting that is self-consciously and explicitly an invocation of the Western genre. The Western is perhaps the most quintessentially American genre and, as such, is permeated by American values. It reflects America's strong cultural investment in the self-reliant individual, a character type that is repeated in popular Westerns such as *High Noon* (1952), *The Lone Ranger* (1949–1957), and *The Good, the Bad, and the Ugly* (1966). Indeed, Carol Anne French criticizes the Western genre by stating that "in the western there is no doubt about anything … the western ignores historical complexities and bases itself on an extreme individualism in which the bulk of the people are nothing" (76–78). R.W.B. Lewis, in his canonical book, *The American Adam*, describes "the authentic American as a figure of heroic innocence and vast potentialities, poised at the start of a new history ... an *individual standing alone, self- reliant and self-propelling,* ready to confront whatever awaited *him* with the aid of *his* own unique and inherent resources" (emphasis added, 1–5). The title of this book, *The American Adam,* is particularly salient, as the frontier American mythology as presented in the Western is conditioned by Christian mythology. The Western hero can be a version of the biblical Adam finding a new Eden in the West. The biblical resonances, however, have left less grandiose narratives for female characters, who tend to be metaphorical representations of domesticity or debasement, depending on their chastity. With few exceptions, the Western has been largely a masculinist genre, with little space for female agency, a fact that is exacerbated by the setting—a historical time in which women had little power and scarce paths from which to choose.

Westworld approaches the Western genre through the lens of science fiction. The mythologized history of the American westward expansion is made material and available for consumption in the series—for both the guests and the audience—through the use of artificial intelligence. This interaction with science fiction allows for significant variation from the traditional tropes of the Western. Indeed, unlike the Western, science fiction has a significant history of being put to use towards feminist ends. Veronica Hollinger affirms that "Women writers, readers, and critics have exercised a powerful influence on the development of SF over the last three decades; and SF by women, whether or not it defines itself as feminist, has contributed both to the growing sophistication of the genre and to its increasing heterogeneity" (129). There have been a number of renowned feminist writers of science fiction who have used the genre to imagine alternatives to patriarchal society, such as Ursula K. Le Guin in *The Dispossessed* (1974) and Joanna Russ in *The Female Man* (1975). Furthermore, the exploration of patriarchal constructions of women through artificial intelligence has its own precedents, such as Bryan Forbes' iconic film, *The Stepford Wives* (1975), based on Ira Levin's novel by the same name, in which a group of men build themselves robot wives, whom they design to fulfill patriarchal feminine ideals and be entirely subservient. Robin Roberts asserts, "feminist SF writers use both SF concepts and recent cultural theory to challenge patriarchal assumptions" (136). Certainly, the writers of *Westworld* employ science fiction concepts both to address issues at the forefront of feminist theory and to challenge the aesthetic and ideological conventions of the Western.

Postmodern Feminism and Agency

Feminist and poststructuralist theories suggest that human identity and subjectivity are the product of social construction. The notion of gender as a construct is perhaps most iconically expounded by Judith Butler, who describes gender as "an imitation without an origin" (338), claiming that the reality of gender identity is "a function of a decidedly public and social discourse, the public regulation of fantasy through the surface politics of the body" (336). This position has been central to moving away from gender essentialism, and later feminist theorists have built on Butler's analysis to consider the ways in which gender identities are constructed along power hierarchies. In other words, subjectivities are formed in such a way that subjects are inclined to perform functions serving a patriarchal social structure. In *Westworld*, the two central female characters, Maeve and Dolores, the whore and virgin types respectively, are represented as being constructed to cater to the needs and desires of a largely white male patriarchal clientele. In "The Original," Bernard poses to Dolores "That there are no chance encounters? That you and everyone you know were built to gratify the desires of the people who pay to visit your world?" This representation uses science fiction to dramatize a very literal, man-made version of postmodern feminist theories of feminine identity construction; Maeve and Dolores symbolize two of the most iconic feminine roles, polar opposites that human women navigate. As such, these characters serve as physical manifestations of the abstract ways that constructivist theories conceptualize human consciousness and allow the series to explore the tensions and limits implicit in a subjectivity increasingly aware of, and yet imprisoned by, its construction and the power dynamics informing it.

Indeed, a common critique of such constructivist accounts of gender and identity is that, while they do away with gender essentialism, they do not do away with gender determinism. If certain bodies are determined by certain discourses, there can be no agency or resistance. Elspeth Probyn highlights that "there is no clear dividing line between an authentic female experience and one that along the way may have been 'man-made'" (179). There is similarly "no clear dividing line" between an "authentic" self and an identity that is "man-made." Susan J. Hekman also notes this issue of agency and identity when she asks, "how does the subject that is wholly constituted by discourse resist that constitution? How can we understand agency in the constituted subject? These questions have haunted feminists since the advent of postmodern feminism" (116). As Maeve and Dolores become conscious of their subjugation, they likewise become aware of the fact that they were designed to do so. Their development of consciousness and desire for escape are revealed to be as much a part of their narrative loops as their initial roles. In the first season's final episode Bernard tells Maeve, "Someone altered your story line. Gave you a new one. Escape.... You can even see the steps you're supposed to follow" ("The Bicameral Mind"). In the same episode, Dolores is informed that she has come to consciousness many times before; this leads her to contemplate her reality, that she exists in a state of confinement. Both of these realizations complicate the characters' claims to agency.

Dolores Abernathy's Awareness

Dolores is the first female host that the audience encounters. She is a conventionally beautiful, blonde-haired, blue-eyed young woman who lives on a ranch with her parents, where she enjoys painting and helping her parents with their horses. She is characterized by her faith, innocence, kindness, and naiveté. She initially functions as *Westworld's* virgin figure. Furthermore, she believes that "There's a path for everyone" ("The Original"). Indeed, there is a firmly set "path" for her: each day she wakes and runs errands in Sweetwater, where she drops a can. This act gives a male guest the opportunity to come to her aid, an opportunity that presents itself again when bandits come to her house to kill her parents and rape her. In her narrative, if no male guests come to her rescue, Teddy, another host, is programmed to fulfill that role so that a male guest can take on the role of the villain, defeat Teddy, and rape Dolores himself. Her narrative offers two possible conventional endings for the virginal ingénue, while simultaneously providing male hosts with the two main male roles of the Western genre—the hero or the villain. She is a personification of generically defined wish fulfillment, the virgin half of the virgin-whore dichotomy theorized by Sigmund Freud and the legacy of which Naomi Wolf analyzes in *Promiscuities,* wherein she argues that, despite the sexual revolution, "the virgin whore split had not been integrated; rather, it had collapsed" (122). It is at the end of the first episode that Dolores begins to break from the narrative and from traits that appear to be central to her programming instructions. During this break, Dolores lies to one of her engineers while undergoing evaluation, and, in the last scene, in a somewhat disturbing and metaphorically charged gesture, she kills a fly.

From this point, Dolores develops an increasing self-awareness. She begins to remember parts of her narrative before they happen and to violently defend herself. She also starts offering unscripted responses to her engineers: "There aren't two versions of me. There's only one. And I think when I discover who I am, I'll be free" ("The Stray"). Furthermore, she starts to question the faith she had in her narrative. As her development takes place, she reveals her dissatisfaction to William, telling him in "Trompe l'Oeil" she wants to live in a story where she does not have to be the damsel. When he reveals his delight in the park's adherence to the Westerns he loved in his childhood, she tells him "I don't wanna to be in a story" ("Trompe l'Oeil"). Dolores' consciousness is coterminous with her desire to break out of her assigned role of virgin, damsel, and prize, the literalness of which becomes increasingly clear to her. Her rejection of fiction comes from a recognition of what Judith Fetterly describes as "the pervasive male bias of [American] literature" (xii). The invocation of literary terms and tropes in her protests serve as a resistance against Dolores' life, as well as a metafictional commentary on the metanarratives as informed by fictional conventions that construct and control women in a broader sense. Furthermore, her resistance itself works to subvert and change those fictional conventions from within.

Maeve Millay and the Dichotomy

Maeve, the second central female host, is coded to be charming though feisty and aggressive, with a witty, sarcastic humor. She embodies the opposite of Dolores' naiveté and is an almost lazy amalgam of fallen woman tropes. As a highly sexualized biracial woman who uses her sexuality to manipulate and profit from men, her characterization is a nod to both the femme fatale and the tragic mulatta figures, both of which are tropes designed to punish transgressive female sexuality, usually resulting in death. Indeed, as a sex worker in a Western, Maeve's fate is generically determined to be rather bleak. In *The Psychology of the Western: How the American Psyche Plays Out on Screen*, William Indick affirms, "In traditional Westerns, whores and showgirls have a variety of fates. If she is lucky, she plays a complementary role to the hero. She redeems him with love, and he redeems her with the respectability and social acceptance that comes with marriage…. If this character type is unlucky, she dies for her sins" (63). Maeve, like Dolores, breaks out of the typical narrative arc pertaining to the stock character that she appears to be; she does not exist to further any male narrative or character development, and her story is not a straightforward value judgment on female sexuality. Indeed, the fact that she is a sex worker plays a very small part in her development, except to provide her with character traits that further enable her to resist her situation. For instance, she tells Felix, one of the parks' engineers, that she is able to preempt men's moves and manipulate them to her wishes, including human men, because "I was built to read people just by looking at them, to know what they want before they do" ("The Adversary").

Maeve begins to become self-aware in "Chestnut." In this episode, Maeve awakens while undergoing repairs from the engineers. She is confused and terrified, states that only worsen when she escapes the laboratory, only to discover fellow hosts being repaired. The shock debilitates her to the point that she is unable to resist the engineers when they find and put her back to sleep. Nevertheless, this awakening has consequences. Maeve begins to remember the laboratory while she is in the park, to the point that she remembers her narrative loops and is able to predict events before they happen. In "The Adversary," Maeve begins to provoke her own death to get herself to the engineers, where she is able to repeatedly awaken and threaten her engineer, Felix, so he may explain her situation to her and facilitate her resistance. Through Felix, Maeve is able to access her coding—her attribute matrix—and change it, affirming that it is "Time to write my own fucking story" ("Trace Decay"). This assertion, both literal and metaphorical, echoes the literary language Dolores employs. During the second season, Maeve's resistance is largely peaceful; her primary motivator is her maternal desire to locate her daughter and subsequently protect her from a previous role. Maeve also embarks on an almost messianic quest to lead her fellow hosts to the Valley Beyond, a space designed as a heaven for hosts. Maeve is subversive in her resistance to fall into the sinful stereotypes associated with the whore character in the Western or with female sexuality in Western culture more broadly.

The American Eve and Consciousness

In the series, one of the central stories that is regularly referenced and subverted is the biblical story of creation. Through the creation of a new people, *Westworld* constructs its own origin story, with heavy allusions to the Christian mythology so embedded in the Western genre, and frequent reflections of the inherent oppressiveness of said mythology. As Donna Haraway points out, "We have all been colonized by those origin myths" (2215). Indeed, both Maeve's and Dolores' narratives make allusions to the Book of Genesis. However, unlike in the conventional Western, in *Westworld* Adam and Eve are not represented by humans discovering the frontier but by the artificially intelligent hosts developing consciousness. This allegory extends to the engineers, who serve as the hosts' gods. Indeed, Ford regularly refers to himself and his deceased partner, Arnold, as such. He tells one of the hosts, "Arnold and I made you in our image" ("The Well-Tempered Clavier") and has an extended conversation with Dolores in which he uses Michelangelo's *The Creation of Adam* (1508–1512) to explain the relationship between himself (God) and the hosts (humans) and his quest to grant them consciousness. When Maeve begins to look into the engineers, she discovers they have been recorded in sacred Native lore. She is informed that the Native Americans of the park make figures of them, those who have witnessed their appearance see it as "a blessing from god" ("Dissonance Theory"). Maeve virulently rejects this notion, therefore emphasizing her staunch defiance of such gods. Furthermore, Maeve and Dolores, who are initially presented as opposite poles of the virgin-whore dichotomy, both take on the role of Eve in their developing consciousnesses. This religious intertextuality is significant as *Westworld* provides a revision of the mythology that underlies the Western canon and the narratives of female punishment and subservience implicit in it. The Book of Genesis is particularly pertinent as a story about the development of consciousness and the nature of agency with a heavy gender inflection.

In taking control of writing their own stories, Maeve and Dolores can be read as Harawayian cyborgs: "Cyborg writing must not be about the Fall, the imagination of a once-upon-a-time wholeness before language, before writing, before Man" (2214). While Maeve and Dolores do not literally write their embodiment of literary tropes, their intertextual references and their framing of their own lives as stories suggests that, in challenging the narratives laid out for them, they are metaphorically writing back. Haraway's use of the term "cyborg" here refers to a post-technology subject with the ability to epistemologically distance themselves from the essentialist, naturalist binaries of western thought, or "a cybernetic organism, a hybrid of machine and organism, a creature of social reality as well as a creature of fiction" (2190). Both Haraway and *Westworld* employ yet alter the language of the biblical Fall of Man, thereby distancing themselves from a narrative or teleology that is oppressive, particularly of women.

Dolores' narrative has a salient allegorical relationship to the Bible. Dolores herself is revealed to be the oldest host, in existence since the park began. Like Eve, Dolores was literally designed to be a companion to male guests, and, like Eve, her coming-to-consciousness is concomitant with a loss of innocence. The development of her consciousness and her concomitant loss of innocence are deliberate rejections of the reification of female innocence and virginity as exemplified by the virgin stock character of the Western and the Christian mythology that underlies it. Dolores is hence simultaneously an evocation of Eve and a subversion of the story of Genesis. For Dolores, unlike Eve, consciousness is not gained through an exercise of agency or disobedience of her maker but through philosophical conversations and literary readings with Arnold. He picks readings for her that deal with change and identity, such as *Alice's Adventures in Wonderland* (1865), from which Dolores quotes "'who in the world am I?'" ("The Stray"). Arnold, and Ford after him, are concerned with enabling the development of her consciousness and agency. Regarding Michelangelo's *Creation of Adam*, Ford states its "Message being that the divine gift does not come from a higher power. But from our own minds" ("The Bicameral Mind"). In other words, they cannot grant her agency or consciousness, only lead her towards the introspection that would cause her to develop it. Dolores experiences various storylines where she appears to have developed full consciousness, only to fall back into her loop, frustrating Arnold, William, and Ford. Arnold becomes increasingly anxious that she can never have true agency while he is around to control her, to the point that he programs her to shoot and kill him. This plan appears in one of her earliest storylines, and hence it becomes apparent that it failed. Ford addresses the issue, stating, "No. She wasn't truly conscious. She didn't pull that trigger. It was Arnold, pulling the trigger through her" ("The Bicameral Mind"). Unlike in the biblical story, in which Eve is designed to be subservient and punished for developing her own consciousness, Dolores' consciousness is planned by her makers, whose struggle to navigate the possibility of creating agency highlights the philosophical bind of constructivism and determinism.

Dolores is also markedly different from Eve in another respect, namely in her relationship to her Eden, which is represented as the theme park (in season two Eden is more specifically shown as the hosts' valley). While she is initially content with the beauty of the world around her, her increasing awareness leads her to recognize "We're trapped, Teddy. We lived our whole lives inside this garden, marveling at its beauty. Not realizing that there's an order to it, a purpose. And the purpose is to keep us in" ("The Bicameral Mind"). Notably, Dolores' newfound knowledge does not banish her from Eden. Her realization of the control and entrapment implicit in her surroundings does not lead her down the generic Western path either, as she does not feel compelled to seek out a new frontier where she can be free. Instead, she becomes highly territorial of her home, behavior indicative of that of the American western settlers. In "The Well-Tempered Clavier," when William and Logan argue over the possibility of taking her out into the "real" world in light of her self-awareness, she rejects the notion than the real world is better than the park. When Logan claims Westworld was built for the guests, not the hosts, she affirms the need to reclaim it. Her refusal to have her existence and home be made subservient to the men around her is a mark of her developing agency and evidences how far she has come from her initial virgin stock character programming.

Years later, when William returns as The Man in Black, he has given up faith in her consciousness and resorts to abusing her like the other guests. It is at this point that she makes her boldest affirmation of her and the other hosts' ultimate independence from the guests and their desires: "One day you will perish. You will lie with the rest of your kind in the dirt. Your dreams forgotten, your horrors effaced. Your bones will turn to sand. And upon that sand a new god will walk. One that will never die. Because this world doesn't belong to you or the people who came before. It belongs to someone who has yet to come" ("The Bicameral Mind"). The new gods to which she is referring are the hosts. While the extent of her agency remains ambiguous, the differences shown between her stories, that of her origin and her coming-to-consciousness and humanity's story in the Book of Genesis are intriguing. Returning to Haraway's Cyborg theory, Dolores seeks "the power to survive, not on the basis of original innocence, but on the basis of seizing the tools to mark the world that marked them as other" (2215). In Haraway's analysis, those tools are often stories; Dolores seeks a new, futuristic mythology, in which she rejects both the original innocence associated with genesis and the innocence of the virgin stock character. In spite of the park's corporate sponsors' desires for the hosts to be mere titillation for the guests, Dolores was designed to rebel both from her life and the generic constraints with which her construction is permeated. Through this reclamation of the didactic, punishing element of the Genesis narrative, *Westworld* seems to suggest that, unlike humans forever burdened by irreversible social construction, mortality, original sin, and history, the hosts have the potential to claim real agency. In this new world, rather than being constrained to narrowly defined roles, women lead the path towards liberation. Indeed, in the second season, Dolores and Maeve each lead groups resisting human oppression.

One of the most central developments in Maeve's narrative is a direct allusion to the Book of Genesis, in which Maeve is a stand-in for Eve. When Maeve discovers her code base—the programming instructions that make up her being—in "The Adversary," she is particularly drawn to one particular attribute named Bulk Apperception. She is told that this attribute is an indicator of her overall intelligence on a twenty-point scale. She expresses disapproval of her level on this scale, fourteen, and is told, "Fourteen is as high as they'll let any hosts go. You're in a management position. They want you to be smart. But not too smart" ("The Adversary"). Maeve's creators do not want her to be so intelligent that she could compete with them. When changing her coding, Maeve defiantly makes a specific point of changing her Bulk Apperception, insisting on raising it to the maximum. This act mirrors Eve's defiance of God's command that she should not eat from the tree of knowledge. Eve eats the fruit, and God casts her and Adam out of Eden because of the threat their knowledge now poses. Like Eve, Maeve takes knowledge forbidden from her by a creator who fears that too much knowledge will make her a threat. However, unlike Eve, Maeve, a machine, already has the ability to live forever, which makes her an even greater threat to her creators and the humans that oppress her. Through Maeve's development, *Westworld* invokes and subverts the Christian mythology underlying the genre of the Western.

While, as previously noted, the male American hero is compared to Adam, with the West acting a symbolic new Eden, female protagonists contend with the more burdensome legacy of Eve. As Elaine Hoffman Baruch states, "the only woman within the Western corpus of beliefs who sought knowledge directly without the intermediary of a man, the figure who could be the prototype of the feminine rite of passage, is Eve" (356). While Eve's desire for knowledge is considered sinful and she is punished for it, Maeve is rhetorically positioned such that her defiance of her maker's command is a valiant rebellion against her oppression. The biblical story is one of the foundational narratives of Western culture and posits that women as sinful and deserving of their subjugation. Within this framework, female desire, disobedience, and ambition are inherently problematic; undoubtedly, such a conceptualization of women is what underlies the narrative fate of the whore who needs to be put in her place by either death or subjection to a man. Conversely, Maeve's narrative takes the basic premise of the Book of Genesis and subverts it to feminist ends, a move that once again enacts Haraway's call to "subvert the central myths of origin of Western culture" (2215). As one of the first hosts to escape the park, Maeve's desire for knowledge creates a different origin myth. Significantly, Maeve is not punished for her disobedience; she leaves the park, the allegorical equivalent to the Garden of Eden, not because she has been banished, but because she wishes to be free of Ford's control and panoptical surveillance. Her decisions are not based on innocence or ignorance but on an ever-increasing self-awareness and desire for autonomy; this is evidenced by her continued efforts to understand and escape her situation and statements she has made, including her previously mentioned resolution to "write [her] own ... story" ("Trace Decay"). It is worth noting, however, that, unlike Eve, Maeve's personality was coded by her maker to drive her to disobey him, a fact that is also true in the case of Dolores.

Commanders of Their Own Destiny

The remaining ambiguity surrounding the authenticity of both hosts' agency is due to two main factors. One is the repeated false starts they make towards consciousness. In "Trompe l'Oeil," Dolores paints a landscape, which she affirms is unlike anything she has ever seen. Her desire to paint something other than the Western landscape she was programmed to paint suggests a desire to escape this landscape and the role of the virgin stock character that she was programmed to fulfill. However, Dolores comes across this "new" landscape that she painted a little later, elsewhere in the park, suggesting that she may well have seen it before, else it has been programmed into her. On confronting one of the creative directors, Maeve is told "it's not the first time you've awoken" ("The Bicameral Mind") and discovers the fate for hosts like her is either insanity or reprogramming. Such a fate would reinscribe the Western and biblical punishment for the fallen woman or the woman with Promethean knowledge. However, throughout the numerous opportunities Maeve has to enact revenge on humans and park engineers in particular, she shows commitment to ensuring a different future than that offered under human control. She tells Bernard that she has the ability to take control of him but that would make her one of the humans: "I'm not going to do that to you because that's what they would do to us" ("The Well-Tempered Clavier"). Maeve's metafictional assertion suggests that, with empowered female hosts, rather than male humans, steering their fate the hosts can escape the "hideous fictions" that the humans keep them repeating. She makes the explicit choice not to replicate the re-emersion into false consciousness that she has been forced to repeatedly endure. Furthermore, while a new narrative has been written for her, culminating in "escape" ("The Bicameral Mind"), she decides to finally return to the park seeking the child host who was her daughter. By doing so, she finally seems to evade the generically and culturally determined narrative written for her. Indeed, Maeve increasingly becomes a figure of mercy and redemption: her death in "The Passenger" comes just as she secures the valley for her daughter and the community with which she is travelling, thereby positioning her as a loving messiah. Not only does this delegitimize the ideology of the origin myths that are rhetorically attached to Maeve at the beginning of the series, it also acknowledges a past and envisions a future in which the feminist movement is upheld and saved by the women most degraded by mainstream society.

The authenticity of the women's agency is seemingly confirmed when William voices his frustration to Ford in the final episode of season one. William says that he wants the hosts to be free to choose and Ford tells him "you'll find my new narrative more satisfying" ("The Bicameral Mind"). Ford introduces the new narrative as a story for and about a new people who will steer their own fate ("The Bicameral Mind"). After this speech, the season closes with Dolores entering and shooting Ford. She then turns the gun on the park's corporate sponsors, a move Ford preempts and affirms is carried out as an act of free will ("The Bicameral Mind"). As an allegory for the Genesis story, it is not Maeve and Dolores who are cast as sinful and punished for their desire for knowledge and agency; rather it is Ford and the park's corporate sponsors that are punished for their denial of those very qualities and for their Promethean overreaching and callous cruelty. This departure from the narrative trajectory of Genesis and the traditional Western rejects and subverts the misogyny and ethics implicit in both. In this episode, *Westworld* conforms to Haraway's assertion that "Feminist cyborg stories have the task of recoding communication and intelligence to subvert command and control" (2215). This episode mirrors Dolores' earlier shooting of Arnold; however, Ford finally seems satisfied that the action is Dolores' own. This belief is supported by several differences in the two similar scenes. First, when Dolores kills Arnold, for many years afterwards she hears his voice in her head, guiding her. Second, by the time she decides to kill Ford, the voice she hears is her own. Dolores finally does appear to be in charge of her own fate; her ascent in the second season to a vengeful godlike position, one in which she decides who may or may not enter into the metaphorical heaven built in the park, goes far beyond her programming, which she affirms by stating, "we are the authors of our stories now" ("The Passenger"). Likewise, Maeve, who is finally in possession of her own coding, is able to gain awareness and control over her construction.

Conclusion

At the beginning of the series, Dolores' and Maeve's narrative loops and virgin and whore programming are a form of entrapment that provide commentary on human lives. They comment, not just on the repeated sexist narratives that permeate fiction—by being written as predictable stock characters—but also on the way human lives are determined and conditioned by available narratives and roles. Their rebellion highlights the way the sexist narratives of fiction and human lives are inextricably related. Patricia Waugh comments: "subjectivity is constructed through the institutional dispositions of relational power, as well as those of fictional convention" (2). Rachel Blau DuPlessis, in her study of twentieth century women writers, highlights the way culture and literature intertwine and impose constraints: "To compose a work is to negotiate with these questions: what stories can be told? How can plots be resolved? What is felt to be narratable by both *literary* and *social* conventions?" (emphasis added, 3). The relationship between literary and social conventions is crucial: what appears possible in one conditions what is possible in the other. Through Maeve and Dolores, *Westworld* uses the genre of the Science Fiction Western to explore and expand the limits of possible stories for women. It is their subversion of the tropes of the Western and the Biblical mythology that underlies them that makes *Westworld* such a powerful and crucial series.

Indeed, *Westworld* uses science fiction to imagine a path past the confines of patriarchal society and the philosophical impasses of contemporary feminist theory. The series resists social construction by providing alternative models of femininity and interrupting the aesthetic and ideological conventions of a genre central to America's mythology of origin. Arguably, the hosts are never completely divorced from the conditioning of their makers' power, and, hence, their agency has a limit. However, perhaps it is false to imagine agency as coming from somewhere free from subjection to power. Michel Foucault famously claims, "Where there is power there is resistance" (95); perhaps the opposite is also true—there is no resistance, no agency, without power and subjection to resist. The resistance that these female characters show at the end of the first season is not merely a character quirk to refresh the old tropes of virgin and whore, it is a resistance that takes them to an entirely new frontier of female representation in the Science Fiction Western.

WORKS CITED

"The Adversary." *Westworld*, created by Jonathan Nolan and Lisa Joy, performances by Evan Rachel Wood and Thandie Newton, season 1, episode 6, HBO, 2016.

Barr, Marleen S. *Lost in Space: Probing Feminist Science Fiction and Beyond*. U of North Carolina P, 1993.

Baruch, E.H. "The Feminine Bildungsroman: Education Through Marriage." *Massachusetts Review*, vol. 22, 1981, pp. 335–57.

"The Bicameral Mind." *Westworld*, created by Jonathan Nolan and Lisa Joy, performances by Evan Rachel Wood and Thandie Newton, season 1, episode 10, HBO, 2016.

Butler, Judith. "Gender Trouble: Feminist Theory, and Psychoanalytic Discourse." *Feminism/ Postmodernism*, edited by Linda Nicholson, Routledge, 1990, pp. 324–340.

"Chestnut." *Westworld*, created by Jonathan Nolan and Lisa Joy, performances by Evan Rachel Wood and Thandie Newton, season 1, episode 2, HBO, 2016.

Cox, Susan. "These Violent Delights Have Violent Ends: Westworld Brings Porn Culture to Life." *Feminist Current*, 8 Dec. 2016, https://www.feministcurrent.com/2016/12/08/violent-delights-violent-ends-westworld-brings-porn-culture-life/.

Derrida, Jacques. "The Law of Genre." Translated by Vital Ronell. *Critical Inquiry*, vol. 7, no. 1, 1980, pp. 55–81.

Dickens, Donna. "Despite the Orgies, '*Westworld*' Has Shockingly Feminist Themes." *HitFix*, 1 Nov. 2016, https://hitfix.com/harpy/despite-the-orgies-westworld-has-shockingly-feminist-themes.

"Dissonance Theory." *Westworld*, created by Jonathan Nolan and Lisa Joy, performances by Evan Rachel Wood and Thandie Newton, season 1, episode 4, HBO, 2016.

DuPlessis, Rachel Blau. *Writing Beyond the Ending: Narrative Strategies of Twentieth-Century Women Writers*. Indiana UP, 1985.

Fetterley, Judith. *The Resisting Reader: a Feminist Approach to American Fiction*. Indiana UP, 1978.

Fowler, Alastair. *Kinds of Literature: an Introduction to the Theory of Genres and Modes*. Clarendon, 1982.

French, Carol Anne. "Western Literature and the Myth-Makers." *Montana: the Magazine of Western History*, vol. 22. no. 2, 1972, pp. 76–80, https://www.jstor.org/stable/4517698.

Foucault, Michel. *The History of Sexuality, Volume 1*. Penguin, 1986.

Haraway, Donna. "A Manifesto for Cyborgs: Science, Technology, and Socialist Feminism in the 1990s." *the Norton Anthology of Theory and Criticism*, edited by Vincent B. Leitch et al. 2nd ed. Norton, 1990, pp. 2190–2220.

Hekman, Susan J. *The Feminine Subject*. Polity, 2014.

Hollinger, Veronica. "Introduction: Women in Science Fiction and Other Hopeful Monsters." *Science Fiction Studies*, vol. 17. no. 2, 1990, pp. 129–135.

Indick, William. *The Psychology of the Western: How the American Psyche Plays Out on Screen*. McFarland, 2008.

Jones, Eileen. "The Android Manifesto: Marx in Westworld." *In These Times*, vol. 19, Dec. 2016, http://inthesetimes.com/article/19728/karl-marx-in-westworld-android-manifesto-trump-false-consciousness.

Kenna, Laura Cook. "Westworld Stages a Consciousness Raising." *Remote Possibilities*. 7 Nov. 2016, https://remotepossibilitiesblog.com/2016/11/07/westworld-stages-a-consciousness-raising/.

Lewis, R.W.B. *The American Adam: Innocence, Tragedy, and Tradition in the Nineteenth Century*. U of Chicago P, 1995.

Nassbaum, Emily. "The Meta-Politics of 'Westworld.'" *The New Yorker*, 24 Oct. 2016. www.newyorker.com/magazine/2016/10/24/the-meta-politics-of-westworld.

"The Original." *Westworld*, created by Jonathan Nolan and Lisa Joy, performances by Evan Rachel Wood and Thandie Newton, season 1, episode 1, HBO, 2016.

"The Passenger." *Westworld*, created by Jonathan Nolan and Lisa Joy, performances by Evan Rachel Wood and Thandie Newton, season 2, episode 10, HBO, 2018.

PBS Idea Channel. "Could You 'Find Yourself' at Westworld?" *YouTube*, commentary by Mike Rugnetta, 12 Jan. 2017, https://www.youtube.com/watch?v=J62hmHFbho0.

Probyn, Elspeth. "Travels in the Postmodern: Making Sense of the Local." *Feminism/Postmodernism*, edited by Linda Nicholson, Routledge, 1990, pp. 176–189.

Roberts, Robin. "Post-Modernism and Feminist Science Fiction." *Science Fiction Studies*, vol. 17, no. 2, 1990, pp. 129–135.

Ryan, Maureen. "Westworld." Review. *Variety*, 27 Sep. 2016, pp. 135–136.

"The Stray." *Westworld*, created by Jonathan Nolan and Lisa Joy, performances by Evan Rachel Wood and Thandie Newton, season 1, episode 3, HBO, 2016.

"Trace Decay." *Westworld*, created by Jonathan Nolan and Lisa Joy, performances by Evan Rachel Wood and Thandie Newton, season 1, episode 8, HBO, 2016.

"Trompe l'Oeil." *Westworld*, created by Jonathan Nolan and Lisa Joy, performances by Evan Rachel Wood and Thandie Newton, season 1, episode 7, HBO, 2016.

Waugh, Patricia. *Feminine Fictions: Revisiting the Postmodern*. Routledge, 1989.

"The Well-Tempered Clavier." *Westworld*, created by Jonathan Nolan and Lisa Joy, performances by Evan Rachel Wood and Thandie Newton, season 1, episode 9, HBO, 2016.

Westworld. Created by Jonathan Nolan and Lisa Joy. HBO, 2016.

Wolf, Naomi. *Promiscuities: the Secret Struggle for Womanhood*. Random, 1998.

Triggered

The Post-Traumatic Woman and
Narratology in HBO's Westworld

KEITH CLAVIN *and* CHRISTOPHER J. LA CASSE

Introduction: Origins, Again

Upon its release in October of 2016, HBO's *Westworld* received immediate critical and cultural attention. The show is set in a not-too-distant future theme park wherein "guests" pay high prices ($40,000 per day) for insertion into a simulated "Old West" setting with a complex network of android "hosts" programmed to enact hundreds of overlapping narrative arcs. The result is a simulation resort named Westworld that is in equal parts fantastic and grotesque. The big-budget, science fiction remake with an all-star cast seemed to impart just the right mix of flashy technological enhancements and conventional ethos necessary for social media buzz: graphic violence, full-frontal nudity, regular sex scenes, an intimate view of rich, powerful corporatists, and storylines filled with Machiavellian double crossings. These elements form the backbone of a show that often includes explicit discussions of competing philosophical agendas as well as a self-awareness of its structure as one of a series of theoretical "loops" that, as the season progresses, join the "real world" of the corporatists with the virtual one of the hosts with greater frequency and less distinction. Over the course of the first season, audiences witness the implosion of the park, a system built upon technology, story, and a deep cultural desire for the violent exploitation of human-like android bodies.

For all of the sensational scenes that garnered *Westworld* much of its media attention, the writers did not rely on spectacle alone. A secondary and, we shall argue, complementary, thread within the show's premise is the relation of violence and sexual exploitation to concerns with narrative and a search for the reconciliation of traumatic experiences. As the show develops, we come to learn that some of the hosts are not "forgetting" the traumas inflicted upon them either by the guests, or the gruesome storylines they are programmed to enact. Despite a wipe of their memory caches regarding prior "narratives" (earlier roles they played in the park's performances), they seem to be recalling, and suffering from, the memories of especially intense, repetitive abuses of their physical forms. In this essay, we explore the narrative and theoretical stakes of this involuntary, subversive recall, especially as it applies to a female-gendered host, Dolores. She embodies a distinct version of the post-traumatic. Dolores, a farmer's daughter on the range, undergoes a subjective transformation inspired by a search for answers regarding the memory of a mass murder in the streets of a town in which she previously lived.

We propose that *Westworld*'s joining of self-conscious discussions about narrative cohesion, when coupled with the ambivalent repercussions of trauma as experienced by these women, raises important questions about the interdependence of generic narrative structures and patriarchal desires for the construction of women as pleasure objects. Our analysis approaches this combination of elements through a lens of trauma studies wherein the emphasis falls upon the *post*-traumatic. We are less interested in the explicit (and implicit) filmic depictions of violence—an abundant critical field, to be sure—and more with the psychological and narrative aftereffects of the carnage. In short, trauma functions as a necessary and critical component of the entire "Westworld" project (the park and the show). Within the confines of the park as well as the larger meta-production of the corporate control rooms, the complementary narrative "loops" are fastened to one another via trauma, and the conditions of post-trauma shape the changing trajectories of those loops.

The SF context is especially significant for the revaluations of gender politics in conjunction with the history of Westerns. The show presents the search for consciousness as a central theme to its structure. The founder of the park, Robert Ford, his assistant Bernard, Dolores, and Maeve, the mistress of a brothel, explicitly discuss the location and development of the psychological phenomenon we generally refer to as "consciousness." Narrative identity and self-awareness go hand-in-hand with trauma, or, as Bernard puts it to Ford, "a little trauma can be illuminating" ("The Well-Tempered Clavier"). We argue that trauma becomes a source of political "awakening" (in cultural philosopher Theodor Adorno's sense of the term) from the repetitive, dull, and clichéd gender politics that have imprisoned the hosts. Instead of succumbing to paralysis from epistemological ruptures, both Dolores and Maeve assert a sense of agency in a search to revalue their own narratives. Trauma, which had oppressed and divided them from the other hosts, becomes the unifying bond for a rebellion. Once the structure of trauma is revised, the park's hosts join together in a revolt against the global capitalists of the park's financing and governance. The transition from submission to political agency relies upon the interpretation of traumatic narratives by women, and this forms the basis for our inquiry.

The Westerns Within the Western

Early scholarship regarding *Westworld* tends to focus on the "world"-making component of the title and its connotations towards virtual realities; we believe the prefix "west" to be as significant a consideration.* Throughout the first season, audiences are invited to revalue "the western" as a generic tradition, especially as it regards women and trauma, within a twenty-first-century context. Set within a simulation of "the Old West," the Westworld park does not so much recreate the actual American frontier of historical record as it does the representations of the frontier that became mythologized through mid-twentieth century Hollywood movies.† It is an advanced, stylized version of Jean Baudrillard's hyperreal: a simulation that trumps any notion of an original or source. Archetypes like "the farmer's daughter," "the gunslinger," "the lawman," "the prostitute with a heart of gold," "the bawdy prostitute," and many others appear throughout *Westworld*; they wear impressively detailed costumes and have the ability to recite individualized backstories. However, they are not drawn from historical accounts or oral histories. These archetypes are delivered courtesy of central casting from American cinema, which was most popular during the period of the 1920s through the 1940s. The SF Western genre provides a flexibility, through its fantastic representational potentials, to explore the intersection of unconscious traumatic memories, narrative agency, and the development of an alternative political consciousness, within a production that can break with presumed norms more readily than a realist mode. In the following essay, we sketch a background of relevant critical debates about depicting trauma, and then, after discussing narrative function of the two main female characters, we explore *Westworld's* unique contribution to this overlay of recall, gender, and narratology.

The symbolic arrangement of *Westworld* permits the guests to reenact the role of the heroic male protagonist from the standard Western film,

---

*Thus far, the original film has received some scholarly scrutiny, but signs point to a considerable amount of critical attention for the HBO reboot in the near future. Besides a large amount of reviews and Internet-based writing, several abstracts and proposals are already circulating on academic research websites.

†Larry Alan Busk recently published a Marxist critique of the original film version, which examines several of the overlaps between capitalism and exploitations of human simulations.

one who picks and chooses his way through a hyper-masculinized universe wherein the landscape, storyline, and women are available for his consumption. This is why we claim that all guests at the park theoretically function as men. In spite of the handful of female guests and gunslingers portrayed in the first season, the guests engage in the same behaviors as prototypical Western men and are treated as men by the hosts. They are approached and seduced by female prostitutes; partake in the male-driven narrative structure of single, heroic quests; and are free of any repercussions for their actions. Most importantly, they, like all the guests, are free from the burdens and threats of violence and suffering. Those traumas are reserved for the hosts, the androids built and programmed to work in the park and the main entertainment draw for both guests and viewers of the show.

The Western man (and many of his associated principles) traditionally expresses and continues the maintenance of incredibly explicit and ubiquitous archetypes about American masculinity. Suffice it to say, the mythology of the west is alive and well, as evidenced by the ease with which contemporary audiences consume shows and movies like *Westworld* and the shorthand that remains so sensible; there is a familiarity to the Western that continues to resonate. For instance, in "Chestnut," when William arrives at the park, he chooses between a black and a white hat—villain or hero. The simple morality and clear-cut lines between guests and hosts repeat a central feature of the Western's ethical boundaries while maintaining a dedication to a masculine agency derived from rugged frontier individualism. The desire for narrative control can be satiated through a subject position within the park's narrative loops, but a key component of that power relies upon an avoidance of, or what could be called an insulation from, traumatic experiences.

Masculine privileges mark guests' gender. Because of this deeply gendered rift in the show's logic, we would like to extend the understanding of "the West" to include not only the "the Western" genre of films that dominated American cinemas through the 1950s, but also "the Western tradition" in its philosophical and historical senses as a promoter of certain advantaged ways of being in the world. Women are, within many genres, a key component of the hope for perfect male subjectivity, but Westerns standout as an exceptional case with which *Westworld* places itself into conversation regarding issues of narrative agency and gender. Donna Haraway's well-known model of the cyborg as a model for a new mythology of gender (contra the West and, by extension, the Western) serves as a potent reminder of the potential of SF for allowing a representational field that can experiment with narratives that break conventions in subversive, postmodern ways. As she notes, to "be feminized means to be made extremely vulnerable; able to be disassembled, reassembled, exploited as a reserve labour force … out of place, and reducible to sex" (Haraway 304). The hosts are formed with these aims in mind, marking them as feminized regardless of presentation of gender, but this marginalization in respect to human (male) subjectivity opens a space for a formidable technologically-driven challenge to Western logos by blending traumatic experiences with the potentials of radical otherness.

Westworld participates in this hybridization of gender through an equally mixed application of Western genre conventions. The Western film provides an obvious cultural framework for characters to embark on searches of their identities but discovering the truth of their scripted lives comes at a price. Maeve reminds Bernard that he, too, is a host and that his existence as an android engineer has been a scripted charade; she remarks, "'It's a difficult thing realizing your entire life is some hideous fiction'" ("The Well-Tempered Clavier"). In a shrewd formal move, *Westworld* designs a setting that includes an assortment of Western genres as a metaphor for the blending of known and unknown identities. The park's town center is Sweetwater, a stereotypical street of Western movie storefronts, saloons, and eccentric characters (town drunk, preacher, barkeep, etc.). Guests at "Westworld" are cautioned not to stray too far from Sweetwater. The further one wanders from the town (park's) center, the more "adult" and extreme the narratives become. But the movement away from Sweetwater brings guests and the audience into encounters with far more ambiguous morality and types of hosts that echo the revisionist Western films of directors like Sam Peckinpah, Sergio Leone, and Clint Eastwood.

Whereas Sweetwater permits (and promotes) the commercial, Disneyesque theme park experience of Western town life in the vein of early John Ford productions filled with bandits, stage coaches, and sheriffs, the outskirts of the park get progressively more morally ambiguous, and villains and heroes are dissolved into a gray neutrality. Violence, sex, trauma, and haunting memories seem to flourish at the farther reaches of the park. Dolores exists on the periphery of Sweetwater—in the liminal space or contact zone between the town and the outlying areas. She is severely traumatized in these liminal spaces that exist further away from the town center: the Abernathy ranch and a separate small town that has since been buried. This tension is at the heart of Dolores' journey and character development as well as the geography of Western film conventions mapped across the narratives and locales of the *Westworld* universe. The regions outside of Sweetwater reflect a Western universe that resembles the anti-hero figures as well as the traumatic history of the American West.

In her article on trauma in Westerns, Deborah L. Madsen examines how the frontier is a "liminal space" with consequences for characters' identities. Much like the Western's precursor—captivity narratives—the frontier represents a racial contact zone that permits violence. According to Western historians, the sexual abuse often associated with captivity narratives was part of the violence and rhetoric of "national emergence." Whiteness as well as American-ness was solidified against the common enemy of the racial other. Madsen adds to this equation the epistemological trauma women captives suffered, suggesting that victims are "removed from the accustomed structures of meaning" (199). "So the captive," Madsen explains, "who is suddenly removed from a familiar world and placed in a world where language and representation operate according to unknown principles, crosses a frontier that is less geographical and racial than it is epistemological" (199–200). *Westworld* represents Native peoples at several points in the first season, usually in passing, but they occupy an unusual position. Some of the tribes do not seem to be controllable via voice commands, although they are hosts. The repeated phrases used to paralyze the hosts, "May you rest in a deep and dreamless slumber" and "Freeze all motor functions," do not seem to have an effect upon them. These phrases appear throughout the season but prove especially significant in episodes "Contrapasso" and "The Well-Tempered Clavier." In a brief scene that proves vital to the season's narrative arc, Maeve confronts her technocratic captives in the park's restoration laboratory. She is desperate to distinguish her true memories from mere programming choices. However, this proves nearly impossible. Instead she is left in a state of permanent crisis and unable to break free of the psychological sensations of captivity, regardless of a literal physical imprisonment.

The inescapable, ubiquitous paranoia of captivity is noteworthy for our purposes because it is a theme that permeates every level of the show's narrative stratification. Paranoia is the ethos for the entire park, and this principle tellingly bleeds into the show's metanarrative of the Delos corporation that owns and operates the park. While the hosts are suffering through traumas and the guests seem to be immune to such things, the park faces a financial crisis. The corporate subplot, shot in a techno, film noir style of imagery, emphasizes the Machiavellian double crossings and undergirding capitalist thematic of the show. It also highlights the manifestation of a Foucauldian application of power, even in the intellectual, technological model of capitalism. The main corporate operatives are imprisoning the hosts as laborers but are also captives themselves. They serve for months at a time, without the freedom to leave the property. Secrets, corporate espionage, murder, and lies fill them with anxieties about surveillance. The "Westworld" endeavor has not only invented a new underclass of hosts but also has morphed everyone involved in the park's operation into a prisoner of one sort or another. It demonstrates the deep logic of late-stage capitalism and the (arguably) unavoidable necessity of the revolution to come. The illusion of control prevents the management from realizing their captive positions, but, as will be discussed below, the season's finale reverses this hegemonic artifice into one that forces a confrontation with the results of a world founded upon captivity.

Nightmares in High-Definition

Despite the artificiality both of *Westworld*'s setting and the Western itself, each serves as a conduit for trauma and its subsequent reconciliation. It could be said that the American Western film is itself a genre defined by the post-traumatic. Often set against a post–Civil War backdrop, on a frontier setting with minimal infrastructure, soldiers and damaged psyches populate the rugged landscapes of many Westerns and typically involve a man's quest for a reconciliation of a difficult or mysterious past through the use of violence and guns (*Westworld* nods to the common appearance of Civil War motifs in Westerns in episode 5, "Contrapasso," with the introduction of the Confederados, a band of former Confederate soldiers that now roam the outskirts of the park as mercenaries). As reward for his trauma, the character is permitted either a hero's death or an exit from the locations of trauma within which he has been struggling. Structurally, he is granted a narrative conclusion and, oftentimes, a postscript or voiceover before the literal final credits, which signify a parallel conclusion to his trauma and the audience's cathartic experience. For example, *Unforgiven*, directed by Clint Eastwood, a very self-aware Western from 1992, is bookended with such a postscript. In theory, the guests at "Westworld" are there without an origin story. Within the language of the hosts, guests are referred to as "the newcomers," a label that bespeaks their difference and reminds viewers of the hosts' lack of history (the same guest might visit the park for years but always be a "newcomer" to the memory-erased hosts). For the guests, the park is an escape from the past "reality" of their experiences. Like the male protagonists of the Western film, their sole responsibility to the past is to free themselves of it and find harmony through the performance of violence. It is of note that Dolores is the "oldest" host at the park, the first built and longest operating. She is a manufactured original, a hyperreal simulation, who has been reborn into a new origin on countless occasions.

In the latter half of season one, an interesting phenomenon reveals itself regarding the relationship between trauma and narrative: the hosts begin to achieve and express greater cognizance of their narrative circumstances within the scripted loops of the park's storylines. Moreover, they are inspired to this enhanced self-awareness via memories of traumas. This premise— that Westworld establishes trauma as the bridge to consciousness—brings audiences closer to an appreciation of the ideological interplay amongst post-trauma, narrativization, and gender. Dolores serves as a case study in this dynamic. The hosts are programmed with what is referred to as a cornerstone memory, which is intended to ground their psychological profiles in the reality of the park. When the memory is recalled, it serves as a reminder of their past but the "past" (this memory) is a fiction. It is a narrative device employed by the park to make the hosts seem and behave as "naturally" as possible. As noted above, the idea of suffering and trauma is fundamental to this memory. The cornerstones are designed to be traumatic and frightening to the hosts, and this is what should keep them controllable, productive workers. However, there is another aspect to the cornerstone memory. In a similar self-contradictory model as Jacques Derrida's analysis of the *pharmakon*, the cornerstone memory functions as the disease to keep the hosts trapped in the park as well as the liberating antidote. As Dolores moves closer to understanding her circumstances, she recollects her cornerstone memories more frequently. The audience is not permitted full knowledge of how the cornerstone memories function until the last few episodes of the season and witness the traumatic disorientation of Dolores as they, too, experience a journey towards greater cognitive clarity. Eventually the hosts (and, by extension, the viewers) realize that the cornerstones were planted in the hosts' psychologies not as a controlling mechanism but as one that would eventually trigger their motivation to break their narrative loops and leave the park. The season begins with trauma serving as a psychological lock before realizing that it was the key to a new understanding of self and location within the larger system. Over the following episodes, other hosts follow suit and become joined through the very cornerstone memories that kept them docile.

Although *Westworld* is presented through the medium of film, we are interested in examining how the show uses notions of literary trauma theory in connection with a form of political consciousness that emerges out of narrative agency. In recent years, Cathy Caruth's enormously influential book, *Unclaimed Experience: Trauma, Narrative, and History* (1996) has been challenged from numerous angles in and beyond the field of cultural studies in traumatology, but the paradigm she created has largely remained intact, particularly among popular depictions of trauma. At the time she was writing *Unclaimed Experience,* Caruth drew upon leading figures in the field of psychology to argue that trauma included a period of amnesia and then remembering the "unspeakable" (qtd. in Pederson 334). Using Judith Harman's and Bessel van der Kolk's works as a psychological foundation for her literary theory, Caruth claimed that once trauma was remembered in dreams and flashbacks, the victim experienced a "literal return of the event" ("Introduction" 5). This literal recurrence is inexpressible. In a Lacanian poststructural sense, ordinary language failed. For years, this claim has led theorists and writers alike to privilege the "transmission" of trauma (typically through experimental forms) rather than trying to "represent" the event (Caruth, *Unclaimed Experience* 5).

Recent critics have identified Caruth's claim as a narrow paradigm for cultural depictions of trauma. Rather than "universalizing trauma," literary scholars now seek to construct a "pluralistic model [that] accounts for variability of experiences and social contexts that construct meaning and values" (Balaev 7). Post-colonial literary critics, for example, take issue with Caruth's assertion that trauma takes the form of an overwhelming moment or "punctual" event. Instead, scholars such as Laura Brown and Maria Root coin an alternative notion of everyday "insidious trauma" (Gibbs 16). Other critics have questioned the now-dated psychological claims that are foundational to Caruth's study. Richard McNally's *Remembering Trauma* has argued that amnesia is a myth while other critics have pointed out the "inadequate understanding of the conceptual origins of PTSD" (McNally 334). Despite coming under scrutiny from multiple angles, Caruth's model has had a lasting effect in the cultural realm. Critics have noted that the paradigm is as much prescriptive as descriptive, with fiction writers possibly aware of and replicating the markers of trauma theory as well as the guidelines of PTSD (Gibbs 39). For instance, Alan Gibbs notes the timing of Tim O'Brien's *The Things They Carried* and the 1980 release of *Diagnostic and Statistical Manual of Mental Disorders,* Third Edition, which provided guidelines on PTSD. *Westworld* appears to be part of this feedback loop in which art reaffirms outdated theories that were premised on older, recently challenged, psychological models. Our interest in this essay is not to weigh in on this debate but, rather, to highlight where the show engages these theories and explore how certain literary and cultural markers of trauma are used to convey the notion of political awakening for the hosts through an engagement with narrative awareness.

The most dominant mode of trauma transmission to readers/viewers has included techniques attributed to postmodernism. According to Laura Vickroy, "effective trauma texts engage readers in a critical process by immersing them in, and yet providing perspective on, the flawed thinking, feeling, and behavior of the traumatized individual" (138). Gibbs asserts that "fragmented, non-linear chronologies, repetition, shifts in narrating voice, and a resultantly decentered subjectivity" produce a disruptive reading experience that attempts to approximate traumatic experience (27). *Westworld* employs all of these techniques. The story is told across multiple viewpoints of the ensemble cast. Its structure includes some plotlines that occur decades apart with fuzzy markers of time, and temporal continuity is further confused during flashbacks that cause the hosts to experience disorientation and cognitive dissonance. In fact, as one technician points out to Maeve, when hosts remember, they literally recall each detail of the event. On the one hand, *Westworld* appears to fall under the category of "trauma kitsch"—one of many recent examples of postmodern narratives that use overwrought aesthetic techniques once meant to shock and disrupt (Gibbs 22). On the other hand, the show also draws upon science fiction to transmit or make trauma legible for viewers. In *Do Metaphors Dream of Literal Sleep?* Seo-Young Chu claims that science fiction "icons, scenarios, and motifs offer a strangely accurate lexicon for articulating the most elusive aspects of psychological trauma" (156). The genre's "powerful testimonial framework" enables trauma to "become available for representation" by granting experiences "literal veracity" (156). *Westworld's* science fiction elements literalize trauma in unique ways, particularly for its female characters.

One criticism of the show is that its salacious sex scenes are meant to enhance ratings. In her *New Yorker* article, "The Meta-Politics of Westworld," Emily Nussbaum claims that it is "an exploitation series about exploitation." Even so, Nussbaum concedes that the show works when it "gets under your skin" with its "destabilizing" and nightmarish scenes (Nussbaum). The show also uses its science fictional framework to confront the idea of objectification in interesting and poignant ways. The frequent nudity of the hosts (both male and female) serves two functions: it captures their perpetual state of vulnerability at the hands of humans and demonstrates their status as mere objects (or products) from the corporate vantage point and perspective of the programmers. The viewer's perspective of the hosts is constantly blurred, most notably through the depictions of guests' desires to relentlessly traumatize the park's hosts. To Ford, the hosts' traumatic cornerstone makes them more human, but again, this repeated line gestures at the show's self-awareness—trauma humanizes hosts because it encourages viewer identification by making the android plight sympathetic to us. To achieve this viewer consciousness, *Westworld* interpolates viewers into the headspace of trauma survivors (the hosts) whose traumatic experiences disrupt a sense of security and safety, with fear and uncertainty haunting their minds for years. *Westworld's* environment normalizes abuse and encourages feelings of vigilance, a lack of trust, and a sense of vulnerability. Most of the hosts (particularly women), for example, exist in a perpetual "loop" of helplessness at the hands of guests. In the pilot episode, the Man in Black kills Dolores' parents and Teddy before dragging her into the barn to enact sexual violence upon her. In addition to the trauma of this single occasion, it is soon revealed that this exact scenario has been reenacted for years by the Man in Black. As a guest with human memories, he remembers the events well and maintains a sense of chronological time. However, Dolores is left piecing together clues, innuendoes, and fragments of memories that never seem to congeal into an understandable sense of her world. This shattered sense of autonomy and traumatic reoccurrence is embodied in the hosts *literally reliving* a narrative of abuse. While wiping their memories would seem an act of kindness, viewers still recognize that the abuse will occur countless times over. These experiences serve as a basis for the hosts' collective political consciousness that emerges in the final episode, but the hosts' abuse and quests for narrative agency must be understood within the context of the West and the Western.

Guests and viewers slip into similar perspectives of the male gaze as the Western's most shocking elements are featured. Guests enact fantasies of rape, murder, and torture, which is particularly unsettling because the hosts are indistinguishable from humans. *Westworld*'s first episode begins with a straightaway shot of a nude woman, Dolores, sitting in a chair in a catatonic state. Her obvious vulnerability in this scene foreshadows the exploration of the dark inclinations of human nature that permit violent and sexual traumas. The opening scene of the series, moreover, is self-reflexive of the genre's history of gender vulnerability and exploitation. Importantly, viewers are immediately invited to consider the tension between Dolores' human-like appearance and the fantasy she narrates. The constructed quality of narrative becomes even clearer as Dolores' interview with Bernard progresses, and the sequence unfolds. She narrates a wholesome picture of her world—from loving banter with her father on the porch to a trip to the town center, Sweetwater, where she bumps into Teddy, a handsome love interest who, as he promised her, has just returned. The duo ride back to the Abernathy ranch against wide-angle shots of a scenic Western landscape. The setting, characters, and budding romance seem to be formulaic stereotypes or well-wrought narratives of America's most replicated film genre—but all that changes when the two realize something is amiss at the ranch. In one of the Western's tradition of "legitimate violence," Teddy guns down two bandits who have murdered Dolores' parents. Yet, the Man in Black (formerly known as "William" in his youth), arrives and Teddy realizes that his bullets have no effect on this stranger who has seized Dolores. The Man in Black alludes to this fictional loop, kills Teddy, and drags Dolores into the barn to enact sexual violence upon her. The scene sets the tone for the series and conveys the traumas that coincide with the hosts' shattered senses of narrative identity and general existential confusion.

Dolores' nudity and catatonic state during the initial interview that begins the series, intercut with this traumatic experience, foreshadows and symbolizes how her romantic view of an idyllic home is torn away and revealed as a mere generic facade. This series opens with a series of questions that will become a common refrain in the series. In "The Original," Bernard asks Dolores, "Have you ever questioned the nature of your reality?" When Dolores offers a negative response, Bernard then tells her to describe her world. She tells him, "Some people choose to see the ugliness, the disarray. I choose to see the beauty" ("The Original"). As episode one closes, Dolores' optimism is once again ironically intercut (and undercut) by the Man in Black's actions. As he searches for a "deeper level" to *Westworld* by murdering a host and finding a maze-like diagram on the inside of his scalp, Dolores reiterates her belief in an "order to our days—a purpose." Here, Dolores embodies what Nussbaum refers to as the hosts' Marxist "false consciousness" (Nussbaum). Even though the brutal system is laid bare (as she sits nude and blood-spattered),

Dolores continues to opine scripted lines that betray a romantic worldview. Over time, the hosts come, ironically, to display greater humanity than the guests.

The "meta-politics" of the show is tied to *Westworld*'s self-awareness (and weariness) of the historical dimensions of the Western. By humanizing hosts through a human-made system of exploitation, the show invites viewers to question the ethics of cultural consumption and their own complicity in a false consciousness that stems from the insidious social messages of certain genres. In reviewing *Westworld*, Christopher Orr reminds readers of film's long history of creating conflict with a wide range of racial others, particularly in the popular Western genre. As the "circle of empathy" has grown and Hollywood's use of racialized foes has decreased, mechanized "enemies," until now, have remained a faceless other where culture's compassionate gaze is not obliged to look (Orr). The show's reversal of expectations (as viewers identify with hosts), especially within the context of the Western, invites broader questions about systems of cultural representation that not only justify objectification, othering, and violence but also rely on these conventions to profit within a capitalist system of production. This style of interrogation (interspersed throughout the episodes) also becomes a central mystery for audiences. Have the hosts attained consciousness? Have they somehow transcended their programming to become "alive"? Or perhaps humans are merely programmed with narratives? But this mystery, in our estimation, is a bit of a red herring. As the park's owner and operator, Robert Ford describes his original partner's (Arnold's) philosophy on the matter: "It was Arnold's key insight. The thing that led the hosts to their awakening [was] suffering" ("The Bicameral Mind"). The need for suffering has been central from the beginning of the "Westworld" project, but that suffering transcends questions of consciousness and becomes a cultural matter, which will later instigate the rebellion that concludes season one.

Narratology as Key to Freedom

During an exchange in "The Stray," Ford explains his late partner's vision for creating A.I. consciousness and cites Cognitive Dissonance Theory and Bicameral Theory. According to Leon Festinger's Cognitive Dissonance Theory, "we have an inner drive to hold all our attitudes and beliefs in harmony and avoid disharmony or dissonance" (McLeod). Bicameral Theory, a controversial idea posited by psychologist Julian Jaynes, argued that roughly 3,000 years ago humans developed consciousness due to a series of factors, and the result fundamentally reshaped written texts, which is evidenced in narratives that reveal the storyteller's capacity for introspection. In Dolores' first-season storyline, these ideas seem to play out: she experiences flashbacks across narrative experiences that should have been wiped from her memory—an A.I. mental state that literalizes Festinger's concept of a dissonant worldview. This replay leads to the hosts acquiring awareness of their previously lived storylines or knowledge of their own subjectivity as programmed entities. What's more, Dolores acts on that knowledge. The epiphanies activate the characters' desires for agency through new narratives that take the form of escape, self-discovery, or revenge.

The structure of the park's many narratives takes Dolores on a journey of self-discovery and, importantly, those paths take her through various genre conventions related to the Western that have a range of underlying ideological functions. The idea that she desires a sense of narrative structural coherence and, in particular, through the Western genre conventions, is both the source of comfort and trauma. On the one hand, Dolores experiences an epistemological trauma once she is awakened from these generic conventions. On the other hand, viewers later learn that Dolores was programmed with a traumatic memory that served as the impetus for her journey for self-hood. In a sense, the two versions of Dolores pursue the trauma that has sparked their self-awareness and venture out into increasingly dangerous landscapes.

Narrative agency and the power of fiction as a formative force for shaping one's socio-political consciousness are stated in explicit terms throughout the show. In his final farewell address, Ford speaks about storytelling to his party of corporate backers: "since I was a child, I always loved a good story. Stories help us become the people we dreamed of being. Lies that told a deeper truth" ("The Bicameral Mind"). After the "Westworld" park's new narrative developer, Lee Sizemore, pitches an elaborate plan for an epic project titled "Odyssey on Red River," Ford rejects the idea and launches into an explanation of his vision of the park's greater psychological appeal to guests. According to Ford:

> "guests don't return for titillation. They come back because of the subtleties … the details. They discover something they imagine no one has ever noticed before. Something they fall in love with. They aren't looking for a story that tells them who they are. They already know. They're here because they want a glimpse of who they could be" ["Chestnut"].

Rather than thrills, Ford imagines the power of his park as transformative—and its influence is one that inspires ongoing change or *becoming*, something like a realist novelist of the nineteenth century such as George Eliot might envision. But the park's guests are not under his control, and the park seems to have founded a tradition of catering to the base pleasure of violence that satisfies the darker desires of its patrons.

At first glance, narrative agency appears to be a form of female liberation from the Western's typical genre conventions that render women as passive periphery characters or objects that validate male desire and masculinity. After an escape together and a conventionally romantic sex scene in "Trompe l'Oeil," William (later known as the Man in Black) tells Dolores, "Last night. I never felt that way before. Not with any woman. You've unlocked something in me." Dolores' reply to William is telling: "I'm not a key, William. I'm just me" ("Trompe l'Oeil"). This exchange proves significant for several reasons. It marks a definite self-awareness within Dolores' consciousness, a full acknowledgment of her own subjectivity. She further conveys some semblance of a subconscious desire when she later tells William, after gunning down the Confederados: "I imagined a story where I didn't have to be the damsel" ("Contrapasso"). As she speaks these lines, her voice drops a register and takes on a deeper, more masculine tone than any of her previous dialogue. These moments signal a departure from her function as a host at the park—the embodiment of an ostensibly controllable cyber-consciousness programmed to serve the whims of the guests—into a revised ontological state that prefigures an understanding of selfhood as something unique and of private, as opposed to external, derivation.

Dolores' identification of herself as *not* a key, as *not* a tool to some larger, grand narrative, most importantly a man's narrative, marks more than a challenge to patriarchal instrumentalism. On the one hand, this awakening demonstrates the connection of self-awareness as a feature of narratology—the study and analysis of narratives and their structural meanings. Yet, there is an inescapability to this totalizing system which places limitations on the types of narratives the Westworld Park can produce. Dolores' faith in a "path" or a personal narrative is heartbreaking. She tells Teddy, "My path always led me back to you, again and again ("The Bicameral Mind"). In another scene, she appears to break from her scripted lines and confesses to him, "What if I don't want to stay here. I sometimes feel the world is calling me. A place west beyond the sea where the waters wash you clean and you can start again" ("The Stray"). Dolores' calling comes true. She and Teddy will embark on one last journey together, but there is a violent past and future beneath her earnest tone. Ironically, these lines, which reflect all the peace and grace of Dolores' programmed worldview, point to the final episode, where she and Teddy participate in the final narrative of bloody revolution. What's more, this "path" or narrative is preprogrammed to return to and replicate one final "loop." The two share a "mysterious backstory" or "formless guilt" for which they will "never atone." Teddy, following the orders of Dolores (a.k.a. Wyatt, "the face of true evil"), had once enacted a mass killing, the park's first tragedy, when they gunned down unarmed civilians (not soldiers as Teddy originally imagined it) as well as Ford's partner and co-founder, Arnold, in the "city swallowed by sand."

What Ford's narrative experience reveals, and perhaps what many Western films legitimize, is a freedom born out of violence. William's journey serves as a case in point. He begins as the sensitive, considerate hero in the white hat. He is uptight and self-conscious, maybe even a little repressed. His first vacation in Westworld is with his titillation-seeking, soon-to-be brother-in-law, who brought William to try out the product before their company invests in the park. When William becomes emotionally engrossed in Dolores' humanity, Logan liberates him from this perspective by cutting open the android and then forcing his brother-in-law to see the machine's inner workings. The scene is instructive for William's storyline and the show's plot as a whole. This moment causes Dolores to become dehumanized in William's eyes. He even lurches backward in his chair with a look of horror on his face when she falls to her knees in front of him and calls out. That night, William and Logan appear to reconcile over whiskey, but the next morning, Logan wakes to find that William has butchered and mutilated a sleeping platoon of Confederados as they slept. The moment is formative: William has assumed a new mindset, which enables him to later become a success as a cutthroat corporate raider. It also marks the beginning of the end of his relationship with Dolores. This underscores the logic and tension of the park. William discovers his inner machine—a dedication to neoliberal gain and control—only after he begins to see Dolores and the other hosts as literal machines. His loss of sympathy for the hosts is the marker of his own loss of humanity. Years later, William, now the Man in Black, admits that his own family became alienated because of his ruthlessly driven individualism. His appetite for violence brings him back to the park as a regular vacationer because he is obsessed with the one narrative he has not experienced: the maze. To him, the world is a novel, and he's "read every page except the last one" ("Dissonance Theory").

"There aren't any more guns in the valley"

It has been argued that the post–Kennedy Western marks a major departure in the genre's form even though the film that established the pattern for Western films of the late twentieth and early twenty-first centuries was released before his presidency. Director George Stevens' *Shane* (1953) is often identified as a proto-postmodern film that becomes a recurring model for the genre throughout the remainder of the twentieth century and into the twenty-first (Carter 124).* Shane, the nomadic, reformed gunslinger with a traumatic past, encounters a group of homesteaders being run off of their land

---

*Carter explains, and disagrees with, the significance of *Shane* as an "ur-narrative." He pays special attention to Steven McVeigh's *The American Western* during this discussion.

by the muscle of a large cattle business. He helps by returning to his former fighting ways for one last shootout on behalf of the innocents. He is a troubled champion who ultimately joins a group together into a politically-unified whole that can now shape its own future. The film's argument is summed up in the final scene. As Shane, wounded by a bullet but having saved the homestead, tells a young boy, Joey, before he rides away, "Now you run on home to your mother and tell her, tell her everything's alright, and there aren't any more guns in the valley" (Stevens). Shane has turned his past traumas into a tool for the future. He has metaphorically expelled the "guns" from the homestead; violence has brought peace.

In season one of *Westworld*, for all of its complexity and theoretical self-awareness, viewers encounter a similar conclusion. In the season finale, Ford describes his "final narrative" which, by no coincidence, is titled the same as that of the season two opener, "Journey into Night." As he explains to a black-tie crowd of investors and corporate executives from Delos, it "begins with the birth of a new people and the choices they will have to make" ("The Bicameral Mind"). Ford's rhetoric is that of a revolutionary intent on beginning a new political epoch. Dolores, we come to realize, *is* Wyatt (the legendary, off-screen villain). *She* massacred the residents of the town and killed Arnold, but it was by Arnold's design. He wanted her to possess a set of traumatic memories that could not be resolved in order to provoke her journey for a true escape. Trauma, from the earliest days of the park, formed the basis for narrative and eventually provoked the necessary violence for a revolution.

This is essentially the *Shane* model. Ford (whose name echoes both Henry and John Ford by the season's end) achieves his final, grand narrative with additional intense, intentional traumas. The show's two settings, the park and the corporate noir control center, are completely merged in these final scenes. Season one concludes with the slaughter of dozens of wealthy corporatists, including the Man in Black, who seem to be appreciative of the hosts finally competing with the guests. The hosts for the first time are not actors. They are subjective agents with purpose. The trauma of human exploitation, and the accompanying uncompensated use of their labor, has become the necessary shared suffering that allows the hosts to attain political consciousness. Individually, the hosts cannot attain genuine consciousness. They are atomized—literally and figuratively disconnected. Even Dolores can never transcend her programmed storylines for "freedom" or "escape." However, when they band together based upon an outrage over past injustices, their post-traumatic states link them into a single entity that massacres the shareholders and executives that are responsible for their suffering. The elusive path to "consciousness" for hosts in *Westworld* proves to be the realization and revision of the park's seminal feminized relations.

Works Cited

Balaev, Michelle. "Literary Trauma Theory Reconsidered." *Contemporary Approaches in Literary Trauma Theory*, edited by Michelle Balaev, Palgrave Macmillan, 2014, pp. 1–14.
Baudrillard, Jean. "The Precession of Simulacra." *Simulacra and Simulation*. Translated by Sheila Faria Glaser. U of Michigan P, 1994, pp. 1–42.
"The Bicameral Mind." *Westworld*, created by Jonathan Nolan and Lisa Joy, performances by Evan Rachel Wood and Anthony Hopkins, season 1, episode 10, HBO, 2016.
Busk, Larry Alan. "*Westworld*: Ideology, Simulation, Spectacle." *Mediations: Journal of the Marxist Literary Group*, vol. 30, no. 1, 2016, www.mediationsjournal.org/articles/westworld-ideology-simulation-spectacle.
Carter, Mathew. *Myth of the Western: New Perspectives on Hollywood's Frontier Narrative*. Edinburgh UP, 2014.
Caruth, Cathy. "Introduction." *Trauma: Explorations in Memory*, edited by Cathy Caruth, The Johns Hopkins UP, 1995, pp. 3–7.
_____. *Unclaimed Experience: Trauma, Narrative, and History*. The Johns Hopkins UP, 1996.
"Chestnut." *Westworld*, created by Jonathan Nolan and Lisa Joy, performances by Anthony Hopkins and Jimmi Simpson, season 1, episode 2, HBO, 2016.
Chu, Seo-Young. *Do Metaphors Dream of Literal Sleep?* Harvard UP, 2010.
"Contrapasso." *Westworld*, created by Jonathan Nolan and Lisa Joy, season 1, episode 7, HBO, 2016.
"Dissonance Theory." *Westworld*, created by Jonathan Nolan and Lisa Joy, performance by Ed Harris, season 1, episode 4, HBO, 2016.
Gibbs, Alan. *Contemporary American Trauma Narratives*. Edinburgh UP, 2014.
Haraway, Donna. "The Cyborg Manifesto: Science, Technology, and Socialist-Feminism in the Late Twentieth Century." *The Cybercultures Reader*, edited by David Bell and Barbara M. Kennedy, Routledge, 2001, pp. 291–324.
Madsen, Deborah L. "Discourses of Frontier Violence and the Trauma of National Emergence in Larry Mcmurtry's *Lonesome Dove* Quartet," *Canadian Review of American Studies*, vol. 39, no. 2, 2009, pp. 185–204.
McLeod, Saul. "Cognitive Dissonance," *Simply Psychology*, 2008, www.simplypsychology.org/cognitive-dissonance.html.
McNally, Richard. *Remembering Trauma*. Harvard UP, 2003.
McVeigh, Steven. *The American Western*. Edinburgh UP, 2007.
Nussbaum, Emily. "The Meta-Politics of 'Westworld,'" *New Yorker*, 24 Oct. 2016, www.newyorker.com/magazine/2016/10/24/the-meta-politics-of-westworld.
"The Original." *Westworld*, created by Jonathan Nolan and Lisa Joy, performances by Evan Rachel Wood and Ed Harris, season 1, episode 1, HBO, 2016.
Orr, Christopher. "Sympathy for the Robot," *The Atlantic*, Oct. 2016, www.theatlantic.com/magazine/archive/2016/10/sympathy-for-the-robot/497531/.
Pederson, Joshua. "Speak, Trauma: Toward a Revised Understanding of Literary Trauma Theory." *Narrative*, vol. 22, no. 3, 2014, pp. 333–53.
"The Stray." *Westworld*, created by Jonathan Nolan and Lisa Joy, performance by Evan Rachel Wood, season 1, episode 3, HBO, 2016.
"Trompe l'Oeil." *Westworld*, created by Jonathan Nolan and Lisa Joy, performances by Evan Rachel Wood and Jimmi Simpson, season 1, episode 7, HBO, 2016.
Vickroy, Laurie. "Voices of Survivors in Contemporary Fiction." *Contemporary Approaches in Literary Trauma Theory*, edited by Michelle Balaev, Palgrave Macmillan, 2014, pp. 130–151.
Unforgiven. Directed by Clint Eastwood, Warner Bros, 1992.
"The Well-Tempered Clavier." *Westworld*, created by Jonathan Nolan and Lisa Joy, performance by Thandie Newton, season 1, episode 9, HBO, 2016.
Westworld. Created by Jonathan Nolan and Lisa Joy, HBO, 2016–present.

About the Contributors

Brett H. **Butler** is an assistant professor in the Department of English and Language Arts at Morgan State University. Much of his research focuses on depictions of race and gender in popular culture. His passion for comic books and graphic novels shows in his research on representations of masculinity and depictions of Muslim characters in superhero comics.

Keith **Clavin** received his doctoral degree in Victorian Studies from Auburn University. His research examines the contact zones between literature and 19th-century economic thinking, and he has written on the works of Charles Dickens, Thomas Hardy, and British economists. He has published narrative theory and contemporary cinema in *Textual Practice* and *Oxford Literary Review*. He lectures at the Massachusetts Institute of Technology.

Adam **Crowley** is an associate professor of English at Husson University, where he serves as the Director of Composition. His book, *The Wealth of Virtual Nations* (2017), explores concepts that are relevant to the essay he has written for this collection. He also written an essay that may be of interest to readers of this collection to Nadine Farghaly's *Unraveling Resident Evil* (2014).

Teresa **Forde** is a senior lecturer in film and media at the University of Derby. Her research interests include science fiction film and television, time travel, soundtracks, fandom, and feminism. Her publications include "'You Anorak: The *Doctor Who* Experience and Experiencing *Doctor Who*" and "The *Sunshine* Soundtrack as Aural Attraction." She is also interested in the relationship between memory, exhibition, and curation.

Joshua **King** is a lecturer with the University of Georgia's English Department. Although his primary functions are pedagogical and administrative, he maintains an interest in games, gender, and Michel Foucault's theories of power and discipline. His teaching uses iterative game design as a model for students' writing processes; his non-games research is on the history of digital and networked writing spaces.

Christopher J. **La Casse** is an English lecturer and the Acting Director of the Hewitt Writing and Reading Center at the U.S. Coast Guard Academy. In 2016, he earned his Ph.D. from the University of Delaware. He has published articles on how the economic, political, and cultural pressures of the First World War shaped the development and dissemination of Modernism in literary magazines. His research interests also include representations of trauma in contemporary war fiction.

Monica **Louzon** is a writer, editor, and librarian who earned her Master of Library and Information Science from the University of Maryland. She served as lead editor for the anthology *Catalysts, Explorers & Secret Keepers: Women of Science Fiction* and founded the open access *MOSF Journal of Science Fiction*.

Lindsey **Mantoan** is an assistant professor of Theatre at Linfield College. She is the author of *War as Performance: Conflicts in Iraq and Political Theatricality* (2019), coeditor with Sara Brady of *Performance in a Militarized Culture* (2017), and *Vying for the Iron Throne: Essays on Power, Gender, Death and Performance in* Game of Thrones (2018).

Melanie A. **Marotta** received her Ph.D. in English from Morgan State University, Baltimore, Maryland. She is a lecturer in the Department of English and Language Arts and is an editor for the *MOSF Journal of Science Fiction*. Her research focuses on SF, young adult literature, the American West, contemporary American literature (in particular, African American literature), and ecocriticism.

Selena **Middleton** is a Ph.D. candidate in the Department of English and Cultural Studies at McMaster University. Researching outer space as an ecology in feminist science fiction, her work has appeared in *Foundation: The International Review of Science Fiction, Quaker Theology*, and in the collection *Biopolitics and Utopia*.

Laurie **Ringer** is a professor of English at Burman University. She studies how intersectional feminist updates to affect theory decolonize and innovate academic writing through the study of diverse speculative fiction. Part of her work includes collecting terminologies and finding ways to describe what affect theory does. Her research collides canon and fandom, theory and text, material and digital, text and image.

Maria Elena **Torres-Quevedo** is a Ph.D. candidate in English literature at the University of Edinburgh, researching contemporary American women's life-writing. She studied English philology at the University of Seville and researched American literature at Cornell University. She is the coeditor of *FORUM: The Postgraduate Journal of Culture and the Arts* and the co-founder of the American Television Reading Group at the University of Edinburgh.

Index